Richard Anderson is Master Cutter and Managing Director of Richard Anderson Ltd., Savile Row's youngest genuine bespoke tailoring house, opened in 2001. He has worked on Savile Row for 27 years.

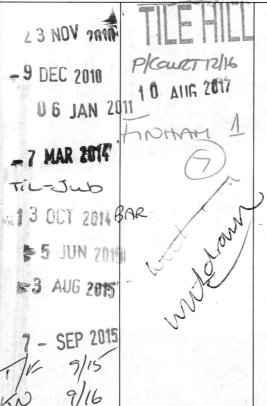

BESPOKE

Richard Anderson quit school to become an apprentice on Savile Row and wound up owning his own shop on the world famous 'Golden Mile'. His clientele includes royalty, politicians and media stars. In February 1982, he started work at Savile Row's Henry Huntsman & Sons, earning just £2,000 a year, but his life changed forever. Richard's apprenticeship, overseen by the debonair Colin Hammick, grumpy eccentric Brian Hall, and the heroically overworked 'leg man' Dick Lakey, was seventeen years of rigorous practice in perfectionism. 'Young Richard' became, at thirty-four, the youngest head cutter in Huntsman's one hundred and fifty year history.

RICHARD ANDERSON

◆

BESPOKE

Complete and Unabridged

ULVERSCROFT
Leicester

First published in Great Britain in 2009 by
Simon & Schuster UK Ltd.
London

First Large Print Edition
published 2010
by arrangement with
Simon & Schuster UK Ltd.
London

The moral right of the author has been asserted

Copyright © 2009 by Richard Anderson

British Library CIP Data

Anderson, Richard.
  Bespoke.
  1. Anderson, Richard. 2. Tailors- -England- -London- -
Biography. 3. Tailoring- -England- -London.
  4. Tailoring- -England- -London- -History.
  5. Large type books.
  I. Title
  687'.044'09421–dc22

  ISBN 978-1-44480-326-6

Published by
F. A. Thorpe (Publishing)
Anstey, Leicestershire

Set by Words & Graphics Ltd.
Anstey, Leicestershire
Printed and bound in Great Britain by
T. J. International Ltd., Padstow, Cornwall

This book is printed on acid-free paper

For

Fran

Mum   Dad

Tom   Molly   George   Mai

Contents

Dispatched

Foreword

One of life's greatest pleasures is to have the opportunity to experience a bespoke suit from a fine English firm such as Richard Anderson's.

I first met Richard when he worked at Huntsman, before he opened his own house on Savile Row eight years ago. To be dressed in a suit cut by Richard gives me empowerment and confidence; I show the world my best side in his exquisite bespoke. Winter or summer, the foundation of my wardrobe remains the same: a navy double-breasted, lined in scarlet, cut by Richard himself. It is wearing his work that I receive my highest accolades as a member of the Best-Dressed Hall of Fame.

The time-honoured tradition of bespoke tailoring is an English institution that for centuries has stood for distinction and discretion. Your cutter knows every nuance of fine, handmade tuning in the expert cut of cloth, as well as the ideal shape for your personal wardrobe. To achieve 'absolute simplicity', as Baudelaire once wrote of true elegance, one's cutter must marshal countless details of individual perspective into the perfect sartorial expression of an accomplished gentleman.

In this compelling personal history of his adventurous rise through the rank and file of Savile Row, Richard tells of one man's journey to establish his own mark through his belief in the highest qualities of fine tailoring, which he upholds not only in London but also in his expansion beyond to the global market. As the age of commuting became the norm, Richard was one of the first to offer personal bi-annual fittings of a customer's complete wardrobe — from dress suits to business attire to dinner clothes, topcoats, blazers, sport jackets and white tie — in all leading capitals of the world. Richard Anderson's very special staff members, and often Richard himself, fly to those customers unable to come to London for the critical choice of fabric and required fittings to make the perfect individual suit.

A well-dressed man approaches his wardrobe the way he reads his financial sheets and gives as much concern to his expression of appropriate distinction through individual choice and the finest handmade skills of Richard Anderson's cutters and ateliers. As the Comte de Buffon, Georges-Louis Leclerc, said: 'The style is the man himself.' Richard Anderson bespoke affords men the best possible style in a world where fine craftsmanship is not a luxury to the individual man, but a requirement of his very existence.

André Leon Talley
September 2009
Editor-at-Large, *Vogue* USA

Some names have been changed.

Young Richard

Reckoning

My first proper job interview was with the Sun Alliance Insurance Company. I failed to show. I cannot remember exactly why — probably in favour of a kickabout with my mates, or furthering my pursuit of Fran O'Connor, arguably the prettiest girl in St Michael's sixth form — but I do remember the swiftly damning letter I received from the firm, thanking me for having wasted its time. It was an inauspicious beginning.

Lest I botch another good prospect, my father took it upon himself to accompany me personally to my next interview. He had seen the job advertised in the *Daily Telegraph* just a week before: 'Wanted,' the advertisement read, 'sixteen- or seventeen-year-old apprentice cutter for Savile Row firm. Energetic . . . intelligent . . . smart appearance . . . ' I was sceptical (what the hell was a cutter?) but Dad made the call and we were granted an appointment at ten the following Tuesday. I had never heard of Huntsman before. For that matter I am not sure I had ever heard of Savile Row.

This was January 1982, and the night

3

before my interview marked the arrival of Greater London's worst snowstorm in a decade. Cascading thickly through the night and well into the next morning, the snow seemed to have brought most of England's train service to a halt. Dad and I managed to squeeze into some standing room on one of the few trains actually making the eighteen-mile journey from Watford Junction to Euston, but by the time we emerged from the Piccadilly underpass into the bright winter glare it was almost midday.

Among the braver members of the West End's workforce we walked briskly up Regent Street, its dramatic tunnelling curve taking us past the Air Street archway, Aquascutum, the Café Royal and Austin Reed. My eyes widened at the unfamiliar splendour and soaring architecture — I had only been to London a handful of times, and usually with my parents, to visit the shops or see a show — but there was no time to linger; we were already two hours late. A left onto Vigo Street followed by a quick right put us at the top end of Savile Row, which except for Dad and me was as empty and bleak as an Alaskan ghost town. Halfway down a series of staid, almost uniform shops, all of them a formidably greyish hue in my memory, stood Number 11, its lower window cloaked with a

4

faded, moss-green curtain. Never before had I approached such an imposing façade. Mounting its snow-swept marble steps on Dad's heels I felt a surge of trepidation.

Dad opened the door and we entered.

As we brushed and stamped snow from our shoulders and boots, two stuffed stag heads stared back at us from over an immense fireplace crackling with flames. Before us on the floor lay a vast Persian rug that was slightly threadbare at the edges. Two long, wooden display tables stood to one side, layered with crinkle-edged cloth swatches in countless colours, weights and textures. Towards the back of the room was a buzz of activity — phones ringing and people grouped in twos and threes to survey catalogues of yet more fabric, deeply engaged in lively debates concerning the materials' sundry qualities and potential.

'Good morning, Sir!'

A middle-aged man in a dark grey suit and green-and-red striped military tie had broken away from one of these conversations to greet us grandly. He strode purposefully, his smart coat and trousers seeming to usher his proud body forth, his receding hair slicked back and made immobile by some kind of pomade. He seemed of a different era.

Dad answered in a slightly tremulous but

businesslike voice I had never heard before. 'Good morning! I'm Tony Anderson and this is my son Richard, who has an interview with you today. We were due at ten, I'm afraid, but the weather — '

The pomaded man waved away Dad's pending apology and indicated for us to follow him further into the shop. He led us into a large fitting room off to the right, a space that easily accommodated three generous leather chairs. On the walls hung several oil paintings in heavy, gilded frames: four hunting scenes and a group portrait of evidently well-to-do gentlemen dressed in pink coats around a banquet table. 'Wait here,' ordered our man. 'I'll get Mr Hall.'

The fitting room contained two immense mirrors, one at each end. Inescapably face-to-face with my reflection — my hair and trouser hems damp from the snow, my navy school blazer looking tattier than ever — I desperately wanted to disappear.

Presently a man strode in with the air and stature of a drill sergeant, but in pinstripes. He had severe blue eyes, an immaculately groomed moustache and an angular jaw. In an authoritative manner, straining for patience — polite as he was, he obviously saw in us a couple of peasants with no concept of where we were or what it was all about — he

6

gave a brief but formidable history of the firm's sartorial sovereignty and then asked a few perfunctory questions of me. I listened carefully and spoke little, responding with a short yes or no whenever possible and mentioning only very shyly my joke of a Saturday job, which was selling jeans at a bargain outfitter called Cheapjack's in Watford Parade. This was my only relevant work experience, and to be fair calling it relevant is a stretch: for the most part I spent my time at Cheapjack's flirting with Fran or having a laugh with my mates, who would drop by and loiter to talk about birds and football more than to buy clothes. 'It is quite different here,' Mr Hall said coolly. Indeed. I was having trouble imagining myself standing under those stag heads and having a chat to John Bailey or Andy Hayes about Watford FC's latest fortunes.

When Mr Hall rose, I expected to be shown the door.

Instead, he asked Dad for the school report we had been instructed to bring and said he wanted us to see 'the workshop'. Report in hand, Mr Hall left to find someone named Toby, who would take us up to the workshop foreman, Mr Coombes. Alone again, Dad and I exchanged glances. I could tell from Dad's eyebrows he was impressed. We certainly were a world away from Hertfordshire.

A young man knocked on the fitting room's door and entered. Tall, handsome, wearing a double-breasted grey flannel suit with brown shoes, he looked about nineteen or twenty. Friendly but also a trifle imperious, he asked us to follow him out of the fitting room towards the back of the shop, passing through a space where five long wooden tables stood in a row, surrounded by the same heavy, dark wood panelling we had encountered in the reception area. Every surface was strewn with lengths of cloth, brown-paper patterns and half-made garments awaiting further assembly or refinement, massive shears like scissors on steroids nestled in their folds. Phones rang ceaselessly while two men examined a pair of trousers, lifting and turning one of its legs to inspect it from every angle. Having just left us, Mr Hall was here now, modelling an unfinished coat in front of a long mirror, a cigarette sticking abruptly out of the corner of his mouth. His tone was different from the one he had used during our interview. Berating a short, scruffy, Mediterranean-looking man, he barked: 'No, you *berk*! I want it like this!' The atmosphere was electric: masculine, loud and aggressive.

I liked it.

'You here for the apprentice cutter job?'

Toby asked, taking a fag from a gold Benson & Hedges packet and igniting it with a silver spring-top Zippo lighter. He did this while taking a flight of stairs two steps at a time. Although fit from playing football twice weekly, I was breathing hard by the time we reached the sixth flight. Behind me Dad gasped noisily. At the top we entered a room brilliant with post-blizzard sunlight streaming through its large windows. There were two dozen people or more at work in this bright, lofty space, most of them elderly and of foreign extraction and who at one moment or another lifted a suspicious eye towards me and Dad. As they worked and chatted over the hum of sewing and pressing machines Toby ushered us briskly through the workshop to introduce us to its foreman.

In utter contrast to the impeccable peacocks in the shop and cutting room downstairs, Mr Coombes was a short, fat, balding and dishevelled man, a pair of half-moon spectacles perched precariously on the end of his red nose. He was warm and ingratiating as he showed us around, and that his enthusiasm for his work ran deep and genuine was obvious as he described how bundles of cloth would arrive from the cutting room to be transformed by his tailors into a coat. 'Coat,' as I heard then for the first time, was the industry term favoured over 'jacket'.

Each coat tailor had his own role among the team: one affixed the collar, another the sleeves, another the lining, and so on — this approach being a departure, Mr Coombes explained, from the more common and less expensive Savile Row practice of having a single tailor assemble an entire suit. Huntsman's sectionalised system ensured consistency of superb quality throughout. We spent half an hour or so with Mr Coombes, looking at pink fox-hunting coats; the large, check-tweed jackets for which Huntsman was famous; and even a vicuña overcoat commissioned by Rex Harrison. 'How much?' Dad ventured, the businesslike tone now gone from his voice. 'Ten thousand pounds,' Mr Coombes replied. Dad blanched. When we had said our thank yous and followed Toby back downstairs (much easier than coming up), Mr Hall asked us what we thought. 'Very impressive,' said Dad, 'especially Mr Harrison's overcoat.' Mr Hall nodded. 'Ten thousand pounds!' Dad added. 'Christ! I paid less than that for my first house.'

Again I thought we were finished and that when I left Savile Row it would be for ever. But after handing my school report back to my father with a dig about how I 'could've done better', Mr Hall installed us once more in our fitting room for an introduction to Huntsman's managing director.

Colin Hammick was a slim man, tall and immaculate, his hair slicked back somewhat less austerely than Mr Hall's, his ruddy face deeply invaded by generous sideburns and twitching with a nervous energy that was contagious. After shaking our hands he sat down, crossed his legs, and eagerly withdrew a cigarette from a pack he then balanced impatiently on his armrest. Proceeding to lift a light to the filter end he became annoyed when the fag wouldn't take, even as the distinctive smell of burning filter filled the room. 'Excuse me,' Dad said tentatively, pointing, 'but you're lighting the wrong end.' I was mortified. 'Oh, how silly,' Mr Hammick tutted, uncrossing and recrossing his legs a couple of times, at last focusing his enormous globes on me and my school blazer and opening his mouth as though to ask a question. He was interrupted by a knock on the door and the gentleman who'd greeted us when we first arrived poked his head in.

'I am sorry to bother you, Mr Hammick, but Mr Zohrabian is here for his fitting and he is in a terrible hurry — '

'Well,' Mr Hammick said, rising for the door, unfazed — or if anything relieved — by

11

this premature conclusion. 'Nice to meet you.' He said this automatically, his mind obviously already onto Mr Zohrabian's affairs. 'What've we got for him, Gerry?' he asked the man lurking in the door. Barely out of our sight, he began bellowing for backup. '*Toby? Toby!!*'

'Phone us on Friday at midday to see if you have the job,' said Mr Hall, stirred by the commotion and standing to shake our hands. 'We still have a number of candidates to see.' He passed me a card and got the receptionist to fetch our overcoats. Back outside, squinting and trudging through the bright snow, Dad and I were silent, our minds and senses still inside, dumbstruck by all we had seen and heard. I caught the slow train back from Euston to Watford on my own while Dad — satisfied, for the moment anyway, that he had chaperoned me some distance in the direction of a career — went straight from the West End to his own job in Acton as a boiler engineer. When my train finally arrived at Watford Junction, I felt like I had arrived home from Mars.

★ ★ ★

At precisely twelve o'clock on the Friday after my interview, having excused myself from a tedious maths lesson, I phoned Huntsman from the school secretary's office.

'Good morning, Huntsman.'

'May I speak to Mr Hall please?'

'I'll just transfer you.'

Long pause.

'Brian Hall speaking.'

'Uh . . . H-h-hello, Mr Hall, this is Richard Anderson. We met last week, last Tuesday. You asked me to ring about the apprentice cutter position?'

'Ah yes. We would like you to start a three-month trial period on Monday, the 1st of February. Nine o'clock. Is that convenient?'

'Yes. Thank you.' Stunned and dry-mouthed, I managed only these words. Hall proposed an annual salary of £2000. I didn't dare try to negotiate. Pride and anticipation but also a bit of unease jangled inside me as I made my way through the locker-lined halls back to class. Could it really be possible that only three weeks remained of this, my school-governed boyhood, and the commencement of proper employment in London's West End? Naively, I imagined working would mean living more or less in the same easygoing way I'd been coasting through life so far, just without the tedium of chalkboards, teachers and exams; I intended perfectly well to continue wooing Fran, playing football for South Oxhey Pavilion, and partying with my mates Bailey, Hayes, Paul Mettam, Pete Kerrison and John Appleford. Unfortunately, not only would the reality of working life prove a rude awakening, any high hopes I had had for a leisurely swan-song were unceremoniously quashed.

Sister Anthony, the head teacher of St Michael's, my comprehensive in Garston, Watford, was a woman as formidable as she was minuscule. In her early sixties, standing (or rather stooping) just under five foot and favouring enormous bugeye glasses through which she scrutinised the goings-on at St Michael's with tiny knowing eyes, she was respected and admired by everyone — not least for stoically accepting her nickname, 'the Ant'. No more than one hour elapsed between my triumphant phone call to Savile Row and the Ant's receipt of my news — that I was off to bright city lights in only three weeks, forgoing the remainder of my education — and by three o'clock the same afternoon I was sitting in her office with my mother, being ordered by the Ant to clean out my locker and leave St Michael's at once. It had been decided (whether by some committee or the Ant alone, it wasn't clear — although the Ant's authority was so

14

absolute no allies would have been necessary) that my hanging around despite having no intention of finishing the year was bound to be a disruptive influence on my peers. I was gutted. No glorious defiant departure, no farewell celebration; far from sailing out on my terms, instead I would be leaving with my tail between my legs — accompanied by my mother! — and that very afternoon, with lessons in full swing. 'Good luck,' the Ant said through a disparaging smile. Her judgement was clear: I was embarking on the wrong path, a foolish and irresponsible future, one I would undoubtedly come to regret.

The next three weeks passed excruciatingly slowly. Effectively I was in limbo and had nothing to do. Mornings I ran seven or eight miles and afternoons I played football with my friends when they got out of school. My father advised that I would need my fitness working in London — as if I were headed not for a tailoring house but the Royal Marines. In the evenings I saw Fran, who herself was enduring some chastisement from the nun squad for dating a cocky dropout. Some days, anxious and idle, I did little more than pound the streets (well, the rural backroads of Hertfordshire) for hours, wracked with worry that in so flagrantly denouncing a life of diplomas and desk jobs I was making an irrevocably ruinous mistake.

One weekend Dad and I decided we needed to kit me out for my big first day and we made for Marks & Spencer, bastion of middle-aged English correctness, where we ludicrously misjudged a blue pinstriped suit I fancied 'too formal'. Instead, we walked away with an ugly, green, worsted single-breasted number and a bland selection of grey, fawn and white shirts — some of them to my horror short-sleeved. Shoes? Plain black slip-ons. The jacket, a thirty-eight regular, was too big, the thirty-inch-waist trousers too short in the leg. It would be no secret that I was a slave to the early eighties teenage fashion of wearing white socks with black shoes, although this was bound to become a short-lived rebellion.

As D-day approached I became evermore apprehensive. I was the eldest of three siblings in the household and so the first to go to work. Just about everyone older on my football team had also left school early, having likewise forsworn higher education and tiresome desk-bound work, but this was to become construction workers, welders or mechanics. My father was an engineer, my mother a housewife; I knew no one whose trade was tailoring and I had no idea what to expect. Although I know now why Huntsman gave me the job — I was young, mouldable, and despite an ill-advised wedge haircut looked the part — during the days leading up to my apprenticeship I felt certain the firm had made a grave mistake, and that within hours of my return to Savile Row on the 1st of February my sheer incongruity and ineptitude would be exposed.

★ ★ ★

It was bone-chillingly cold as I stood on the train platform at ten past seven on that pitch-black Monday morning. There were only six of us waiting for the branch line to take us from Park Street into Watford Junction, where I would then catch a commuter train to Euston followed by the Victoria Line two quick stops to Oxford Circus. (Dad and I had made a successful dummy run a few days before.) Finally the two-carriage Abbey Flyer appeared around the corner from St Albans and entered the station. Its horn was shrill and bleak. Numbed by the cold, we six punters politely alighted and I found an empty seat in the corner of the second carriage. I remember the 'décor', soon to become a reliably grim feature of my weekday commute: blue- and black-checked upholstered seats that were

17

threadbare and decrepit, exposing broken springs. A group of teenage schoolgirls in green blazers and matching hats shrieked and laughed across the aisle — taking the mick out of the straighter members of our carriage, I suspected, myself included. I felt very self-conscious of my middle-aged suit and Tupperware sandwich box packed by my mum, but managed to keep my cool for the duration of the twelve-minute journey, gluing my gaze to the Hertfordshire countryside slowly brightening outside. Only when the ticket collector came by — a cool, young, black-bearded guy with faux gold hoop earrings and chains around his neck — did I relax the tiniest bit, for his wild gypsy look momentarily rid me of the green blazers' attention.

After disembarking the Flyer I successfully negotiated my way onto the fast train from Watford platform nine to Euston Station. This was a different story: the platform was packed, mostly with bona fide middle-aged men in dark suits, some making small talk but more with their noses in the *Sun* or *Daily Mail*. My quest for a seat was in vain and I spent the following twenty minutes hanging one-armed from the cold metal overhead luggage rack. Again, the journey passed insufferably slowly. The carriage was crowded but virtually silent; Walkmans were not yet ubiquitous and Discmans, mobiles, iPods and Blackberries remained phenomena of the future.

I arrived at Oxford Circus bang on time. The Seiko Quartz clock at the top of the creaking escalators read eight twenty-five.

Perfect.

Now: which exit?

Predictably, I chose the wrong one and wound up turned the wrong way on Regent Street — facing the BBC building, rather than Piccadilly — and it wasn't until I had marched decisively in this direction for several minutes that I realised my mistake. No need to panic, I told myself. Everyone knows Savile Row; just ask. But the Indian road sweeper looked at me blankly, as did a pretty girl about my age, neither of them expressing even a modicum of sympathy to my worsening plight.

Eight forty-five. Panic mounting, ill-fitting suit flapping, I ran the half-mile back to Oxford Circus and down the stairs to the main concourse, searching frantically for a point of reference. None. The station was crowded with people striding confidently for their destinations. It was midwinter and although I wasn't wearing an overcoat, just a jumper under my suit coat, I was sweating

19

buckets, my brand new Marks & Spencer shirt becoming damp and tight.

Eight fifty-two.

And then I saw him: a tall bloke in a navy overcoat lighting a Benson & Hedges with a silver Zippo's enormous flame. It was the apprentice who had shown me and Dad up to the workshop three long weeks ago. Saved! With a thumping heart I ran to catch up with him — What was his name? Not Tony . . . Toby? Toby! — as he strode casually towards the south exit, knocking the slow and inferior out of his way as he went. 'I'm so glad to see you!' I gasped. 'I took the wrong exit, and got lost — ' The smile Toby gave me when he turned around and looked me up and down was one I would come to know well. 'Dickhead,' it said. Cowed into silence, I shut my mouth and followed Toby's calm, unhindered, smoke-wreathed progression straight to Savile Row. We reached Number 11 at eight fifty-nine.

★ ★ ★

My first three months at Huntsman caused me relentless mental and emotional chaos.

Mercifully making no mention of having saved my skin at Oxford Circus, Toby introduced me around my first day — though it would be weeks before anyone other than Toby would address me directly. Mr Hammick, the managing director, and Mr Hall, who had hired me, now roundly ignored my presence, and if anyone else on the 120-person staff wanted some insufferable or degrading task done, it would fall to Toby, who — delighted finally to have his own minion — would turn around and delegate it to me. I quickly learned that working at Huntsman was not unlike being in the army, where one must resist being broken down; no one missed an opportunity to remind me that I was at the bottom of the food chain, the lowest of the low. Endlessly, I carried clothing in different stages of make, or production, up and down the six flights of stairs between the cutting room and the coat workshop. Each day I made dozens of trips to the vending machines or local cafés for sandwiches, chocolate bars, cups of tea, cigarettes and whatever else my superiors (everyone) desired. In time my tasks became ever-so-slightly more important — I might be asked to deliver a finished suit to a client's hotel, but early on this was rare. My basic daily duties were to courier goods internally, fetch staff sustenance, and shadow Toby, my sartorial elder brother. All of this I was expected to do as inconspicuously as humanly possible.

Despite the tangential nature of my role, the actual suit-making process gradually revealed itself to me, if only in the most rudimentary terms.

After discussing with the client his specifications and desires, a master cutter would make the necessary measurements and then construct and cut a paper pattern consisting of five templates: three for the jacket (a back, a forepart and a sleeve) and two for the trousers (a topside, for the front of the leg, and an underside, for the back). Every client had his own pattern, cut not only to accommodate his dimensions but also to flatter the overall figure and complement his individual style. The paper pattern would then be arranged meticulously in a 'lay' on the material that had been selected by the customer, and its perimeter marked out with a piece of chalk shaped something like an oversized guitar pick. This had to be done not only accurately but also in the most economical way, so as to waste as little fabric as possible. The 'striker' would then strike, or cut, the fabric around the pattern and (nine times out of ten) hand these pieces over to the company basters, who would baste them together, which means to assemble them provisionally with long, loose, easily removable white stitches for the first fitting. If the customer's pattern were certain to be current and correct, the cut fabric would be turned directly over to the Heddon Street team for a more advanced assembly.

As I learned on my first day, over a hamburger and Huntsman hierarchy briefing in the Wimpy bar overlooking Piccadilly Circus, Toby had been with the firm for about a year. He had completed a three-year degree from the London College of Fashion, followed by some unpaid work experience next door at Ten Savile Row, Dege & Skinner. Granted a salaried position at Huntsman, he soon established himself as its primary striker for the three chief pattern cutters — Colin Hammick, Brian Hall and Richard Lakey. (Two Richards was temporarily problematic; this was why I became known as 'Young Richard' or, when Hammick was particularly exasperated with me, 'Just William'.) Hammick and Hall each oversaw his own coat department while Lakey cut all of the company's trousers. As my would-be apprentice cutter position put me in their proximity much of the time, and although for the most part they acted as though I were invisible, the main characters in the daily drama of my new existence were Toby and these three men.

Hammick was in his mid-fifties and every day unfailingly maintained the same immaculate appearance I had admired during my interview. In a navy mohair or grey flannel suit, usually over a pale blue shirt and navy polka-dot tie, he chain-smoked, seemingly both to contend with and perpetuate his nervous energy, charming but lethal. Above all Hammick was an artist, obsessed with perfection, his standards defining the superior quality of what Huntsman produced company-wide.

Hall was also a director, though a fraction below Hammick in the rankings, and in contrast to Hammick Hall had a more menacing military air, a manner especially aggressive and formidable when he was grumpy or disappointed, which was most of the time. If Hammick was the idealistic artist, Hall was the methodical workman, and their respective coat-cutting departments — which, annually, would produce about 600 garments — each reflected to an extent this difference in temperament. Whereas Hammick's customers were the gems — Gianni Agnelli, the Rothschilds, Cayzers and Palumbos (not that *I* had a clue who these people were then) — Hall's customers on the whole were of a less glamorous tier, for Hammick had first refusal and made a habit of keeping the ritzier and better-figured ones for himself. Even in my early days in the cutting room it became evident that although Hall was unfairly rarely recognised as having Hammick's 'artistry' he nevertheless was a technically brilliant cutter whose customers, or at least some of them, came to rely upon his oddities. While with his clients Hammick took a more clubbable, overindulgent, softly-softly approach, Hall was cool, verging on rude. A begrudging 'good morning' or 'good afternoon' prefaced Hall's fittings, during which he would speak only if his customer forced conversation upon him. When done he would say simply, 'That's all I need today, Sir', and, while still retrieving the coat from the customer's back: 'We'll send a card when we're ready for you again.' Then, as soon as he could — never mind whether the client was out the door — Hall would beat a fast retreat to the sanctuary of cutting tables, where his private dissection of the fitting's findings would begin.

The trousers cutter, Richard Lakey, also in his mid-fifties, was something of a hero to me, for according to shop lore he had had a promising football career with Tottenham Hotspur until an irreparable knee injury cut it short. He was fourteen at the time, and at his father's urging sought to learn a trade. The choice came down to tailoring or hair-dressing and in the interest of some subtle notion of masculinity Lakey plumped for a job with Horne Brothers and within a year was making trousers and breeches in a heavily bomb-damaged workshop in the West End.

Huntsman took Lakey on in 1960, and although he flourished in his new, more prestigious post, the mounting workload dealt him a series of ailments requiring temporary leaves. And yet for all the pressure Lakey was under, having time and again manfully returned — he was still solely responsible for cutting upwards of two thousand pairs of legwear per year, and managed this despite chronic back pain from years bent diligently over his board — I found him the most friendly and approachable of the three cutters. He was never rude, never imperious, and never held a single one of my countless obtuse questions against me.

In addition to these three men the cutting room was blessed with the occasional presence of Fred Lintott, who, although only in his late fifties, had been at Huntsman for forty-four years, having risen from a 14-year-old cutting apprentice to joint managing director, alongside Hammick. While Hammick presided over the technical side of things, Lintott managed the business — not only at Huntsman but at affiliated children's clothing and shoe shops in Mayfair as well.

Hammick's elder by only a couple of years, Lintott nevertheless held seniority in the hallowed boardroom and sole authority over Huntsman's fabric selection, export and wholesale operations. For years he had been the firm's chief international representative — spending as many as seven months of each year abroad, collecting orders from those of our European and American clients whose busy schedules would not accommodate a sudden journey to London. His experience with children — and not only in the professional sense, for in addition to five of his own he had five adopted children as well — undoubtedly contributed to his warm and friendly nature, even with those of us forever spinning around the bottom of the totem pole, whom he treated like colleagues of long-time affection and esteem. A Member of the Order of the Empire for his work on behalf of tailoring's export business, he was a superb salesman and an immensely popular figurehead. And his charm and good humour, welcome counters to Hammick's perfectionist demands and the ever-dour grumbling of Sergeant Hall, had even once landed him an impromptu appearance filling in for an absentee on *The Tonight Show* with Johnny Carson — a Hollywood stint that did wonders for Savile Row's stateside trade.

The paper patterns that Hammick, Hall and Lakey created for each client would be delivered to Toby's cutting board, a beautiful oak slab twenty-two feet long and three wide, at the very back of the cutting room. In front of this cutting board stood a similar one for Lakey and in front of his was Hall's. Three short steps down was Hammick's department, comprising two more cutting boards and serving as the threshold that divided the cutting room from what we called 'the front shop'. This was the staghead-and-fireplace reception room my father and I had found so impressive on interview day. It exuded formality and rectitude. As a rule (there were innumerable rules; my head spun trying to remember them all), at no time should the front shop feature any fewer than three salesmen plus a receptionist to field calls and greet clientele. Existing customers were addressed by name or title. New customers were called 'Sir' or 'Madam'. No matter how high the temperature, it was imperative to wear a coat in the front shop; salesmen were allowed to disrobe down to their shirtsleeves only beyond Hammick's cutting board, where they would be out of customers' view. Likewise, cutters were allowed to work in their shirts provided they stayed well behind the Hammick threshold until suiting up. Of course, this strictly regulated space was not immune to squalls of panic. Very often a customer would swan in unannounced, expecting a fitting; worse, the garment would be ready but nowhere to be found. More often than not, and usually regardless of whether we were personally responsible for such crises, Toby and I would find ourselves on the receiving end of an ongoing bollocking as we ran from workshop to hanging room and back again, searching racks and board-tops in a frenzy.

When I wasn't bearing the brunt of a bollocking — or being told, as I seemed to be every other day, to get a haircut — I spent my three-month trial period, which spanned the late winter and early spring of 1982, watching Toby. This was my training in how to arrange lays on fabric for all of the pattern possibilities: three-piece suits, coats and trousers, overcoats, hunting coats, morning and dress coats — each of which, as I mentioned, had to be laid out and struck so as to waste as little of the precious cloth as possible. Each lay would be checked by the corresponding pattern cutter before the cloth order was confirmed, giving rise to healthy competitions as to who could achieve the most economical positioning. Hammick, Hall and Lakey were always trumping Toby. One had to take into consideration checks, adding in an extra four inches to allow for matching them up, and one-way cloths had to be cut with all parts of the pattern facing the same way, to avoid shading. Lightweight fabrics such as linens, cottons and silks also had to be cut in the same direction but with an extra allowance for shrinkage. Even at this early stage, each garment's individuality and the attention to detail required were formidably apparent. I was allowed to practise with old patterns and the gargantuan fifteen-inch striking shears, marking and cutting up pieces of mungo, a tailoring term for cheap or leftover fabric. At over a kilo the shears were heavy to lift, let alone cut in a straight and accurate line. All those miles I had run, all those football matches played in favour of fitness — in no way had they prepared me for wielding those massive double-bladed swords.

By the time my trial period neared its conclusion, I had established a routine whereby at ten each morning I would take a shopping list around to Lakey, Hall and Hammick and ask what they wanted from the café up the street. A cheese roll for Lakey ('keep the change,' he would quip, handing over exactly enough); forty Embassy Number 1s for Hall and forty Piccadilly cigarettes plus a fried egg or cheese and cucumber on white for Hammick. 'It is vital, Young Richard,' Hammick told me a hundred times, if once, 'that you watch while they put the salt and pepper on.' Crikey. No one could be trusted to get it right.

'Getting it right' according to Hammick's sky-high standards was not, in those first few weeks, something for which I had natural flair. The frustration I felt when reprimanded for even the tiniest botch or blunder — from failing to fetch the right colour cloth to burdening my master with an oversalted sandwich — was severe, and I frequently wondered whether in accepting this job I had made the right decision. Sitting on the train from Watford Junction to Euston every morning as it rolled sleepily out of platform nine, I could just make out Bailey, Hayes and other assorted contemporaries laughing over some joke of which I ached to be a part while they waited for the 321 bus to take them in the opposite direction to St Michael's. Where I was heading was not safe or fun; it was hard and demoralising. It was also character-building, of course — I know this now. But at cheeky seventeen, what did I know or care about building character?

After one particularly harrowing week during which I seemed to have failed spectacularly at every task flung my way,

Hammick called me into fitting room number 4 and stared me down with disappointed eyes, as ever a lit fag between his lips. It was a Friday afternoon.

'Young Richard,' he said gravely. 'We are not confident this is the trade for you. Why not have a think, and discuss it with your parents, and come back to me at the end of next week to let me know whether you really want to stay.' Punctuated by drags on his fag, delivered with just the right combination of pity, sadness and aggression, it was a classy dressing down that made me feel like putting my head in an oven. I nodded and said nothing.

'Nice weekend,' Hammick said on his way out.

Nice weekend Christ.

I elected not to tell my parents and Fran about this little hiccup. Working the floor at Cheapjack's the following afternoon — I had kept on with this job, which hour for hour paid twice as much as working at Huntsman, where I earned a paltry forty quid a week — I saw Watford through a new lens. I did not want to work at Cheapjack's for the rest of my life. I missed my former life of leisure, working minimally at getting passable school marks and seeing my mates every day — and yet something had happened since my contretemps with the Ant, and since the blank three weeks I had then spent idly waiting for my future to start. I had become interested. *Ambitious*. I wanted to know what I could achieve. And already, just *thinking* about leaving Huntsman, I missed its sounds, its smells, its energy and its characters, however hatter-mad they were. I missed Hammick and Hall's unflagging work ethic, of which I had only just begun to feel an inkling of pride for my small involvement. I missed the whole West End experience, which without my Huntsman employment would have seemed superior to me, a suburb-bound failure. I even missed my meagre salary, without which I would have been hard-pressed to take Fran out for anything other than a glass of water. And fine, being an apprentice cutter was not the same as being a professional footballer, or a rock star, dreams I had harboured for nearly a decade, but working for Huntsman, widely considered the best tailoring house in the world, was *real*, within my grasp, and had a glamour all its own. I could not just walk away. Hammick's gauntlet-throwing had precisely the effect he no doubt intended it to have. The mere suggestion that I might jack it in made my pride surge and my indignation boil over. And when this inner tantrum subsided I resolved to succeed.

Monday morning I returned to work a little earlier than usual and with refreshed enthusiasm set about running my errands, chalking out Toby's striking jobs with speed and precision, and endeavouring heroically to suppress my anger and disappointment when spoken to like a dog. I could sense Hammick's and Hall's eyes on me incessantly, waiting for a slip. The consensus must have been that I would come back just long enough to resign — or perhaps that I wouldn't show my sorry face again at all. But I was determined not to be bullied out. When on Friday, my day of reckoning, I asked Hammick whether he wanted to see me, he looked harassed and confused. What the hell are you on about, boy? I could see him thinking. Either he had forgotten about our conversation the previous week — the interim for me having been a week of persistent self-consciousness and worry — or I had already sufficiently redeemed myself and it was not his style to stand on ceremony with a lad in a cheap baggy coat. But I wanted clarity. Resolution. Replacing his dying cigarette with a fresh one, Hammick shuffled behind me into fitting room 4 and looked at me expectantly.

'I thought about what you said last week,

34

Mr Hammick. And honestly I wasn't sure I was cut out for the job. But I've thought about it and if it's all right with you I'd like to stay.'

Hammick drew leisurely on his fag and studied me carefully. My stomach lurched. Finally he nodded, slowly, and exhaled.

'OK.'

Phew!

At the door he turned round to face me again.

'Young Richard,' he said. 'Was that cutting remark supposed to be some sort of pun?'

'No, Sir,' I said. 'I hadn't even thought of it.'

Hammick looked disappointed.

'All right then,' he said. 'See you next week.'

Just William

The said Apprentice his Master shall faithfully serve, his Secrets keep, his lawful commands every where gladly do.
                              The 1808 tailoring indentures of
                                              George Adeney

Shortly after my gruelling tête-à-têtes with Hammick, Fred Lintott had a stroke in the boardroom and died.

I had just couriered something upstairs to the workshop when its phone rang and Hammick told Coombes the news.

After replacing the receiver, Coombes ceremoniously tapped his shears on his worktable three times, summoning a curious lull in the room's whirr and chatter. 'Mr Lintott has died,' he said, unable to look a single one of the two dozen or so bewildered tailors in the eye. The unanimous reaction was a moving display of incredulity and grief. Whereas between the workshop staff and the managers or cutters of a tailoring house there often prevails a mutually alienating sense of it being 'them versus us', this had never been the case with lovely Lintott, who had made it his habit to establish a personal, friendly and equal relationship with everyone on staff, from Hammick right down to the tea boy. What would the abrupt vanishing of this great equalizing force mean?

After Lintott's funeral, Hammick became sole managing director and effected a slight restructuring. Among other adjustments, it was decided that for one day each week I should assist up in the workshop alongside Coombes and Carmelo Reina, head of the finishing team, to supplement what I was learning about measuring and fitting customers downstairs with some practical sewing basics. Meanwhile, Hall, our minister of efficiency and organization, likewise exercising his own small inheritance of authority, took it upon himself to combat what he considered Huntsman's most egregious weakness — that Toby and I were regularly being caught on the hop by customers who'd popped round by surprise — by devising a system whereby every coat's whereabouts could, at least in theory, be determined at all times.

Each customer was appointed his own little pink cutter card, to be filed alphabetically. Here the order's details were written: a unique job number, a description of the garment ('single-breasted blue fresco blazer', for example) followed by a row of boxes indicating the different stages of make the garment would go through, and by whose hands:

* * *

A tick under ALT or TICKETS meant the customer had met with the company's credit criteria, triggering a ticket issued from the finance office signalling that the making of the garment could commence.

A tick under IN CUT meant that a paper pattern had been created by the master cutter and laid out on cloth by his striker, who would have physically cut the cloth pieces, now ready for provisional assembly.

The initials under BASTER identified which of the company's tailors would be responsible for the basting phase. (When I started, Huntsman had two full-time basters, each of whom was proficient enough to baste together two coats a day.) No pockets or linings were put in at the basting stage; the idea was to create a simple, accurate cloth representation of the paper pattern in pure form. What basting did require was establishing a balanced relationship between the coat's back and foreparts while also accounting preliminarily for what I would come to know as figuration: the master cutter's notes on the customer's bodily idiosyncrasies, such as a slight stoop or uneven shoulder blades. A mock collar made of canvas would be shaped around the neck and more canvas inserted in the chest to give the coat some body. For a new customer it would not be unusual to undergo two or three fittings at this provisional stage to finalise the paper pattern before moving on to the more advanced tailoring, when alterations to the resulting garments could be considerably more costly and time-consuming.

When both customer and, more importantly, his cutter were happy with the baste and ready to proceed, the under-cutter would rip it down — disassemble the coat using a penknife or bodkin, being extremely careful not to damage the material — and then smooth it out for the next phase. The paper pattern would be revised as necessary and placed again on the chosen cloth for re-marking and re-cutting. The resulting pieces would be delivered up to the workshop in a bundle for reassembly initially by Fred Coombes's team. Included along with the basic pieces at this stage would be all the trimmings, to be added eventually by the assembly line of finishing tailors, each responsible for attaching a different facet: Ermazine, Silesia or silk lining; collar canvas and melton; tropical syddo, white felt, horsehair and lapthair canvases for the front body panels; hand silk for fine stitching; buttons and buttonhole twist. The adjusted paper pattern would also be included, for the tailors' reference. This phase of more formal assembly generally took approximately two to three weeks and then the coat would be returned to the master cutter now looking much more like the finished article. The shoulders would have been finished by hand; the side seams, facings and pockets machined securely in; and the hand-padded body canvas and handmade shoulder pads inserted — but still there would be no top collar and the sleeve and body linings would be only basted into place. A tick under FWD indicated that this phase was now complete.

40

When the forward fitting had then taken place, the garment would be returned to Carmelo Reina's team for any remaining adjustments and finishing. Adjustments at this point were expected to be minimal: raising the collar ever-so-slightly, wadding in the shoulders a bit more, lengthening or shortening the sleeves, taking in or letting out the side seams. When these alterations had been made the garment would be turned over to fine-fingered tailoresses who would 'fell', or stitch, the delicate lining to the coat and perform other detailed handwork, such as lining the pockets and stitching buttonholes. Then the suit would be pressed, a highly specialised and underrated stage in itself (a bad press could go some way to undoing all of the work done up to this point), and, finally, the buttons sewn on. When all of this had been done, a tick could at last be made under FIN.

As for the fittings themselves, their dates and times would be scribbled on the card's reverse, and whereas Hammick might more solicitously *ask* one of his clients when he wanted to come in, Hall gave out appointments as though they were court-ordered punishments. 'We'll send you a card in three weeks,' he barked. In addition to being recorded on the back of the client's card, the confirmed date would also be entered in the company diary to ensure the deadline would be met.

Foolproof?

Not exactly.

★ ★ ★

Meticulous and well meaning though it was, Hall's card system was ultimately only as good as the humans executing each of its stages, and in my new capacity as a part-time apprentice to the workshop team I had ample opportunity to prove myself its weakest link.

Every Wednesday I exchanged my shapeless Marks & Spencer suit and dress shoes for a pair of jeans, moccasins and a jumper, and upon arriving at work bypassed the cutting room to head directly up to the Heddon Street workshop — named as such for having an official address on the H-shaped alley between Regent Street and Savile Row — and where things started a little earlier: eight thirty instead of nine. The heavy double doors one encountered at the base of the 19–21 Heddon Street stairwell were the same ones David Bowie had stood next to for the album cover of *Ziggy Stardust* — a coincidence which served merely to remind me that my erstwhile dream of becoming a rock star was now just that: an erstwhile dream. Five flights later loomed the large loft Toby had shown me and my father the day of my interview — where Coombes had proudly wheeled out Rex Harrison's £10,000 coat. Approximately 3,500–4,000 square feet, lined with large windows that gave out onto a sprawling view of West End rooftops, the space was brilliant with a combination of copious natural light and fluorescent tubes suspended above each tailor's board. My post, it was elected, would be smack at the room's centre, directly opposite Coombes and adjacent to Reina: in not one firing line but two, where I could get away with nothing.

Having finally become somewhat accustomed to the bustling atmosphere of the front shop and cutting room — where the pace was fierce, phones rang incessantly, and the cutters and salesmen and office staff were always dashing around, a passionate nervous energy uniting the troops — I found the Heddon Street workshop quiet. Too quiet. The majority of the tailors and tailoresses up there were already beyond retirement age, and those that weren't were certainly heading in that direction. A forty-year Huntsman veteran, Coombes himself was so old that every lunch hour, which began at one fifteen, after gobbling down whatever Mrs Coombes

43

had packed into an old brown Tupperware tub, he would climb onto his cutting board and, using his pressing cushion as a pillow, be asleep by one thirty. His success rate at waking up in time to oversee the punctual resumption of work at two was only about 80 per cent, and yet no one ever bothered to rouse him. It was too much fun when Hammick or Hall would pay a visit to find their foreman still flat out and snoring at three thirty.

Indeed, the only young blood with whom I might bond were a cheerful apprentice named Patrick Hislop, well into his fourth year at the company, and two of the tailoresses: a quiet girl named Dorothy Alvarez, a year or so older than I, and Jane Dawson, about the same age, but whose superiority over yours truly in the pecking order was unmistakable. Working alongside them only one day a week, I enjoyed little camaraderie with these three — who if they had any of Toby's fondness for jokes and hijinks did not find fit to share it with me.

My first training was in ripping apart the basted coats so they could be remarked and recut according to the pattern adjusted as a result of the first fitting. As many as thirty bastes would be hauled up those five punishing flights of stairs either by Toby or myself over the course of a week. Coombes bestowed upon me my own bodkin: a small plastic instrument shaped like a pen with a soft pointed end and used for removing the stitches of a basted garment. The critical trick was to do this at top speed ('Twenty minutes to rip down and smooth a coat,' I had heard Hall bark more than once. 'That's all it should take') without tearing or causing any other damage to the cloth.

The collar came off first, followed by the sleeves. Then the back had to be split down the centre, the makeshift canvas and pads withdrawn from the foreparts, all dead stitches spotted and removed, chalk marks brushed out, and then the garment would be handed first to the presser to be smoothed and finally to the fixer to be remarked for forward assembly. A bundle of a dozen or so basted coats in need of ripping down awaited me each Wednesday as I pushed through the Ziggy Stardust doors and began my ascent skyward. Climbing onto my heavy wooden work-board to sit with my legs dangling a good eighteen inches above the floor, I would begin to rip manically, bodkin flying, as various elderly continental Europeans ambled to and fro, clutching half-made garments, some nodding politely or glowering in my direction, others behaving as though I did not exist.

Ripping down bastes wasn't my only training up in the Heddon Street nursing home. Another early port of call for any aspiring tailor is to pick up hand speed by padding collars and canvases. In fact, in those days it was common for an apprentice to spend a couple of years on these tasks alone before being allowed to progress further.

To pad a collar you would be given what is called an undercollar, which typically measures five by twenty-two inches and is cut on the bias at an angle of thirty-three degrees. Undercollar canvas is wool with light pores throughout, strong yet flexible enough to respond to an iron. On top of the canvas undercollar you would then baste in another undercollar, of melton: a soft fabric in a colour matching the jacket it would eventually adorn. The melton undercollar is what is visible when you lift the collar at the nape and look at its underside.

Regimented rows of tiny angled stitches would give the collar canvas a slight curl, so that once connected to the coat it would lay naturally around the neck. Putting these stitches in was boring, methodical work, but being able to decrease the time it took me to finish one collar from two-and-a-half hours to thirty minutes was pretty satisfying. I was alone in my ambition to pick up the workshop's pace: the tailors who had been working there for decades had no incentive to move faster or increase production. They were geared up to produce twenty-five forward coats plus twenty-five finished coats a week — that was all. No amount of cajoling from downstairs was going to up the ante. And yet it would be contrary to my own work ethic today if I were to fail to acknowledge the quality of the coats that left that room: every last one of them was first class.

As with the collar, the insertion of materials into the chest of a coat to give it shape also demanded extreme care and attention. There would be a length of wool syddo, heavy or light depending on the weight of fabric used for the coat itself, a piece of white felt and a piece of natural horsehair canvas. The syddo would have to spend a night in the Heddon Street sink to shrink, then be left to dry before being pressed. The forepart pattern would then be placed onto the canvas and each side cut. The canvas would run the length of the coat, filling the whole shoulder before angling down through the chest and finishing just inside the front dart. On the forepart a puff cut would be taken to the top of the canvas at the

47

shoulder's midpoint and cut to approximately five inches down. This helps prevent the shoulder from stringing, or acquiring a corrugated look, later in the coat's life.

Then the horsehair would be basted to the chest and the white felt placed on top. Now a dozen or so intricate rows of hand stitches would attach the three types of canvas together and a fourteen-pound iron applied to the layers to finish a light but pliable chest area that over time would actually mould to the unique body underneath.

So for the next couple of months I spent Wednesday mornings ripping down and smoothing coat bastes and Wednesday afternoons working on my hand speed and canvasing technique. Of course, this routine remained punctuated by several daily trips up and down the five flights of stairs, conveying jobs or reporting to the cutting room for my next bollocking.

★　★　★

Soon after I had begun working in the Heddon Street workshop on Wednesdays I was downstairs in the cutting room one Friday morning when the black Bakelite phone to the left of Hall's cutting board gave a shrill ring. Agitated at having been jolted to such an early start, Hall tutted, set down his cup of vending-machine coffee and stretched a long, pinstriped arm around the phone post to extract the receiver from its cradle.

'Extension twenty-six, good morning, cutting room,' he growled, cigarette bouncing up and down in his mouth as he spoke.

It was Mr Reina.

'Holes?' Hall barked. 'How many?'

Without looking up I could feel Hall's uneasy gaze turn to settle on me.

'Ah yes. The one-day-a-week man. I see. Well, send them down.'

Hall slammed down the phone and strode the two paces to his cutting board, then turned around a full 180 degrees to stand with his back to his board, his eyes burning holes in my direction. I did my best to continue marking out a pair of grey flannel trousers while appearing manfully unperturbed.

Thirty seconds later young Patrick Hislop crept into the cutting room wearing an apologetic look. He felt, I imagined, just as self-conscious as I did, if not more. He was only twenty at the time, and one of Huntsman's very few black employees. In his arms he held various limp-looking scraps.

'What's all this?' Hall shouted as though his phone conversation with Reina hadn't taken place less than a minute before.

Poor Patrick, he was just the messenger. It was the first time I'd seen a black man blush. Overawed by the cutting room's formality and Hall's vicious tone, he meekly laid the offending articles — various foreparts, backs and sleeves — before our fearsome director.

'There are tears and holes in all these coats, Sir. Mr Reina thought you should see them.'

Hall's cigarette hadn't moved from the left side of his mouth, and his left eye was now screwed shut against the rising smoke. With right eye alone he glared at both me and Patrick simultaneously.

'Where are the job tickets?'

'Mr Reina didn't send them down,' said Patrick.

'Young Richard, get me Mr Reina on the phone!'

I slinked round to the phone post and dialled the workshop's extension, heart beating, face hot with shame.

'Extension two-one-nine,' answered Reina's voice.

'Good morning, Mr Reina,' I said weakly. 'I've got Mr Hall for you.'

Hall took the phone and thanked me in a voice wracked with disappointment. To Reina he said that new cloth would have to be ordered and so could the job tickets please be sent down so the front shop could organise this. With any luck, enough of the same fabrics would still be available, or the company would have to ring the customers concerned and confess our mistake. 'And I would suggest,' he added before letting Reina go, 'that Young Richard do no more ripping until you're fully satisfied he can be relied upon in this area.'

When Hall had sent poor Patrick back upstairs and turned his full attention to me, he said, 'This isn't good enough, old fruit. There're six jobs here full of holes. *Holes*.' He was right, of course. The coats I'd been ripping down lay before us in what looked like a moth-eaten heap.

'And get a haircut!'

My track record with Hammick was not much better.

'Can you send Young Richard down?' Hammick cooed one Wednesday up the inter-company phone. Coombes and Reina immediately loaded me up with forward and finished coats, eager to take full advantage of my descent.

'Here he is!' Lakey the trousers cutter shouted good-naturedly as I entered, breathless and agonisingly self-conscious of my casual workshop clothes. 'Be careful!' Hall moaned as I struggled to hang a slew of coats on his and Hammick's rails in the right order. 'They've just been pressed!' Then my arms were loaded up again with bundles of new jobs to be ripped down and forwarded or finished. Even as I stood there, waiting to be dismissed from behind a small mountain of tweed, Hammick began to describe for me in excruciating detail the alterations required on a forward double-breasted Prince of Wales check coat spread between us on his board.

'Now, Young Richard,' he said. 'I want you to give this to Mr Reina and tell him I need it for the fourteenth.'

'OK.'

'We need to narrow the shoulders an eighth. The collar needs to be raised a small quarter in the centre back and made tighter and, of course, shorter on the right-hand side accordingly. One extra ply of wadding on the right side and I want one ply of wadding and soft canvas at the front — the front of the left scye.'

He paused to light a Piccadilly from one of the six packets lined up on his board before continuing.

'The left side seam needs to be taken in a small quarter on the double in the waist to nothing at the top. I want the right side seam let out a quarter on the single all the way through . . . '

Toby stood directly behind Hammick, just within my line of vision, distracting me with various comedic hand gestures and face-pulling.

' . . . and I need the right-sleeve pitch to be lowered a quarter, both sleeves lengthened three-eighths, and we'll finish the cuffs with four buttons, three real and one dummy. And lastly but very importantly I want to lower the front buttons a quarter. Now, have you got all that, young man?' He asked this through a heavy drag on his fag, neck muscles twitching and eyes wandering disappointedly over my attire.

'Yes, Sir.'

I made to take the coat from the board.

'Not so fast. Would you like to repeat back to me what we intend to do to the coat?'

Stepping back from his board, closing in on the butt of his cigarette, Hammick gazed at his stuffed alteration rail, as though his mind were already onto the next task, though we all knew an affirmative and flawless response from me was anything but a foregone conclusion.

'Ummm . . . '

The marks on the coat were useless as I struggled to remember word-for-word what had been said. Still behind Hammick, Toby was going purple trying to suppress his laughter. Seconds ticked away while I looked forlornly at the coat in front of me, saying nothing.

'We need to narrow the shoulders . . . ' I finally ventured hesitantly.

'How much?'

'A quarter of an inch.' I tried to sound confident.

'An eighth,' Hammick corrected me. His tone was curt and incredulous. He turned the coat around to inspect it anew while I stumbled forth.

'And we need to let the side seams out half an inch . . . '

'No, that's not right either, Young Richard. We need to take in the left side seam a small quarter on the double at the waist to nothing at the top and the right side seam needs to be let out a quarter on the single all the way through. Can you remember anything else?'

'We need to move the front buttons . . . '

'Which way?'

'Up?'

'No, Richard; we need to lower them a quarter. And you haven't mentioned the wadding needed on top of the right shoulder and on the front of the left. You haven't said anything about the sleeve pitch or lengths.

54

Next time you can't remember everything, *ask*. And write it down. Now take this up to Mr Reina and ask him to see me down here at two.'

As I left the cutting room licking my wounds from this latest defeat I could see Toby bent double behind his board, laughing uncontrollably.

'I'm not sure I should be doing this,' I said to him one afternoon soon afterwards. We were sitting at a small Formica slab next to the coffee machine in the corridor linking the cutting room and Heddon Street stairs.

'What?'

'Ripping down bastes! Padding collars! They're jobs for retired tailoresses! They're for someone nearing the end of a career, not an assistant cutter just starting out!'

This was a bad attitude and I was rewarded accordingly.

In due time my masters deemed me better-suited to working downstairs — which in theory was perfectly fine with me, except that my new appointment was to take over trimmings-supply duties from our current trimmer, Lia Ricci. Miss Ricci was a 75-year-old Italian who after forty years working for Huntsman would be retiring in a couple of months. Arthritis had worked its way into her talented fingers and she wanted

55

to spend the remainder of her years sunning in Sicily with her sister. 'As a progression of your apprenticeship,' Hall said gravely (how else?), 'we feel the trimming position is one that could be condensed into two, maybe three mornings a week after Miss Ricci's retirement. Until then we want you to work with Miss Ricci on Tuesday and Thursday mornings. OK, old fruit?'

Of course, I had to agree, much as it seemed a sideways move into an old lady's job.

About three yards square and situated just to the right of Hall's board in the corner of the cutting room, the closet-like space in which I worked with rotund Miss Ricci was ludicrously cramped for two. Columns of cubbyholes containing various trimming materials overlooked above a single square-yard board on which we were expected to measure out a garment's various linings. Bolts of Ermazine, Silesia, linen edging and melton comprised a spectrum representing every imaginable shade of blue, grey, brown, fawn and lovat, the side-by-side semitones blending together — and, of course, lots of black, white and the trademark Huntsman stripe. Buttonhole twist stood proudly on two-inch wooden cobs, tiny skeins of hand silk slept in drawers, and then there were the buttons, thousands of buttons, in black, dark and light grey, and three shades of fawn, each stocked in three sizes: line forty for overcoats, line thirty for coat fronts, line twenty-three for cuffs. Another Huntsman trademark was the two-hole button. Virtually every other Savile Row firm favoured four-hole buttons, but long ago Hammick had deemed two more elegant and never looked back.

These were the main ingredients for coat trimming, and my job, under Miss Ricci's tutelage, was something like that of a restaurant's sous chef: to collect and prepare them in the correct quantities, qualities and measurements for assembly by someone else. Cutting the lining accurately was the most difficult aspect of this, followed by the painstaking process of reviewing with Miss Ricci each job against its corresponding ticket. For the trousers: six inches of flax canvas to strengthen the waistband? Check. Striped curtain lining for inside the waistband? Check. Silesia for pocketing, more Silesia plus linen to strengthen the fly and fork? Check, check. Once the linen had been cut, the piece would be affixed with a clasp and bar for fastening at the top of the fly; these came in silver and grey oxidised, likewise buckles if needed for the hip straps, again in silver and grey oxidised. Strap buttons (usually two) for the bearer, hip-pocket buttons in flat pearl, fly buttons or zip, in each instance colour and size matching the job ticket's specifications exactly. Add to these a bit of tape or leather, if applicable, to go around the heels; plus two skeins of hand silk, one white for felling the waistband and one to match the cloth; and for a suit with a button fly, a full yard and a half of buttonhole twist.

Once the trimmings for a coat or pair of trousers had been measured out and bundled up, they would be handed back to the respective cutter, who would then assign the coats to the Heddon Street workshop and the trousers to one of the trousers tailors for assembly. Whenever I handed such a bundle to Hammick at the end of a day he would reply with a courteous, 'Thank you, Young Richard.' Lakey would tease me amiably: 'Is this all you've done all day?' Hall invariably grabbed his jobs from me without a word, tossing them to the far end of his board, irritated by their very presence.

When Miss Ricci retired, I was alone in holding down the trimmings fort, three mornings a week. Hammick advised all tailors that no trimming would be given out apart from on the designated days, within the designated times. This rule was nigh on impossible to enforce, with tailors needing various bits of lining, threads and buttons throughout each working day. Dispensing the goods I felt something like the proprietor of a lemonade stand in the Sahara.

Hammick himself had run Huntsman's trimmings room when he was a teenager and the stint had instilled in him a bugbear as to the cost of its supplies. He was frugal to an extreme, and took great delight in opening up a bag I had just filled with the requested goods and determining that I had been too generous with the silk or buttonhole twist. With that dreaded furrow of disappointment over his eyes, he would lay the forepart and back pattern pieces of the coat in question onto the lining I had prepared and chastise me for doling out two inches more than necessary.

One morning, one of Lakey's trousers-alteration tailors came to see me while I was on trimmings duty.

From Mauritius, Markus Berkovic was an excellent tailor who always made the effort to look smart, often working in a dark-grey worsted suit he had fitted and made for himself. Owing to Berkovic's classy demeanour and deft fingerwork, Lakey tended to use him for his most difficult customers' alterations. Berkovic had nonchalantly saved Lakey's skin many times over and generally had the entire staff's admiration and respect.

'Morning, Markus,' I said.

'Morning, Richard.' Berkovic produced a small pattern of a smart fawn-and-red overcheck wool worsted. 'I need some lining to match this cloth.'

'How much?' I surveyed our fawn selection, flipping the lining onto the table, extracting the elastic bands and unrolling some ready-to-cut.

'A yard and an eighth, please.'

'Certainly.'

It was only when the lining had been measured out, cut and handed over — more than a yard of it, enough to line a coat, to a *trousers-alteration tailor* — that the penny dropped.

'Thanks very much,' said Berkovic, winking at me as he pulled a crisp five-pound note from his pocket. He laid it on the sill of the trimmings closet — and suddenly my lemonade stand felt like a drug den. Berkovic folded the fawn lining into a tiny square and carefully stuffed it into his pocket, where it all but disappeared.

'Cheers.' He patted me on the shoulder before walking away.

My salary, at that time, amounted to less than a pound per hour. A much less favourable rate than I had just been offered to hand over company lining in fewer seconds than it took Berkovic to climb the stairs back up to the second floor.

The Mayfair Man

Call him 'milord' and charge him extra. Show him only your soberest patterns but let the material be of the best — that is his main interest. Be deferential (you may even rub your hands) and always escort him to the door. Give him every consideration. Because he is very rich you will have great difficulty in getting your money from him (or perhaps it is because you have such great difficulty in getting your money that he is so very rich). He will complain at *all* fittings as a matter of form. Be prepared for this. If he points out a mythical fault, agree with him and make a technical looking chalk mark. When he has gone, brush off the mark and hang up the garment until the next fitting. He'll take it.

'Profile of the Mayfair Man',
Tailor & Cutter, 1947

Not only was Hall's card system powerless in the face of ineptitudes such as mine, it had no solution for grossly overworked employees

— especially those pushed to the limit by onerous customers.

Dick Lakey, our former would-be Tottenham Hotspurs player, in heading up the trousers department found himself under increasing pressure, receiving countless blasts from Hall and Hammick for failing to meet fitting deadlines and not being able to locate trouser orders when customers came in. In his defence, his workload had become enormous. Certainly it was more than any Savile Row worker would be asked to manage today. While Hammick and Hall each oversaw half the coat production, approximately 600 garments annually apiece, Lakey by this time was responsible for 100 per cent of legwear: in the area of 1200 pairs of suit trousers plus breeches *and* all the odd trousers as well, bringing his unit total to about 2000 pairs a year. On top of this he had to service all of the trousers that came back to us from time to time for alteration. It was far too much for one man alone, never mind a man with a permanent backache from bending over a board half his height.

Around the end of my trial period it had been decided that Lakey needed assistance and that on my non-Heddon Street days I would be his apprentice. Although I was happy enough working with Lakey, who was popular among the staff for his Eric Morecambe-style sense of humour, it meant moving from the backmost cutting board I had been sharing with Toby to the middle board, where I began to work at Lakey's right elbow, directly behind Hall. No more wisecracking. With four rails stuffed with Hall's coats to one side and the pressing iron and damp rag directly behind me, I felt a bit shut in; moreover, the clear, fine view of the front shop I had previously enjoyed was now obscured. Of course, I had so much work to do I had little time for gazing dreamily: my new job was to strike all of the suit trousers Toby gave me, along with all of the odd-trouser orders: the grey flannels, cavalry twills, whipcords, etc. No more practising. I was striking upwards of ten pairs a day, plus delivering the jobs to the trousers tailors as well as trying to keep some semblance of order. The frenzied trousers department defied Hall's little pink cards; we were swimming against too strong a tide.

Trousers underwent only a single baste; then they were fitted on the customer, finished, and fitted once more. Most of the trousers team worked in a separate workshop on the first floor of Heddon Street in a light, airy room headed up by Steve Bikzo, a mad Hungarian. Bikzo oversaw his protégé and apprentice Frank Myers, who like Bikzo basted and sewed, along with the trousers presser, Guy Tanner. When the basting was done, Lakey would fit the trousers on the customer, marking any necessary alterations and changing the pattern so that future orders would not need the same adjustments. They would then be given back to Bikzo or Myers, who in turn would ready them to be finished. The finishers were usually elderly Greek or Cypriot women who would fell the waistband and curtains and create button-holes for the fly and hip pockets. Then Tanner would press them and, *voilà*: they would be ready for a final fitting.

Bikzo was a large, jovial man who enjoyed his work almost as much as he enjoyed a drink. Thick-set, with sloping shoulders and a bushy monobrow, he took great delight in sending up anyone he could, much to the amusement of Myers and Tanner — most of his ribbing, it has to be said, was directed at me. With a perfectly straight face he once asked me to pop round to our trimming stockists, Richard James Weldon, and ask for 'a long weight'. Another day he sent me out for a 'packet of black buttonholes' — and this time I fell for it. 'Sorry,' the Weldon team informed me through conspiring smiles. 'We're all out of stock.' It was not until I returned to Bikzo's shop to find Bikzo, Myers and Tanner breathless with laughter that I realised I had just asked to buy a packet of air.

In addition to me, Lakey and the tailors and presser on the first floor of Heddon Street, the trousers department included another tailor named John Laming, a proper English gent in his sixties who seemed to stand with his feet permanently splayed at ten to two. He had a stoop, small beady eyes and a moustache, and he fancied himself an intellectual. He was always itching to tell everyone how badly the company was run. In fact, the very first time I was introduced to Laming, he said, witheringly, 'I don't know what you're doing here. There'll be no trade in three years.' Laming had been at Huntsman for the best part of three decades and was now 'just waiting to retire'. His work was excellent but slow, and his fastidiousness drove Lakey wild — which was why, while the rest of the trousers team worked together, Laming was relegated to his own out-of-the-way workshop upstairs. His greatest thrill was to descend imperiously to the main shop and accuse Lakey or Toby of having cut a pair of trousers badly. A lengthy technical discussion would ensue, with cutter and tailor both defensively poring over the trousers in question, excitedly pointing out evidence of who was to blame for their flagrant flaws. It was little more than a point-scoring session, of course; more often than not some vague compromise would be reached within a quarter of an hour, each man managing to claim for himself some subtle victory. When it went on any longer than this, Hall, who could endure no more, would turn briskly from his board and bark, 'What's the problem, Dick?!' Then Hall himself would inspect the trousers and issue his own swift and forceful diagnosis. With an air of triumph, Laming would take the trousers back upstairs, feeling confident he had made his point in front of Hall, while Lakey returned to work relieved that Laming had gone away, or at least till next time, and that he would not have to order additional cloth through the casualty book. If Hall felt any relief it was merely that this latest miserable wittering session was over.

★   ★   ★

I had seen enough by now to know that Huntsman's clientele was society's *crème de la crème*, a cast of luminaries that over the years included Gianni Agnelli, Katharine Hepburn, Dirk Bogarde, J.J. Cartier, Omar

Sharif, Sir Douglas Fairbanks Jr, Gregory Peck, Bill Blass, Sir Laurence Olivier, Peter Sellars, Bing Crosby, Paul Newman, Henry Kissinger and Sir Rex Harrison. For the majority, money was no object, and in any case the price was immaterial, factors crucial to the sustainability of Huntsman's superior work ethic: perfection of a garment no matter what the expense. Most of Huntsman's clients had already auditioned every other tailoring house on the Row and precisely because Huntsman was not only the best but also the most expensive, its customers became loyal, knowing they could not demand better elsewhere. Of course, high price tags breed high maintenance, and some customers demanded near-miracles. These were people aspiring to be (or stay) at the top of their game; whether that was business, entertainment, seduction or sport — nothing less than perfection would do. When they liked what they saw, they charmed you to the moon. When they did not, they became brutal.

Among Huntsman's leading practitioners of brutality during my day was a man named Alexander Jarvis. From his prestigious family, owners of the country's largest jewellery business, Jarvis had inherited an enormous fortune with which he maintained a home in

Belgravia Square as well as various supplementary residences in the country and overseas. He had joined his family's firm as a young man, but was so disruptive that his father (also a Huntsman patron, one of the many who would bring his son into the shop when Junior was in his late teens) had had to dismiss him after only two years, following which the disgraced heir had ample time to terrorise London's restaurants, hair salons, and, perhaps most enthusiastically, Huntsman. No other tailoring house would have stood for the bastard. Square-shouldered and wide-hipped, his clean-shaven, tortoiseshell-bespectacled face tipped aggressively forward, hair slicked back and parted on the side in a thirties throwback, Jarvis the Younger went on to become a fixture at Huntsman: intolerable enough first thing in the morning, a monstrosity from lunchtime on, when the Châteauneuf du Pape and Courvoisier began to flow. (It was not uncommon for him to be drunk in the mornings, as well; more than once I arrived at work to find his chauffeur parked on the corner while Jarvis slept it off in the back seat.) If Gerry Cummings, the front shop salesman, dared wish Jarvis good afternoon when he came through the door, Jarvis would respond with a growl and commence a rant gaining in volume and obscenity with each step towards the cutting room, where we tried frantically to detour him into one of the four fitting rooms, away from the other customers. Hammick, Jarvis's coat cutter, treated him with disdain, always relegating his tickets to the back of his clip so that Jarvis had to wait twice as long as everyone else to return for a fitting or finished order. This, of course, only exacerbated Jarvis's ire, and in retaliation he would make a point of waiting until five minutes before closing time to lurch in and, for an hour or more, keep the lot of us prisoner to his wrath. It was the same every time.

Lakey suffered Jarvis the most. Fancying himself a keen sportsman, Jarvis was always ordering tennis shorts and trousers or shooting britches, twelve at a time. In addition, Lakey had to alter all of Jarvis's old trousers, which Jarvis was constantly bringing in for adjustment on the back of some crash diet or binge. When his black Silver Shadow Rolls Royce would pull up, there would be an audible intake of breath in the shop and someone would run to the door to try to gauge the extent of his petulance. 'It's bad,' Cummings would advise us more often than not as a red-cheeked Jarvis stumbled onto the pavement while berating his long-suffering second wife or chauffeur. (One of Jarvis's chauffeurs once came into the shop, shaking, to tell us he had become so fed up with Jarvis that he had driven him all the way out to the middle of Whitehall and left him there.) And while our superiors indulged Jarvis's suggestion that everyone come out to admire his car, with perspiration beading on our brows Toby and I would dash to the hanging room to bring up whatever of Jarvis's was ready for fitting or review.

One day must stand out in Lakey's memory as the worst. He was fitting Jarvis with an order of six pairs of grey flannel trousers. All had been cut with belt loops, rather than with an extension band and strap and buckle at the hip. Naturally, Jarvis claimed to have ordered all six with a strap and buckle and became increasingly agitated as he tried each pair on, expletive after expletive ratcheting up the fitting room's tension, poor Lakey taking it all on the chin. By the time he had donned the fifth pair Jarvis was incandescent with rage and abruptly set about ripping the trousers to strips. Tearing the legs from fork to bottom he threw them at Lakey with full force, fly buttons and all, until an eternal tirade later Lakey looked like a half-wrapped flannel mummy scrambling on the floor to claw back what remained of his dignity.

It would have been enough to put anyone over the edge.

Tommy Jermyn was a customer with a temperament at the other end of the spectrum. In his sixties, he was polite and stylish, his near-daily uniform a double-breasted coat cut by Hammick and full pleated trousers with heavy two-inch turn-ups. Both Hammick and Lakey enjoyed fitting him. His confidence in them was absolute, which allowed us all to achieve satisfactory end results with no gratuitous mollycoddling. Jermyn had a home in Antigua, where of course lightweight clothing is a must, and he was often ordering summer jackets and trousers in weights of nine ounces[1] or less. One particular order was for ten pairs of eight-ounce trousers in white cotton. An order for anything white, coat or trousers, always raised eyebrows in the cutting room, for fear of soiling and marking during the making process. Accordingly, having established Jermyn's trousers pattern, Lakey elected to finish all ten pairs completely out, with no baste, to minimise the possibility of stains.

Gingerly, I struck all ten, checking between each slice of the shears that my hands, blades

---

[1] Per square yard

72

and board were spotless. Lakey painstakingly scrutinised every pair when I was done. Having passed inspection, they were then wrapped ceremoniously in tissue paper and passed to our trimmer, who after a thorough scrubbing of her hands matched up the curtain linings, pocket bags, zips, sewing thread and buttons — every last detail snow-white. Then, but only after much deliberation on Lakey's part, all ten pairs were given to Laming, on the basis that he had a slightly finer tailoring hand than Bikzo, and therefore would be less likely to blemish them during making.

Wrong. On each pair that came back over the following three-week period, small spots could be seen here and there — nothing drastic but still unsuitable for any client, never mind Jermyn, whom we loved. Laming vehemently blamed the finisher — who blamed Laming, of course. There was nothing we could do but send the whole lot to the cleaners.

Two days later all ten pairs were back on the rail, ready to be pressed, gleaming white. Also white, however, went Lakey's face when he double-checked the measurements: the cleaners had shrunk the trousers a half inch in the waist and length. A catastrophe. Now they would have to be altered back to the initial measurements, a costly endeavour that, of course, stood to re-mark or soil the cloth, but unfortunately Lakey had no choice, and speed was of the essence. When all ten pairs were sent back to Laming for letting out in the waist and hems, Hammick and Hall were none the wiser.

Laming heroically turned the trousers around in just a couple of days, and all ten pairs came back to perfect measure — but now the chalk marks Lakey had originally made on the waistband and hems were visible. We couldn't send them back to the cleaners; having been shrunk once they would now retain their size, but a second dry-cleaning bill would mean explaining everything to Hammick and enduring the gaze of those massive sad eyes.

'I'll take them home and run them through the washing machine,' Lakey whispered to me out of Hammick and Hall's earshot. 'They're all-cotton, trimmed in cotton . . . they'll be fine.' And so all ten pairs were packed furtively into a large Huntsman carrier bag and lugged home to Sidcup, where Mrs Lakey did the honours.

The next morning I noticed the bag back in the cutting room. I gave Lakey an enquiring look, to which he mumbled something unintelligible and changed the subject.

In those days Huntsman shut for lunch every day between one and two. The front shop lights went out, the doors were locked, and almost everyone on staff (save Cummings or his fellow salesman Alan Crawford, who took turns fielding lunchtime telephone queries) would leave the premises. Though it occasionally proved a minor inconvenience to some customers, most of them knew and respected this quaint tradition. When Toby and I had devoured the lunches packed by our mums, we would head off for the West End to browse the clothes shops and compare cutting room traumas or the weekend gone by and the one to come. At roughly quarter to two we would return to fortify ourselves for the afternoon with some coffee and a couple of fags. On this particular day, I was on my way to the loo just before lights-up and was startled to see Lakey in the corner of the dispatch department, huddled over a pair of white trousers. On the table in front of him were a saltcellar, two lemon halves and a juicer.

He looked unhappy to see me.

'What's up?' I said.

The metal zips had run in the washing machine, leaving dark heavy stains down the front of each pair.

'Salt and lemon, that's the ticket!' Lakey was saying nervously, trying to convince himself as well as me that a miracle was under way. Frantically he plunged the lemon half onto the squeezer and then sprinkled juice onto the trousers' crotch, following this with a liberal sprinkling of salt. I thought I was in a chip shop. The stains did not seem to be shifting; in fact, it looked as though we were adding a nice yellow one around the grey sludge. But, undeterred, Lakey continued applying his lemon-squeezing and seasoning to all ten pairs and then hung them up like cured meat to dry away from prying eyes, in the room behind the dispatch department where all of Huntsman's old or cancelled garments and models were kept.

The results were not good. Early the following morning Lakey and I stood together in the dispatch room viewing his work in silence. The trouser fronts, particularly around the fly, were mottled with various shades of grey, black, yellow and gold stains. There was also a curious hardness to the material in places — corrugation caused by the salt. Ashen-faced, Lakey racked his brains for yet another solution. To my astonishment, for anyone else would have admitted defeat by now, he announced he was going to give the trousers another ride in his washing machine in Sidcup.

The term 'remake' is one greatly suffered by any tailor, and even more so by the garment's cutter. No matter why the remake is necessary — even if the customer's dissatisfaction is owed to poor tailoring, rather than a bad cut — it is the cutter's responsibility when a job is killed and the garment or cloth, in whatever stage of make, relegated to the designated sad rack of rejects, the Pork Rail. ('Jermyn's trousers? Oh, didn't you hear? They've been porked.') Indeed, Huntsman's cutters so prided themselves on their rarity of remakes that whenever one was necessary the mood in the cutting room for days was as though someone had died. Watching Lakey pack Jermyn's increasingly old-looking trousers into a carrier bag for the second time I could tell his mind was heading that way (together with the trousers) but neither of us could bear to say it. For the remainder of the day Lakey looked miserable.

The next morning, however, he was in euphoric mood. Arriving at the shop a shade tardy he laughed and joked with Hall about the unreliability of Kentish trains and bantered good-naturedly with Bikzo as though he hadn't a care in the world.

77

'Everything's OK!' he whispered happily to me when Hall had left the cutting room for a fitting. 'No more stains. Well, hardly . . . We did one wash and they were mostly gone. One more today and they'll be fine.' As he said this he stood in front of the mirror at the end of my board and retied his Windsor knot with satisfaction.

But the following morning Lakey came in with his head down and asked Hall to view the contents of his bag. One by one all ten pairs were brought out ceremoniously, each one muddier and more tattered than the last. Some had no legs, others no seats, some long gashes down the sides and flies. They looked like they had been dragged through a thorny hedge.

They had.

'What in the bloody hell is all this?' Hall seethed.

'Morning, Brian! Morning, Richard!' Hammick trilled, crossing the cutting room for the office, trailing smoke. 'Good heavens. What a mess. Is this patching? Can we get it out of here as quickly as possible please?'

'No, Mr Hammick,' Lakey said. 'Unfortunately these are Mr Jermyn's white trousers.'

Silence.

'The order for ten placed a fortnight ago?' Hammick said finally.

Lakey nodded.

'What in God's name happened, Richard?'

'The foxes ate them.'

'The foxes ate them,' Hammick and Hall repeated in unison.

'Yes,' Lakey said. 'I took them home to put them through the washing machine after we incurred a few stains during making. But while they were drying on the line in the garden last night, the foxes tore them down and ate them.'

Hand on hip, Piccadilly twitching between index and forefinger, Hammick stared at Lakey, his eyes wide and white. The cutting room, usually noisy with phones and conversation, was eerily quiet.

'What's this yellow and grey on the flies?'

'That's from the salt and lemon.'

To this Hammick and Hall could say nothing.

I knew, if not yet from experience then from shop lore, that there were three official bollocking chambers at Huntsman, all other rooms being too close to the front shop for such scenes. In order of increasing severity, these were fitting room no. 3, fitting room no. 4 (where Hammick and I had rendezvoused twice) and the boardroom.

'Got a sec in the boardroom, Richard?' Hammick said quietly.

79

* ★ *

Jermyn's trousers were duly remade at top speed, under Hall's painstaking supervision. Lakey proceeded manfully with me and Laming helping as best as we could. The order and thus the customer were salvaged, but the ordeal nevertheless took its toll on Lakey, who in the ensuing weeks became paranoid and defensive. 'There're two parts to a suit!' he would shout at the salesmen when they would apprise the respective coat cutter of a customer's appointment without telling us poor bods in the trousers department. And more and more frequently one would see Lakey standing at his board, one hand on his aching back, staring vacantly towards the front of the shop, lost in another world until someone managed to bring his attention back to the unfinished trousers stacking up: bastes just fitted, bastes to go back for finishing, alteration trousers to be booked in, alteration trousers to be put in hand, finished pairs ready for fitting. The piles were so high that at times Lakey could not be seen behind them.

One morning Cummings strode into the cutting room with a bale of navy-stripe tweed cloth on his shoulder, his legs bowing under the weight. 'Lord Keith's coming in after lunch,' he shouted as Lakey stared into the front shop.

'Strawberries,' Lakey replied. 'I haven't got any strawberries.'

Hall turned slowly to look at him.

Cummings halted. 'Dick,' he said gently. 'I said Lord Kenneth Keith will be in to see you this afternoon.'

'I haven't picked any strawberries for months,' Lakey said defiantly.

Convalescence from his latest bout with back pain would take him away from us for three months.

Legwork

Lakey's sabbatical provoked a bit of panic on Hammick's part. We had no trousers cover, no alternative. Long-time coat cutters both, neither Hammick nor Hall had any practical experience cutting legwear.

'At least this will give us a chance to get organised,' said Hall, almost cheerfully — he was a sucker for regimen — as he surveyed the board littered with dozens of pairs of trousers. Never one for bookkeeping, Lakey had always worked from a haphazardly kept diary or, more often, his precariously overfull brain. Hall declared his card system the new modus operandi of the trousers department, effective immediately — but with green cards instead of pink. Lots more writing for me, but at least (in theory) we would know where a pair of trousers was at any time. I was granted the luxury of some rail space of my own on which to hang newly cut and basted trousers and trousers awaiting alteration, and after a week of sorting through the backlog, for the first time in years the large trousers-cutting board was virtually cleared.

Now all we needed was a trousers cutter.

Hammick recruited Arthur Kato, a former Huntsman trousers cutter who had retired several years earlier. It was agreed that Kato would work part-time, cutting patterns for new customers and fitting any customers whose orders could not wait. The more important customers would be fitted by Hammick and Hall and then the alterations passed on to Kato to be seen through the workshop.

Kato was a gentle man, tall and wiry with a large nose and black rectangular glasses. He had conceded to return to work for us three days a week, from nine thirty till four. Not exactly a gruelling schedule, but then Hammick and Hall were in no position to crack a whip, as Kato was doing us a favour and would have been just as happy to stay home watching telly. His arrival worked magic on the cutting room's atmosphere: no longer was it so fearsomely charged; even a word or two of praise could be heard granted Kato after a good fitting or when an alteration had gone well. Praise!? Crikey. I could not believe my ears. Never, not once in my admittedly brief but action-packed tenure, had I heard Hammick or Hall utter a single syllable of commendation to one of their employees. I think I would have been less surprised to find an actual pig flying off with the Pork Rail. These men whose standards and demeanours in concert generally deemed a job no better than acceptable (and more often downright rubbish) were now treating Kato to great shows of admiration. There would be jovial chats among the three men — or rather between Hammick and Kato, with Hall interjecting from time to time somewhat less sourly than usual. Technical discussions were given time and attention previously not afforded and allowances were made and accepted in equal measure. It was as though Hammick and Hall had poor Lakey in mind and were now doing their best to atone — or that there was something inherently defeating about trousers cutting and they were determined not to send another legwear man Lakey's beleaguered way.

For my part I was enjoying the change. Kato was a warm and charming man with nothing to prove, so he was less proprietary with tricks of the trade than Hammick or Hall. With Kato on board, my learning curve took a steep climb. And what with our Hallian card system now underway in the trousers department, things were generally more organised: every morning I would check the diary to ensure we would be prepared for the customers due to come in, and then, an hour before the end of each day, I would log the status of all pending trousers into the green cards and hang the pairs up in their rightful places. I now faced each day with a new confidence and vigour — and spent much less time scrambling around for garments gone missing and more time observing the firm's front axle: the cutting room and front shop, where every job began.

* * *

Every new order for a genuinely bespoke garment begins with the customer choosing his cloth. This is the origin of the term 'bespoke': the customer was understood to have 'spoken for' his fabric.

Several factors go into cloth selection. If a customer does not come in already strongly inclined (or, as once was customary and occasionally happens still, with an already selected and purchased piece of cloth in hand), his cutter will make a series of queries about the garment in question. When and where will it be worn? London in the winter? South Africa in the summer? A December wedding in Dubai? Is it just for a small handful of special occasions, or more frequent wear? Often a cutter will advise a first-timer to start with a cloth that has a bit of weight to it, such as a medium-weight wool, so the first garment made according to the pattern will most accurately and lastingly hold the desired silhouette. If a customer begins to make noises in favour of a fabric his cutter thinks will prove a disastrous match for his purpose or build, the cutter might speak up (it is generally inadvisable, for example, for large people to wear big checks, wide pinstripes and bright colours; and grey- and white-haired men should usually choose a bold blue over a pale grey, as the grey will wash them out), but at the end of the day, it is the customer's suit, and if he wants something clownish or bland, his cutter must oblige.

Choosing cloth does not always call for so much fuss. The fourth-wealthiest man in England once walked into a shop on Savile Row and said he wanted to order some overcoats. The salesman on duty presented the customer with a book of cashmere swatch samples from which to choose. The customer began flipping through the swatches, occasionally earmarking one, until he had been through the entire catalogue, which contained about a hundred samples. When he was done, the customer handed it back to the salesman with four samples pulled aside. Chuffed, naturally, for an order of four cashmere overcoats would make any salesman's day, the salesman said, 'Very good, Sir. Those are the four you want?' To which the customer replied, 'No. Those are the four I *don't* want.'

But for punters who cannot afford to buy cashmere coats as though they are penny sweets, choosing cloth is a very difficult, protracted event — a process often involving wives, husbands, girlfriends, boyfriends, horoscopes, coin flips, dice rolls and middle-of-the-night misgivings. If sufficient yardage is present in-house, a cutter or salesman can always drape a good length of something toga-style over the customer's shoulders to give a sense of what being awash in the contemplated colour and texture will do to one's complexion and frame. Unfortunately, owing to the rising cost of materials and transport, it is no longer common for a house to order and stock such amounts. Today one must generally choose from swatch books, although a cutter can always take his most ambivalent customers round to one of the few remaining local cloth suppliers, such as Scabal or William Bill or Holland & Sherry, for the toga treatment.

As for lining: Huntsman's signature white silk with purple stripes of varying widths was used to line the coat-sleeves and waistband, whereas the rest of the suit would be lined with silk or Ermazine chosen on an individual basis. It became common among bespoke tailors to use a different lining in the sleeves because clothes in earlier times were necessarily very heavy. There was no central heating, of course, and a good majority of bespoke tailoring's clientele lived in draughty castles. The cloth and body linings they would select for their suits were heavy, perspiration-absorbent materials — namely alpaca, which was popular until shortly after the Second World War. But heavy lining limited arm mobility, so many houses went in for a specially commissioned lighter lining used exclusively in sleeves — and occasionally in pockets and trouser waistbands as well, indeed wherever 'thermal' lining was unnecessary — and the signature embellishments made for a smart touch.

Back in my early Huntsman days, Hammick, Hall and the company's proprietors would design and order several fabrics and lining by the sixty-yard bolt for storage in our basement stockroom, a massive space running almost the length of the building, from Savile Row to the rear of the cutting room. The advantage to commissioning certain fabrics prior to receiving orders for them was twofold: the cloth patterns were exclusive to

Huntsman and thus perpetuated its distinctiveness; more practically, it was less costly to purchase cloth directly from the Yorkshire and Scottish mills than to go round to one of the West End cloth shops and buy smaller, already cut lengths. Consequently, Huntsman became known for the striped and large-check tweeds its directors favoured — six-inch overplaids that on the bolt looked unwearably garish but which when paired with the right lining and transformed into an elegant suit worked beautifully. Also down in our massive cloth dungeon were: navy serge for blazers; black herringbone for morning wear; hunting fabrics in dozens of weights and colours, from traditional pink melton to dark-grey; yellow doeskin and heavy wool checks for waistcoats; cavalry twill, Bedford cord, stretch nylon for breeches and jodhpurs — all of these in a range of weights and kept company by miles of cotton for shirting and silk for lining and ties. During manufacture, as they were spun and woven, fabrics consistently received heat and then were smoothed, pressed and rolled tightly onto a bale. As soon as you began to work with it, the fabric would start to relax, meaning that eventual shrinkage would have to be taken into account. Robert Packer, Huntsman's owner from 1932 till 1966, decreed during his reign that a new bolt should lie on our stockroom shelves for at least six months before its cloth could be cut, to allow the fabric to 'settle' naturally. (This practice would be commercially unviable these days; fortunately cloth manufacturing has evolved such that there is less changeability in many of the fabrics used today, and when working with fabrics still sensitive to climate and age tailors take measures — sometimes literally — to compensate for this.) Once one of these sixty-yard pieces had benefited from its hibernation, a seven-yard sample would be cut for display in the front shop while the remaining 53 yards would remain downstairs until selected by a customer.

During any rare lulls in all my meticulous organising, maintaining Hall's cracking card system and running up and down endless stairs, Kato allowed me to alter some of his trousers patterns — under his careful supervision, of course. I was taught how to let out the waist, seat and fork, as well as how to lengthen the legs by feathering (tearing) a piece of paper and carefully gluing said extension onto the existing pattern to achieve the correct measure. Similarly, when a customer had lost weight, we would make the pattern smaller to accord with the new measurements of his seat and waist. If a customer gained back the weight he had lost, the trimmed patterns would be 'let out' again with more feathered extensions and a glue stick.

This painstaking practice was my first opportunity to cut pattern paper, which is a completely different game from cutting cloth. Each cutter had his different shears for cutting paper and for cutting cloth — the paper shears being much smaller, their blades approximately seven inches long whereas cloth blades are ten. And while you might well ask what could be simpler than cutting paper and playing with glue sticks (even I paid attention in primary school), fashioning a highly accurate brown paper pattern with seven-inch shears does not come easily. For days I had to practise just achieving straight lines before I could progress to trimming or extending actual paper legs. Kato diligently checked everything I did, examining the pattern from both sides and running his forefinger along its edge to ensure all was smooth to the touch.

Each time a new customer placed his or her first order with Huntsman, the customer was allocated a number that his cutter would write onto the corresponding pattern. And as I have said: over the years a customer's pattern could change, depending on any balance and weight fluctuations and accounting for evolutions in taste and expanding wardrobes. Huntsman's patterns — which in my day must have numbered in the area of 20,000 — were stored in a large stone basement, down rickety stairs situated just to the left of Hammick's cutting board. Here, across a musty hall from the cloth stockroom, were rails and rails of pieces of brown paper looped together by thick white string threaded through diamond-shaped holes and hung from hooks like sides of beef, three tiers high around a room with a vault-like door. And as many of these patterns packed so tightly together swelled from twelve to eighteen or twenty inches over the years, their owners having grown wide on ale and pie, space for pattern-retention is a problem for tailors, some of whom elect to cut patterns on thinner paper and then fold them to save space. The susceptibility of thinner paper to wrinkling and tearing has always dissuaded me from going this route — a bespoke pattern is meant to be a work of art, after all.

The guard and fetcher presiding exclusively over Huntsman's reliquary of brown paper ghosts was David Pepper, 'The Pattern Man'.

Owing to his decrepitude — by the time I came on board he was in his eighties, and had a lumpy bald cranium with tiny tufts of white hair — Pepper worked part-time, from ten till four. Mid-morning, shortly before our first tea break of the day, the half-mahogany, half-glass door that led from Huntsman's back entrance on Heddon Street into the cutting room would swing slowly open as if by magic — Pepper being too low to the ground when he pushed on the bottom half of the door to be seen from within. Then there would be a pause as he pulled himself up to his full height of five feet and, by way of greeting, wiped the ever-present dewdrop from his nose and surveyed the scene.

'Here he is,' Lakey would singsong.

'Straighten up, Pepper,' Hall grumbled.

'Good morning, David.' Hammick, of course.

Shuffling the twelve or so feet to the clocking-in machine in front of Hall's board, poor old Pepper would again pull himself up, extract his clock card from the metal box on the wall, punch it, return it to the box, and then relax again into his normal stance. All this while Hammick, Hall and Lakey would be feeding Pepper's free hand with scraps of paper on which they'd written the numbers of the patterns they needed for the day's business. This fistful Pepper would then take downstairs — along with the pile of yesterday's patterns to be re-filed — and half an hour later reappear, doubled over as ever, clutching the requested patterns and serving them ceremoniously upon the eager cutters one by one. The rest of the day he would spend in his little subterranean kingdom, solitarily filing and re-filing patterns and bringing up the odd request, one painstaking step up those rickety stairs at a time, face forever floorward. He must have had every bloody scuff and divot on those steps memorised.

'Never lost a pattern in sixty years,' Pepper used to insist, disregarding the half dozen or so he misfiled every week and for which he was teased at every opportunity.

I learned later that Pepper lived a miserly existence, renting a shoebox-sized room off Baker Street and spending a pittance on food and drink; the majority of his wage packets went unopened and remained stashed in a drawer for years. His elder brother was a high flyer, an Oxford graduate and master of physics who had written books and lectured worldwide. Pepper was evidently cut from different cloth. All his life he looked after the patterns at 11 Savile Row, his only other duty having been — prior to the installation of our vending machines, at Hall's initiative — pushing an unwieldy tea trolley and urn around the firm, a task requiring two hours in the morning followed by another two in the afternoon and which I imagine had something to do with the old man's postural fate.

When Hammick, Hall or Lakey needed a pattern urgently, Toby and I would try to outdo each other as to who could be the noisiest going down the stairs and then frighten nearly deaf Pepper out of his shoes by shouting the pattern number in question. 'What did you say?' Pepper would ask, jolted from his pattern-filing reverie, wiping his nose. Toby or I would repeat the number and then be treated to the priceless sight of Pepper picking up and repositioning his step-ladder in the vicinity of where he expected that number's pattern to be. Now came a suspenseful moment. Never mind Pepper's precarious perch: if the pattern in question was not in its rightful place, the crumpling expression on his face was heartbreaking. 'Lost another one, eh Pepper?' Lakey and Hall would taunt him when he came up to confirm the news — but not before having quadruple-checked his charges. Lakey once went so far as to hang an old pattern outside, on the iron gate along the street, and when Pepper arrived through the back door Lakey asked him to fetch no. 4826 from downstairs. Pepper spent the best part of an hour ruffling around in his vault before

Hammick called down: 'Oh, David? There's a pattern on the pavement. Might it be yours?'

I remember watching Pepper making his way to retrieve it and thinking to myself that, perhaps from being down in that musty old basement for so many years, wearing his faded brown overalls and creased in half, he had come to resemble a pattern himself.

When a pattern had been cut by Hammick, Hall, Lakey or Kato, and the complete paper doll turned over either to me or Toby for cutting the cloth, the fabric in question would be delivered to us usually by Cummings, who, trying to make the job look easy, would rise from the basement with the large bale on his shoulder, legs as ever bowing under its weight, and thump it like a corpse onto my or Toby's board to be struck. It would then be returned to Pepper's neighbour in the basement, a grumpy old Indian named Mr Desai. Desai wore a large surgical boot and callipers on his right foot, for his right leg was considerably shorter than his left. It would be nice to report that Desai took as much pride in looking after the cloth in his protectorate as dear old Pepper did with his patterns, but alas this was not the case. Desai was accurate enough with his cutting, and diligent in keeping the ledgers up to date, but like an angel of death he took every visit from anyone upstairs as an opportunity to let us know what a 'junk company' we worked for. He took every last second of paid sick leave afforded by his contract and by five thirty on the dot he would be off, moving as fast as his gimpy leg would allow up Regent Street, stopping only to extract the evening papers from the litter bins situated on his way to the Tube.

Working downstairs under Kato also meant more time with the alteration tailors. In addition to the Heddon Street workspace there were two alteration workshops at 12 Savile Row, reached via a door in Number 11 and a flight of stairs up to the first floor. Most tailors' workshops are fairly quiet places, aside from a peaceful buzz of machines and limited small talk. Twelve Savile Row, however, was raucous with humour and debate — most of which stemmed from the relationship between the workshop manager Reno Inglima and the presser Michael Granger.

Inglima was a short, middle-aged Italian with lank dark hair and a serious work ethic. He was a brilliant tailor whose talents had been recognised early by Hammick after Inglima's initial trial on Heddon Street, where he spent a couple of days basting with Coombes. Instead of joining in the main team of either forward-makers or finishers, Inglima was tapped to work closely with Hammick as his main alteration tailor. Any alterations, new or return, pertaining to Hammick's customers went through Inglima and his small tailoring team. He was a godsend to Hammick. Significant alterations to finished coats can be dangerous. One needs an extremely skilled hand to alter shoulders or collars and in some cases to save an order from being cancelled altogether by an unhappy customer. Inglima was of a rare breed of conscientious workmen for whom no alteration was too difficult or too much.

Inglima's sparring partner was Granger, one of the very few of Huntsman's tailors still under forty. Stockily built, moustached, sporting a seventies footballer's perm, he was definitely the Joker in the pack — the first face you would see as you pushed through the heavy brown double doors of the first-floor workshop and, in my case, walked into a volley of good-natured abuse. Granger had joined Huntsman five years earlier, having trained under and eventually taken over from Jack Collander, top presser for nearly forty years. Granger was extremely keen to notify everyone of his own top-presser status, his confidence dented not even when hauled over the coals by Inglima for failing to press a sleeve-head flat or allowing too much roll on a lapel. Hammick, too, regularly berated Granger, summoning him down to the cutting room with a dour 'pop down old chap'. Granger would arrive at Hammick's board with the look of a naughty schoolboy who has been caught with his hand in the biscuit jar; duly he would be taken into my old friend fitting room no. 4 to endure a lecture about how this coat, and this one, *and* this one, failed to meet Hammick's exacting standards. All had to be re-pressed. To Granger's credit, he always took these tellings-off well, agreeing with Hammick that he probably 'wasn't concentrating' or 'was talking too much'. Arms laden with the rejected coats he would trudge back to the first floor where a giddy Inglima would jump on the wagon to take him to task.

Directly above this motley crew was the second alteration workshop housed in Number 12, slightly smaller with just enough space for five tailors.

The leading bully in this room was Michael Downey, an Irishman who was charming when sober but, when drunk, became a mad rascal capable of picking a fight with a spool of thread. Many mornings, after walking tardily past Hammick's board with cracked glasses and blackened eyes owing to another contentious night in the pub, Downey would ease into his workday by climbing atop his tailoring board to pontificate slurringly, usually on politics or religion. Swearing and ranting while everyone else struggled to keep his head down and get on, Downey could spend an hour or more effing and blinding each hapless sewer in turn. Barely five feet, sporting a slight paunch and a faint odour of whisky and urine, he was like a fugitive leprechaun. He was given all our old jobs, jobs the other tailors refused: cumbersome hunt coats to be let out, relined and repaired; dirty old coats needing half-moon elbow patches or leather piping along a frayed front edge. Much of Downey's value as an employee was in his willingness (once he sobered up) to do such work. In fact, the older and grubbier a garment, the more he enjoyed resuscitating it, usually while chewing on sandwiches he had grilled with his pressing iron.

Mr Hall Will See You Now

By the time the prognosis from Sidcup came through — Lakey's latest recuperation was nearing completion and he would be returning at summer's end — I had been deemed proficient enough to strike all of Hall's jobs. I can now recognise this appointment as a blessing critical to my technical development (and organisational capabilities) but at the time I felt woefully put out.

Although I could see it was not all roses, I envied Toby's relationship with Hammick. Hammick knew everything about his customers, from pending orders to permanent idiosyncrasies — how many coats Mr Newman had on the go, which cloths Mr Agnelli was likely to fancy, whether Mr Peck was a single- or double-breasted man. But all of this was kept in his head. To Hall's chronic consternation, Hammick had no daily diary to work from and considered Hall's precious card system a bureaucratic bore, so if Hammick was out of the shop or in a fitting when one of his customers turned up unannounced, we were stuffed. Hammick's drafting in of Toby to do all his striking while also becoming privy to the style and tactile preferences of the firm's swankier clientele conferred on Toby an unofficial head boy status I coveted sorely.

And yet, it has to be said, Hammick's reputation with understudies was not good — at least not from the understudies' point of view. Trade-wide, Hammick was notorious for being a reluctant teacher, cryptic and stingy with praise. The four or five apprentices who preceded Toby had all given loyal service for three, four, five or even six years each — but when it came time to step up and cut a pattern, they fell. All of them were presentable, stylish, intelligent and conscientious. They were certainly more than good enough to run five flights up to Heddon Street every ten minutes and keep Hammick in well-seasoned fried-egg sandwiches and Piccadillies. Some of them were even good enough to strike what is called 'noble', our most expensive yardage, from cashmere to vicuña. But Hammick wore them down. After three, four, five, six years of this — of feeling permanently stalled, of there being no perceptible movement whatsoever towards the Promised Land of Pattern Creation — they would quit. In Hammick's defence, I am sure he would say that if any one of them had demonstrated sufficient aptitude and enthusiasm, he would have jumped to give the lad a chance — but no lad ever did.

Toby, however, seemed to have got over this hump. He surpassed his predecessors and after just a few months of working with Hammick was acknowledged good enough to alter his patterns, much in the same way I had been allowed to adjust Kato's patterns after a fitting deemed it necessary. But in the Huntsman hierarchy Arthur Kato was no Colin Hammick. None of Toby's predecessors had been entrusted with Hammick's patterns except to lay them down on a piece of cloth and cut *around* them, leaving their exquisite edges untouched. But with Toby, once Hammick had fitted a customer at the baste stage and noted the alterations he wished to make to the paper pattern, he would mark it up and hand it over to Toby to execute the changes. 'Now Toby,' I would hear Hammick intone as though walking an aspiring surgeon through a lobotomy, 'we need to take a good eighth off the front edge, we need to deepen the scye a quarter, we need to lengthen the back balance three-eighths, and we need to shorten the right sleeve a sixteenth.' That's right. Hammick worked to the *sixteenth* of an inch. Show me a lobotomist who can work to the sixteenth of

103

an inch using ten-inch shears.

After the new pattern was cut, it would be placed over the old pattern to double-check that all the ordered alterations had been made. Sometimes it would be days before Toby produced an altered pattern that met with Hammick's satisfaction. When one finally did, the customer's style details would then be noted and pinned to the pattern's forepart for the tailors' reference and Toby would move on to the next alteration.

While all of this bonding between teacher and pupil (or master and servant) was going on between Toby and Hammick, I was trying to form a similar working relationship with Hall, without much success.

Working for Hall was like training for the SAS. Spurred on by his barking orders, I rushed from workshop to workshop, tailor to tailor, delivering, retrieving and enquiring about the status of jobs. Nothing was ever done right. *Ever.* Hall made a convincing show of hating every last tailor, every last human abacus on the office staff — hell, every last person in sight. Especially me. Usually for having done no worse than relay the news of someone else's cock-up, I was treated to a constant stream of verbal abuse.

And yet even more despicable than I to the eternally put-upon Hall were his customers.

Woe betide the salesman who took a call from a customer who wanted to come in after four — or, for that matter, during lunch or either of the day's fifteen-minute tea breaks. Or first thing in the morning. This left a very brief window of time — about forty-five minutes in the early afternoon — for a customer to come in for a fitting with Hall without having to suffer his oft-practised look of death.

Another luckless messenger was our receptionist, June Glasspool.

From the cutting room we would hear the switchboard ring and June answer.

'Ah yes. You would like to come in this afternoon, Sir? Let me just check with Mr Hall . . . '

The switchboard was near the front of the shop, encased in mahogany and frosted glass, and it was a long walk from the switchboard to Hall's station.

June had a curious gait — her knees preceded the rest of her by several inches — and whenever she spoke to anyone, even our most timid customers, she blushed violently. Leaving the safety of her confessional-like cubicle to approach Hall she would clutch her notepad to her chest and lower her head meekly. By the time she had trooped up the three small steps that served as the threshold between the shop and the cutting room — Hall's lifted eyes boring into her, daring her to speak — her cheeks and ears would have very nearly flushed to match her burgundy-dyed hair.

Trembling, she consulted her notepad.

'Excuse me, Mr Hall, Mr Theodore would like to come in this afternoon.'

Now Hall kept his eyes on his work. 'Which Mr Theodore?'

'Oh. I'll just check.'

June clumped back to the switchboard and returned a moment later, clutching her notepad as if it were a bullet-proof vest.

'Mr S. Theodore,' she said.

'Junior or Senior?'

'Oh. Let me just check.'

A moment later, a little out of breath now, our beetroot receptionist approached Hall for the third time.

'Mr S. G. Theodore the Third!'

'When does he want to come in?'

'This afternoon.'

'What time this afternoon?'

'Oh. I'll just check.'

Toby began to snigger.

'Between four and five,' June returned to say.

'Where from?'

Silence.

'*Where is he coming from?!*'

'I don't know!'

106

'Well *ask* him!'

Again, June went to the phone, this time to ask one of the most prestigious names in finance where he would be coming from. Meanwhile, irritated as hell, Hall turned to Kato.

'You ready, Arthur?'

'I'm ready with the grey stripe.'

'What? Why? I'm ready with the navy mohair. Why did you get the grey ready? It's a lightweight.'

'I thought it was the stronger of the two.'

'Christ.'

June returned, breathless and nearly doubled over on the stairs. 'Mr Theodore is coming from the country and expects to be with you at four thirty, traffic permitting.'

'Tell him we're not ready.'

Hammick was as indulgent and patient with his customers as Hall was intolerant and brusque. This applied even to our most trying patrons, perpetuating a vicious circle: Hammick's indulgence encouraged their trying behaviour, much as indulging a child breeds a brat. In fact, I often wondered whether it was possible that Hammick's and Hall's contrasting client manners came down to the fact that Hall had children and Hammick did not. Hall used to say that it so annoyed him to be awoken on Christmas morning he would doctor the calendar so his children would be unaware of when Christmas morning was.

As for Hammick's indulgences, an especially vivid specimen was The Impossible Oppenheim. A Bavarian-born financier with houses in Switzerland and France, Olivier Oppenheim had been a customer of Huntsman's since the sixties and had such sway over Hammick, whose fastidiousness he latched onto with a vengeance, that all of Huntsman's other production would be halted for the benefit of his clothing. He would visit London approximately four times a year, staying a week at a time, during which panic and confusion would reign over 11 Savile Row. Oppenheim would always have five or six garments on the go at once, but he so enjoyed being the beneficiary of Hammick's relentless pursuits of perfection that he often left a garment with us for years, so that over time it would have to be re-cut according to slightly different patterns, adjusted to account for weight and balance fluctuations, and flights of fancy, and fickleness . . . In short: there was no end to the fiddling with them in sight. Add to this that Oppenheim invariably arrived for his fittings with an armful of old Huntsman-made items for 'improvements' and Hammick's sessions in the fitting room with him could last four hours at a time.

Hammick was the only person at Huntsman Oppenheim would speak to. Our fine front shop stewards, faithful Cummings and Crawford, knew when Oppenheim barrelled in not to expect even a nod or a grunt, never mind a good morning or good afternoon. Whoever was on duty would simply turn on his heels and walk to the back of the shop to let Hammick know his time was no longer his own. Hammick's round orange ashtray always had two or three cigarettes smouldering in it at any one time, but the announcement of Oppenheim's arrival was a cue to light a fresh one and inhale it down to the butt in a matter of seconds — his last hit for some time. Jacket on and buttoned, sleeve cuffs yanked into position by a quick forward fling of the arms, Hammick would give a reluctant parting glance to his Piccadillies, grab Oppenheim's latest pile of bastes, forward fittings and forward-forward fittings, and head for fitting room no. 1. Fitting room no. 1 was our grandest by far, off-limits to any other customer when Oppenheim was in town. Had Jesus Christ himself dropped in for a fitting at the same time as Oppenheim I think Hammick would have stuck him with Hall in poky fitting room no. 4.

Oppenheim's trouser fittings were a moot point. Lakey, who by now had returned from his three months of recuperation (to find me, or so he said, sitting in exactly the same place as when he left), was no exception to the everyone-but-Hammick-is-invisible rule, so when it came time for Oppenheim to try on trousers Hammick had to join Lakey in the fitting room and act like an interpreter for the United Nations. 'Tell him,' Oppenheim would order Hammick, in reference to Lakey, who was standing two feet away, 'that the trousers are too short and too large in the waist and I don't like the way these pleats fall. And this material, Mr Hammick — is it the same as I've had before? It seems a little lighter in weight . . . ' 'Yes,' Hammick would pander, embarrassed and probably a trifle anxious to be treating our tenuous Lakey in this way. 'Yes, yes, he's got that, Sir — he's going to take the waist in about half an inch and lengthen the legs a good one-eighth at the front, to a small three-eighths at the heel on the right, and lengthen the heel just a quarter on the left leg . . . And we'll see to that fullness between the pleats, won't we, Mr Lakey?'

'Yes, Mr Hammick.'

Mrs Oppenheim would always accompany her master, believing herself equally above addressing anyone other than Hammick. She had a penchant for massive hats that came down well below her eyes, bowing out saucer-style so that with her waifish figure she looked like a floor lamp. Her 'shade' proved something of a hindrance in the fitting room, where she fancied herself a good judge of the proceedings but in actuality could not have been able to see much other than the Oriental rug — the rug and Lakey, anonymously scrabbling around on it to adjust and readjust her husband's turn-ups.

When the Oppenheims finally took their leave, Hammick, flushed with exhaustion and shaking from nicotine withdrawal, would return to his board to repeat his cartoon Piccadilly trick and then instruct me or Toby to clear the fitting room of its wreckage while he summoned Inglima down from the alteration workshop.

Inglima, knowing who had been on the premises, appeared trepidatiously at Hammick's board.

'Mr Inglima. Who are you working on at the moment?'

'The sleeve pitches and float you wanted for Mr Colbert's three coats. You said you needed them tomorrow morning by ten.'

'Leave them, old chap. I want these done for Mr Oppenheim.'

When Inglima had duly received instructions from Hammick on how the coats should be altered — a process involving the trying on, by Hammick, of each and every coat himself — Hammick would then turn to Hall, who for his part would have been doing his best to appear indifferent to this farce, though he knew perfectly well what was coming.

'Oh, Brian,' Hammick would coo. 'Any chance I could use Chris for some alterations on Mr Colbert's coats? They're quite straightforward. It's just that Mr Oppenheim has gone and done his usual and brought back a load for altering . . . '

Sitting quietly on his stool, Hall grimaced at the prospect of losing his only coat alteration tailor for the best part of a day.

'Chris is chock-a-block, I'm afraid,' Hall would reply. 'I've got two full relines for Al Said, plus Doctor Walz's three dinner jackets to let out for the weekend.'

'It's only Tuesday, Brian. I'm sure Doctor Walz doesn't need all three for the weekend. Why don't you phone him and I'll get Chris down and explain what I need done to Mr Colbert's coats.'

As if poaching one of his tailors were not enough, Hammick would pinch one of Hall's Embassy Number 1s on the way back to his

112

own board. Once he even had the gall to ask Hall for a light.

Hammick's complaisance with him knowing no bounds, Oppenheim's hold over Huntsman extended to non-tailoring matters. Hammick would organise Oppenheim's entire London stays — which galleries to visit, which exhibitions to see, which plays to take in, where to dine. When the staff and management at Claridge's were so insulted by his behaviour that they threw Oppenheim out of his suite, it fell to Hammick to spend the best part of a month wining and dining Bill Gustave, head of the hotel, in order to get Oppenheim back in his good graces. And the closest Oppenheim came to thanking Hammick was to call and ask him to order some food for Mrs Oppenheim's dog.

Savile Row West

In 1956, at the age of just sixteen, Brian Lishak set foot on Savile Row for the first time and never left. Having studied textile technology at college he was waiting for a place at Leeds University and needed a job to earn his keep. He responded to a newspaper advertisement for a junior sales assistant at Huntsman and within a week of pitching up had fallen in love with the company's clothes, clientele and perfectionist strivings. He trained selling ties and socks while also dabbling in a bit of shirt-cutting and after a few months was promoted to the front shop, where he assisted Fred Lintott in showing customers the various cloths at their disposal and taking orders for suits.

At this time Huntsman was still owned by Robert Packer, a human dynamo who had built up the business enormously since taking it over in 1932, when the Great Depression had New Yorkers jumping off ledges and the international tailoring trade was floundering. Packer was a Row-trained cutter himself, but he was also a seasoned businessman, having owned a successful company in St James's with his half-brother. He was practical, ambitious, charismatic, and could sell stripes to a zebra. Particularly shrewd in arranging a viable marriage of efficiency and craft, he insisted upon a profitable rate of production without allowing the quality of his employees' output to slip. By the time Brian came on board, Packer was eighty, and would continue to run Huntsman actively and on-site for another ten years — until four weeks before his death, at ninety.

It was in part Packer's ownership that elevated Huntsman's reputation from that of merely a reliable gaiter and britches maker to a glamorous bespoke fashion house unrivalled except perhaps by Anderson & Sheppard for the world's most illustrious patronage. Parisian designers came over *pour le weekend* to see what new cloths their Huntsman contenders had put in stock and found themselves face to face with Yul Brynner, Julie Andrews, Marlene Dietrich or Yehudi Menuhin; one of the Kelloggs, Florsheims or Hearsts; a Maharajah of Jaipur or Jodhpur, or the President of the Central Bank of Iran. Such an ego parade would cause any 16-year-old from Meopham to feel out of his depth, but Packer, recognising Brian's promise, took the boy under his wing, advising him as to how to deal with this or that Lord or

Lady and even (more than once) defending Brian against a long-time customer's unwarranted wrath. Bowling in one afternoon, one such high flyer ignored Brian's greeting and tried to push past him for the back shop. Brian detained the man by asking his name — prompting the customer to explode in an unintelligible hollering fit until Packer came gliding down the shop to intervene, saying with just the right combination of courtesy and chastisement: 'You really shouldn't have a go at this good lad — he's never seen you before. He couldn't possibly have known your name.' The customer backpedalled at once. His name? Simon Christopher Joseph Fraser, Fifteenth Lord Lovat and Fourth Baron Lovat, after whose estate the colour itself came to be called. Brian has not forgotten it since.

It was a Dickensian-esque era when cutters and salesmen still wore uniforms of black coats, stiff collars and striped trousers, and not only Huntsman's customers but its employees as well were addressed by title and surname — all but Brian, so young everyone called him by his Christian name, usually as in 'Brian, where's this?' and 'Brian, fetch us that.' Aristocrats tended to be Savile Row's most egregious offenders in the overdue-payment department and more often than not it fell to Brian to approach Viscount or Milord with an outstanding invoice and request to discuss 'a rather delicate matter'. And, of course, there were the Oppenheims of the day, holier-than-thous who spoke only to Packer or Hammick's predecessor, Cecil Pressland, looking at the front shop boy as though he were a rodent — if they deigned to look at him at all.

But, as we know, every new boy on Savile Row must pay his dues. And Brian's hazing paid off. To his father's disgust, he scrapped the idea of going to university altogether, and by the time another young salesman, six years Brian's senior, lost his travelling privileges for spending too much time on the road chatting up girls, Brian had so distinguished himself with his poise and precocious salesmanship that he was offered the gigolo's ticket to go to America instead. He was only seventeen.

As with many other houses in and around Savile Row, as much as 60 per cent of Huntsman's business was done in America. The most fruitful zone was the Eastern Seaboard, from Boston to Virginia, although there was considerable business to be reaped throughout the rest of the country as well: in New Orleans, Chicago, Kansas City, Denver, Houston, San Francisco and, of course, Los Angeles, where the rise of the movie business had studio execs referring stars and starlets to their British tailors with orders to smarten up. In the late fifties such trips to and around America were made entirely by boat and train, which meant that the average sojourn for anyone wanting to give the vast country a good scouring lasted at least four months.

With Lintott, Brian began his first journey from London to Southampton to board one of the Queens, which proceeded then to sail to Le Havre to pick up more passengers — by which time Brian had exchanged his travelling suit for his bathing trunks and was trying out the luxury liner's swimming pool. Upon entering the Bay of Biscay, infamous for its fierce weather, the Queen hit turbulence that left Brian standing in less than a foot of water, the rest of it having lurched out of the pool and onto the deck. A massive storm kept the ship stationary for thirty-six hours, all engines on full just to maintain position — and a journey that in good weather took an average of five days stretched to eight. The SS *France*, twelve hours ahead, was so badly damaged she had to turn around for repairs. And when the Queen finally did creak into New York Harbor there was a convoy of ambulances waiting at the dock to attend to casualties.

Bad weather would send a ship's crew

scurrying to rig its massive stairwells with ropes the passengers could grip for stabilisation. But in late December and early January, when tailoring missionaries generally made their annual pilgrimage abroad, a typical ship would have carried far fewer passengers than its capacity, and for the most part the stairwells and common areas would be nearly empty. Of the travellers one *did* see milling about, the majority were tailors: seasoned seamen who had mastered sailing without getting green about the gills. As a matter of pride in the newest member of their guild, Brian's colleagues ordered him not to be sick: get lots of exercise, they said, by walking around the interior promenade; drink copious amounts of port and brandy; and eat hearty meals. Whether thanks to this advice or some native robustness, Brian never did get sick — not on his inaugural voyage to America nor on any of the dozens of transatlantic crossings he would make on Savile Row's behalf thereafter.

Most of the tailors travelled in cabin class, something like the equivalent of business class today, while there were also first-class cabins and, of course, steerage, which during Brian's youth was lively with American troops travelling to and from their peacetime stations. On smaller boats, many tailors were able to afford first class, and lived grandly for a week in palatial suites with sunken lounges and crystal chandeliers. If you wanted lobster for breakfast, lunch and dinner, you had it — although many of the travelling tailors drank the majority of their food allowances, liquor going some way to alleviate the loneliness (or perhaps enhance the relief) of so many months away from sweethearts and families back home.

Even after docking, the tailors remained a close-knit crowd. In New York they would stay together in either the Roosevelt, still today at Forty-fifth and Madison, conveniently just north-west of Grand Central, or at the erstwhile Murray Hill or Biltmore. The latter became so well known for accommodating British tailors that if a policeman making late rounds on the corner of Forty-third and Madison ran into a well-dressed drunkard with an English accent he'd steer him straight up to the hotel's twenty-first floor — aka Savile Row West. After about a month in New York, the tailors would move on. Many went to Philadelphia, where they would stay at the Bellevue-Stratford — the Tiffany- and Lalique-bejewelled 'Great Dame of Broad Street' and eventual birthplace of Legionnaires' disease — and then west to Chicago. Amtrak, a government-subsidised rail network conceived and authorised by Nixon in 1970, was still a monopoly of the future, so the tailors' interstate travel was via privately owned and highly romanticised railroads, with the now-extinct Railway Express providing the luxury service of picking up your luggage from a hotel in one city and delivering it direct to your destination in another. Travelling luggage-free was a considerable bonus for Britain's tailoring reps, who had to tote so many essential wares: trunks stuffed tightly with cloth swatches, a duplicate of every pattern available back in London, and sufficient model coats to fit and attract every possible prospective new order: lounge coats, over-coats, dinner jackets, waistcoats, riding and hunt coats for both men and women — and not just one sample of each design but multiple models to fit a wide range of sizes and display each master cutter's distinctive style. Add to these dozens of models and blocks a motley array of ties, handkerchiefs, cufflinks and socks with which to dress Americans from Wall Street to the Hollywood Hills and you had much more than a tailor (none of us known particularly for our brawn) could lug through a dozen cities America-wide on his own.

'America is one long expectoration,' said

Oscar Wilde, and indeed while many Americans were very rich many of them were also uncouth to the point of punctuating fittings in fine hotels with tobacco-and-saliva fires into a spittoon. They looked up to their English tailors. It was an honour to be received by these dandies in bowler hats and pearl stickpins and shown not only how to dress but also how to behave according to British etiquette. One dour old Scot representing a tailoring house on the Row used to treat his American customers with complete and utter disdain — and for this they adored him. He was an exoticism, after all: he carried a silver-topped cane, dressed in the old de rigueur black jacket and striped trousers and even a top hat, and either did not know or care for the old adage about the customer always being right. One day he had finished his work at one of the Manhattan hotels and was turning his mind towards the evening's eating and drinking when there came a knock on his door. When he opened it the man standing there said he wanted to order some suits. 'Do you realise what time it is?' sneered the Scot. 'Yes,' said the American, 'it's five-oh-five. I was held up a little but I'm here now for my five o'clock appointment.' 'I'm sorry,' the Scot replied haughtily, 'I don't see anyone after five o'clock.' 'But I want to order some suits!' the customer cried. '*Sixteen* of them!' Unfazed, the Scot told his latecomer to ring at nine thirty the following morning to see if he could be fitted in — and shut the door.

From Chicago the tailors would take the California Zephyr through Kansas City, stay there for two or three days, then continue on to Denver, then Oakland, then San Francisco — and then back east, but via the south: Los Angeles to Phoenix, Houston, New Orleans and Middleburg, Virginia, where a single crossroads served as the town centre and there were only two hotels: the Red Fox, which purported to be the oldest inn in America, and across the street the Old Colonial, where well into the fifties there was no electricity and the youngest of the all-male waiting staff was eighty-five. (The tailors who stayed there went down the road to conduct business at the local lamp-lit saddlery shop.) If a black man approached you on the street he would take care to cross to the other side. Backwardness aside, Middleburg was a gold mine for Savile Row, particularly Huntsman, for many of the wealthy politicians and socialites who gallivanted there seemed to have decided that Huntsman and Huntsman alone could dress them to their satisfaction. Moreover, the headmistress of a fancy girls' school in the area insisted that if her young charges wanted to ride horses they had to do so in proper English style, keeping Huntsman in orders for ladies' riding jackets and britches for years.

Unlike at Huntsman, or indeed on the tailors' more urban stops in America, everyone was on a first-name basis in Middleburg. In the evenings their customers invited the tailors out for hobnobbing and drinks (bootleg, for Virginia had not repealed Prohibition) — and it was like an episode of *Peyton Place*, a country club swarming with supremely wealthy luminaries, affairs conducted unabashedly left and right. Everywhere you looked you saw Mrs So-and-So with Mr So-and-So-Somebody-Else (although, perhaps needless to say, philandering wasn't limited to the Americans: more than one travelling tailor managed to secure for himself a wife on each side of the Atlantic) and the general mood was clubby almost to the point of familial. Brian once arrived at the Red Fox to be told they could not give him a room, although he had reserved one weeks before. A prominent political figure had come down from New York, the manager explained apologetically, and needed several rooms for himself and his entourage. The manager had not been able to say no. He offered Brian the hotel's lounge in which to display his coats and cloths, but Brian would have to find somewhere else to sleep. As Brian stood in the lobby considering his options — which were meagre, for in those days if you were visiting Middleburg you either slept at the Red Fox, the dim Colonial or on a bench by the side of the road — Franklin Delano Roosevelt the Third walked in, spotted Brian, and his face lit up.

'Brian!' he exclaimed. 'How are you? I had no idea you'd be here!'

'Well,' said Brian, 'I'm here all right, and in fact you've done me a very bad turn. I've got no rooms because of you.'

'Oh, don't worry about that. I'll get a couple of the girls to double up!'

The length and infrequency of trips to America by representatives of Savile Row meant, of course, that American customers had either to be satisfied with fewer fittings or wait years for their orders to be done. When journeys to America were made by boat, the travelling salesman would take an order abroad and the cutters and tailors back in London would finish the suit straight out and send it to the States with no fittings in between. Results were not always ideal. Photographing one's customers abroad is common practice today, but for surprisingly long it was unheard of. Brian, on his second trip to America, became one of the first, probably *the* first, to take a camera along — a massive, bulky camera, with a flashbulb that had to be changed after every shot. Standing approximately five feet away from the customer (and, if necessary, toeing the spittoon out of the frame), he would take both a front and back view plus one from each side to capture the coat's balance and sleeve pitch. New customers would also be photographed in their shirtsleeves, to convey an accurate sense of natural posture and provide a point of comparison to the effect of the block coat. Then the trousers: again from the front, back and each side. All of this documentation made it much more difficult for the cutters back in London to blame any imperfections on their salesman's 'inadequate' measurements and notes.

The advent of air travel heralded the end of many tailors' glorious transatlantic sailings. By the time Hammick was in charge of Huntsman's bespoke division, six-to-eight-hour flights had replaced week-long boat crossings, facilitating multiple trips per year, which allowed for multiple fittings between when a foreign customer's measurements would be taken and when he or she would receive the finished product. By the seventies, Brian and Lintott were splitting the American trips, starting together in New York for a week at the Biltmore and then heading off in separate directions, one west, via Chicago, and the other south, via Baltimore. After six weeks they would meet up back at the Biltmore for a further week to catch the New Yorkers who had been out of town the first time around. Two of these eight-week trips were made religiously every year, and what with travelling throughout Europe as well, Lintott and Brian were often away from Huntsman for up to six months annually. When Lintott's health began to fail, it was left to Brian to plough the furrow abroad alone.

★ ★ ★

As a 'reward' for his efficiency and organisation, Hall was on the receiving end of the vast majority of the orders Brian would bring by the ledgerful back from America. American orders were something of an allergy to Hammick: usually, given an American order he would drag his heels for months. Too many times Brian and Lintott were taken to task by some irate American who had planned a transatlantic trip entirely around his much-anticipated Savile Row fitting only to arrive at Number 11 and be told we were 'not quite ready'. Hammick relegated his American orders to the very back of his ever-bulging ticket-clip in favour of his more prestigious pets. A New Yorker once placed an order for a black cashmere overcoat, but Hammick failed twice to prepare himself for the requested fitting date, forcing old Mr Packer to wheel out the usual apologies: 'I'm afraid we're *still* not quite ready, Sir. He is an *artist*, you know; I promise it will be well worth the wait.' The customer stormed out, reappearing three years later to enquire whether the overcoat he ordered nearly four years earlier was finally ready for its first fitting. Brian was away and panic gripped the cutting room as Cummings enquired if anyone knew a Mr Aiken.

'Not one of mine,' said Hall, strumming confidently through his pink index cards.

Smelling trouble, Cummings ducked into the office and a couple of minutes later emerged white as a ghost to approach Hammick.

Hammick, on the other hand, was cool as ice. 'I don't think he's one of mine, Gerry. Have you heard anything from the Oppenheims? They're supposed to be in next week.'

'Er, no, Mr Hammick, but I'm afraid Mr Aiken is quite irate — he says he ordered his overcoat four years ago and we've never been ready for a fitting. Pearl says the order was indeed made and paid for four years ago

'. . . and that it was booked to yourself, Sir.'

In due course, a bundle of black cashmere was extracted from underneath Hammick's cutting board, grey with dust.

'I'm afraid we're not quite ready, Sir,' we heard Cummings murmur up front. 'Could you come back next week?'

Needless to say, Hammick's perfectionist ethic was not much of a viable business tactic if conducted in a vacuum and reserved for favourites. For all his respect of Hammick's work, Brian suffered great frustration, working diligently to secure orders on the company's behalf only to have them scuppered by Hammick's obstinacy. The final straw came when an American visiting from New York arrived at the shop with his two strapping sons. They had been referred to Huntsman by another client, and Brian spent over two hours with the three men, in the process managing to double their order from one suit apiece to one suit *and* a casual coat *and* a pair of trousers apiece. While the eager trio waited in the front shop for confirmation of their first fitting, Brian went proudly to Hammick's board and announced that the Torkelsons — three new customers in one go — had ordered three two-piece lounge suits in plain grey and navy worsteds plus three single-breasted tweed sport coats and three pairs of trousers, all from shop stock. The men were staying at the Connaught and wanted to come back at the end of the week for their first fitting and carry out the rest with Brian when he would next be in New York.

By any measure, the sale was a coup, but the prospect of cutting three new patterns and getting them basted inside a week prompted Hammick simultaneously to extinguish one Piccadilly and light another while eyeing his stuffed clips of orders waiting to be cut. He inhaled slowly.

'I'm sorry, Brian. I just can't do it. I'm up to my limit. I can't get a baste done for three weeks.'

'But I've got three new customers here — two of them in their early twenties, potential customers for fifty years, hell of a nice family, recommended by one of our best clients . . . '

'I'm *sorry*, Brian. I can't do it.'

When Brian trudged back to tell the Torkelsons that the earliest Huntsman could achieve a first fitting would be the best part of three weeks, the Torkelsons went next door to see if Poole's could be more accommodating.

By this time Brian was an institution more or less on equal footing with Hammick and Hall. But Edward Packer, who had inherited

Huntsman from his father, was disinclined to relinquish any shares in the company, leaving his two master coat cutters and premier salesman out of the loop. The decision was particularly disillusioning for Brian, who after twenty-seven years of dedicated service felt he deserved at least a small stake in the fruits of his labour. Never mind that Brian had minimal control over whether the company would keep a promise he had made to a single client on Huntsman's behalf — he had no control over any of the greater business decisions being made, including the very real possibility that Packer Junior, having no children of his own and already well into his fifties, could cash in by selling the company whenever and to whomever he chose.

Reluctantly, Brian began asking around and eventually left to become a partner of Wells of Mayfair, around the corner on Maddox Street. Not one of Savile Row's big guns, Wells nevertheless had a prestigious history, a solid clientele, and beautiful premises spread throughout four floors, including its own on-site workshops. Wells produced just as many garments as Huntsman was putting out at the time, and while the quality and consistency of the work was not quite in the same league, Wells had a loyal following and some genuinely talented cutters. The company's owner admired Brian's aspirations and passion for the trade and swiftly agreed to make him an equal partner as well as manager of all overseas travel and marketing.

I, for one, was crestfallen by Brian's departure. The defection of Huntsman's most prolific salesman for a rival firm left a gaping hole not only in our ordering but also among the managing personnel, whose righteous quirks (Hammick) and rudeness (Hall) would no longer be mercifully offset by Brian's smiling, buoyant, can-do personality.

The development did give rise to an interesting question, however: who would take over Brian's travelling duties? He and Lintott had built up so many confidences and friendships with their overseas clientele over the decades it seemed impossible that anyone could effect a smooth transition.

Packer Junior, Hammick and Hall decided that just one annual visit to America should be undertaken — in January, for two weeks — and that the company should bother only with the East Coast, staying one week in New York and a couple of days in Boston and Washington each. Hammick's track record with the Yanks having been taken into account, it was further determined that Hall should be the one to take over from Brian — with Toby in tow to help.

Envy's warriors screamed like banshees in my ears. Never mind the unappealing notion of being bunkmates with Hall, I would have been willing to suffer bunking with a thousand Halls to be called up to such a prestigious position. Making matters even more excruciating, the States-bound boys were permitted to choose some new free togs for their inaugural trip — Brian Lishak's long-time devotees had to be won over and retained, after all; his successors had better look stylish — which meant that from my perch at the end of his miserable board I had to watch Hall cut himself a beautiful fourteen-ounce single-breasted navy mohair coat and trousers *and* a gorgeous single-breasted thirty-ounce fly-front black-and-white herringbone overcoat. 'Perfect,' Hall said with what passed for excitement in his repertoire, 'for those bitter January days in New York.' Toby was permitted to select two suits from the company's ready-to-wear selection. He chose the very dark-grey chalk-stripe double-breasted I had been eyeing for months as well as a heavy navy serge that if I had not wanted previously I certainly wanted now. These beauties would be fitted and altered by none other than Lakey and Hammick, whom Toby even had the audacity to ask if the plastic buttons could be exchanged for the horn ones used in bespoke.

It seemed to me that everything happening in the shop now was geared to the forthcoming trip, with Toby's relationship to Hall fast becoming the cheeky filial one I had tried for so long and failed to achieve. It was almost as though they were about to go on holiday together, the way Hall eagerly pored over his bloody cards and maps and Toby strutted around in his horn buttons. Flights and hotels were booked (smoking accommodations all round), updated calling cards sent out to all our American clients, value estimations made for the customs form that needed filling out, smart new models in four different chest sizes cut and run up to and from the workshop by yours truly. Toby had also inherited the role of company photographer and spent a good portion of each day 'getting the hang of' Brian's old 35mm Nikon by running around the shop snapping subjects as though he were David Bailey. It was almost enough for me to throw in my bodkin and run round to Maddox Street myself for a job.

Hall and Toby's plans had one advantage for me, despite my lagging well behind in the local popularity stakes. Toby had to learn basic fitting from Hall, lest they find themselves having to handle two customers at once. Toby needed to know (at the very least) how to put a coat on a customer properly and how to record basic balance and figuration adjustments, and I was invited to stand in on these lessons. They took place at lunchtime, when all lights in the front shop went out and Toby and I, stomachs grumbling, would head for fitting room no. 1, where Hall, annoyed to the hilt at being denied twenty minutes of his own hard-earned lunch hour, would begrudgingly 'borrow' either Cummings or Crawford, our stay-behind alternates on the lunchtime phones.

'First,' Hall instructed, 'bid your customer good morning or good afternoon.' (Hall himself was never very convincing with such pleasantries, but never mind.)

'Then, if the customer has come in wearing a coat, help him out of it and hang it properly on a hanger.

'Now take a careful look at the figure before you.'

At this point Hall began circling Cummings to point out his various defections.

'Note the sloping milk-bottle shoulders, the slight paunch, how the head is carried slightly too far forward, how prominent the seat is, the bow legs . . . ' Cummings, taking one for the team, did his best to look like a bona-fide punter, staring straight ahead into the mirror. Toby and I scribbled in our notebooks furiously. Hall then ran a tape around Cummings's chest — forty-one inches, let us say — and asked me to fetch a single-breasted 42 block model which he then put on Cummings himself.

'You cannot simply 'throw' a coat onto a customer. You must hold it carefully on either side of the collar, along the crease edge, and, standing behind him as he lifts his arms, guide the coat all the way on until it sits comfortably on the back of the neck. Then you move round to the front and, facing the customer, put your hands inside the coat's shoulders to pull the customer's shirt back into its natural position. Double-check that the coat's shoulders are lying as naturally as possible. A poorly positioned coat will prompt pointless alterations and hide the critical figural flaws you need to address.

'Now let your eyes fall to the coat's front bottom edge and decide where the button or buttons should be. To pin the front edge into place, drag the left forepart over the right, ensuring the girth is neither too tight nor too loose and also bearing in mind that the customer might have failed to stand still since you checked the shoulders . . . '

A block coat that was slightly too big for

the customer would be chosen, precisely because of its adjustability. Wearing the 42 I had fetched, Cummings's deficiencies became wincingly apparent. His sloping shoulders caused the coat to 'break', or come loose from the body at the ends, while its collar fell low around the neck, almost below the shirt collar. At this point, Hall explained, it was a coat woefully out of balance, no better than an off-the-peg.

With his white chalk, Hall began to mark the coat where it needed adjustment. Everywhere, evidently. He decorated its surface thoroughly with hash signs, single horizontal lines, single vertical lines, single lines crossed by double lines, double lines crossed by single lines, triangles, and two murderous slashes across the back of Cummings's neck. He then removed the coat from Cummings's back and dismissed Cummings with a sigh-laden thank you for his ridiculous frame.

Next victim.

At forty, Crawford was the junior-most member of our sales team, a cheery Scot with a body about as opposite to Cummings's as you could get. He was tall and bony and had a dropped right shoulder, a large right hip, a protruding left shoulder blade and a flat seat. For some reason Hall enjoyed terrorising

Crawford even more than most of his interlocutors, and so seemed actually to brighten up a little for this particular mock consultation, which quickly had Crawford grimacing meekly. When Crawford's chest had been measured Toby fetched from the stockroom a 40-long coat in which Crawford's top left shoulder fit perfectly but his right disappeared. The back of the coat kicked out, straining against the prominent left shoulder blade. The right sleeve twisted and the side seam pulled tightly, belying Crawford's large right hip. Starting again at the back, Hall moved round the coat, marking its collar and side seams before bending down to check the sides and sleeves and then crouching to see if the bottom front and back lines were parallel and the single button in its rightful position. As he dashed his chalk this way and that all over Crawford's arms and torso — finishing with an angry-looking scribble on one shoulder — his eyes never made contact with his 'customer's', instead remaining always on the coat. One assumed this suited Crawford just fine.

To sum up, Hall advised me and Toby that this cripple, too, would never look passable in off-the-peg or ready-to-wear; bespoke was the only safe option for such an unfortunate figure. When Crawford had been relieved of this humiliating pageant and slinked off, Hall turned to the two coats he had marked up and began to explain each of his chalk signifiers.

First, the coat fitted on Cummings.

Hall explained that there were two ways to deal with Cummings's low collar and sloping, 'milk-bottle' shoulders: either by inserting more wadding and canvas into the shoulder to build it up and ripping off the top collar and raising it up by a good half-inch, onto the inlay left at the top of the back neck — or, in more dramatic cases, by ripping open the back's side seams in order to 'pass them up' and picking up the shoulder ends from 'nothing at the neck point'. In Cummings's instance, Hall had elected for the first measure, which was slightly easier and less costly.

Overall, the coat itself was a little large, so Hall suggested reducing the side seams by a quarter-inch each while also reducing the front edge by three-eighths each side — each trim indicated by a single line where the new edge should be. Finally, the sleeves both needed to be shortened by five-eighths, again indicated by precisely positioned single lines.

Now Crawford's coat.

The right shoulder needed to be picked up

and 'crookened on' — indicated by the angry-looking scribble — and the shoulder seam needed to be opened out, picked up three-eighths 'on the double', and the seam passed over a good one-quarter in order to stop the collar from falling away from the neck. On the left back Hall had drawn a hash-key sign, indicating that the left side seam would have to be ripped open and passed up to give more length over the prominent left shoulder blade while the right side seam had to be let out half an inch over the hip from 'nothing at the top'. Finally, the right sleeve needed to be taken out and repitched back a quarter and both sleeves lengthened by a good one-quarter.

'Good,' Hall said when the front shop lights came on, signalling the end of lunch. Toby and I were still struggling to get down all he had said. 'That's enough for today. Brush the chalk out of these coats and put them back on the rails. Next time we'll put you two fruits into some coats and see how you look.'

Every day during lunch, trying out our various new manoeuvres under Hall's displeased glare, Toby and I both became all thumbs. But we kept at it, practising with ready-to-wears, bastes, and forwards from the hanging room, working our way through the staff's motley range of 'cripples', Toby taking photos at each stage. The art of pinning the front edge alone took weeks to master. The pin had to be inserted at a forty-five-degree angle through the left forepart just enough to catch the right forepart such that its bottom edge would lie flush with the left's. Then a turn of the pin to bring it back out again, leaving a good quarter-inch of silver gleaming on the left forepart. Then take your chalk out of your own coat pocket, choose your button position and mark it with a clean white mark.

Chewing his lunch, Hall would check in regularly to rubbish our efforts, jutting his chin at the mirror to point out that the already pinned forepart was significantly lower than its mate, a classic indicator of the coat having been 'thrown on', or an incompetent pinning of the front edge — or both. 'Practise on the goddamn dummies, you prats,' he would say helpfully on his way out. 'They don't move.'

At last I was learning something tangible in the fitting department, but at the same time it was a gruelling game. All the more so because whereas Toby was off to America for the real deal with state senators and Wall Street moguls, my own immediate future was likely to involve little more excitement than listening to Cummings and Crawford compare lunchboxes.

The Friday before Hall and Toby left, Toby and I were having our mid-morning coffee and fag break around the little Formica thing that passed for a table in the Heddon Street corridor when the cleaning lady passed us on her way out.

'See you next week!' she called.

'Not me,' Toby crowed. 'I'm off to America.'

The cleaning lady asked why I was not going as well.

'Because he's not good enough,' Toby said.

Which maybe I wasn't.

Not yet.

Three Guys

Reverberations

When 14-year-old Lakey joined the sartorial ranks in 1943, London was still smoking from the Blitz. His father accompanied him into town from Hackney for an apprentice sewer interview at Horne Brothers. After about a year learning how to thread buttons, cross stitch and back tack, Lakey confided in an older colleague that he enjoyed the nature of the work but was eager to progress. The colleague pulled him aside.

'Listen,' he said, 'if you really want to get on, go up to the West End. Here you'll learn sewing; *there* you'll learn *tailoring*.'

Good advice — in theory. Prestige aside, wartime tailoring was a brutal calling that only the halest and most frugal contenders survived. Decades of immigration by highly skilled Cypriots, Italians and Swedes yielded fierce competition for too few jobs. (Arguably the best tailor of the late nineteenth century was a Swede named Scholte, who Robert Packer used to say 'made the best shoulder in London'.) In 1912, the trade's struggling journeymen organised a wage strike, which was plotted in the local pubs and would involve some street-marching to the 'Marseillaise'. However, their employers retaliated in part by simply recruiting new workers — including the East End Jews, reportedly willing to work for one penny less an hour — and five weeks later the strike collapsed. Three or four tailors, each working for a different house, would share the rent to work together in one little room — often a windowless, dimly lit and poorly ventilated dungeon with insufficient counter space and a sole sewing machine. What was known as a 'jumper', a specialised machine worker, would 'jump' from workshop to workshop to do all of the machine work: side seams on trousers and long seams on coats. The jumper had to be good and quick and would be paid by the tailors, who in turn were paid by their houses — but in dribs and drabs for piecework, not a steady wage. The houses did not care how or by whom the work was done, just that it was done properly, and, except for the long seams, entirely by hand.

And then there were the bombs.

Still, all Lakey knew at fifteen was that he liked to sew but did not want to be a dressmaker. He won a new job as an apprentice britches tailor with Moss Brothers, whose tailors worked out of various workshops throughout Soho and the West

146

End. One of these was struck by a V-1 flying bomb while Lakey worked on the top floor — the doodlebug bounced off the roof just before detonating, obliterating the building next door. Another shop was on Dean Street, in an old Georgian house near the Royalty Theatre, and had already been blasted to tatters. The balustrade to a massive spiralling staircase had crumbled away such that grown men ascended on all fours to minimise vertigo and their chances of taking a five-storey fall down its core. Here Lakey worked with half a dozen other tailors around a discarded bumping table, one of precious few surfaces not thick with ash and dust. A tailor stationed on the floor above had a wooden leg — everyone always knew when he was in — and sometimes would bang his pegleg on the floor, causing debris to rain down on the men below. 'Have you got any white basting cotton?' he would shout, and little Lakey would climb up to stand on the table and pass the thread through a hole in the ceiling.

To further his prospects, Lakey paid for evening tailoring classes he attended three nights a week, nine months a year, for the next four years. After a further two years in Scotland fulfilling his obligation to the Royal Air Force, he returned to the West End but a decade later was fed up with tailoring. Working in bomb-damaged buildings, ten tailors to a toilet, everyone arguing over who was going to pay for a cleaner — it was a dismal life. Suicides were common and daytime drinking so popular that if a cutter popped round to a workshop to find one of his tailors not there his workmates would say: 'Check the White Horse, and if he's not in the White Horse, check the Windmill, and if he's not in the Windmill, check the Blue Posts . . . ' During the slow seasons of winter and summer there was too little work to go around, and in the busy months of autumn and spring tailors could not afford to decline assignments even if it meant sleeping on one's board to save commuting time. Occasionally, one's indignation at such thankless servitude overwhelmed, as when one of Lakey's superiors tracked him down on a Friday evening and loaded him up with britches to be finished by first thing Monday morning. Lakey took the britches, threw them in the cutter's face, and, wearing his sole bespoke suit — a brown birdseye he made for himself in his evening classes — went round to Huntsman to ask Robert Packer if he might need a new junior cutter.

Until the early twentieth century, the tailoring houses on Savile Row and in the immediate vicinity, the trade's so-called Golden Square Mile, were primarily regimental outfitters. Each British lad who joined the top military regiments was required to be dressed by an official regimental tailor and each tailoring house had its own speciality. Huntsman, founded in 1849 by Henry Huntsman, had incorporated a 'gaiter and breeches maker' dating back to 1809 — thus, Huntsman's regimental contribution would be riding britches. It was a fortunate speciality, on at least two counts: first, britches came in so many different styles and colours to accommodate every anticipated purpose — dressage, defence, polo, ceremonial dress, wear in colonies where lightweight material was preferable, and so on — that in the ledger you would often see an order for as many as fifty pairs of britches for just one soldier. Second, an expertise in britches easily evolved to include fine recreational country and sporting wear, soon winning Huntsman the first three of many eventual royal appointments — to the Prince of Wales in 1865, the Duke of Edinburgh in 1876 and Queen Victoria in 1888. By the turn of the century, Huntsman's six fitting rooms were always full. At one point, the demand for fine equestrian wear raised the company's overall production rate of military britches and mufti, the term for civilian clothes, to more than 2500 units a year.

After Frank and Harry Huntsman joined their father's business and the company moved to Savile Row from Bond Street in 1919,[1] this massive britches operation was headed up by a cutter named McSweeney (the father, coincidentally, of Brian Lishak's eventual business partner at Wells of Mayfair). McSweeney's partner in crime was Bill Short, aka Shortie, a less proficient but more prolific cutter who wore a pearl stickpin to work and fancied himself God's gift to the ladies. By the time Lakey joined these two in 1960, britches were, of course, no longer a major military requirement — the army had long been building itself up with tanks in lieu of horses — but the firm still filled the occasional recreational order until McSweeney and

---

[1] The company moved into Number 11, originally built as a private residence in 1773, when Piccadilly's population had grown such that the private gardens of Burlington House had to be given over to the construction of new accommodations. The upper floors of the Georgian townhouse remained a private residence for many years; for a spell I believe they were home to Richard Bright, who gave his name to Bright's disease, a general historical classification for kidney ailments.

150

Shortie retired. Years later a man came into Huntsman and announced that all his life he had been saving to buy himself a pair of Huntsman's britches — and now here he was, money in hand, ready to be measured up. It was down to poor Lakey to say that he was sorry, the company no longer made them — all of the cutters and workshop tailors sufficiently skilled in making britches had retired or died off. 'Finally I can afford them,' the man wept — actually cried! — 'and you don't make them any more!' Lakey recommended Kilgour, next door, but the poor chap was inconsolable.

Still, with britches' demise came a new era of renown for Huntsman legwear, favoured by the likes of David Niven, Peter Sellars, Peter Ustinov, Merle Oberon, Benny Goodman and Hardy Amies, owner of his own tailoring house along the street. Yet more luminaries crossed the Atlantic, including Clark Gable, Bing Crosby, Paul Newman, James Coburn, Charles Bronson, Gregory Peck, Rex Harrison, Stewart Grainger, the first Mr Judy Garland, at least two Mr Elizabeth Taylors and Katharine Hepburn. Elizabeth Taylor used to send Lakey photographs of her husbands' waistbands pinned as she would have preferred them. Peter Sellars once brought his son in and when Lakey picked him up and put him on the old britches saddle the little boy grabbed the tape measure round Lakey's neck and yanked its ends, nearly strangling him. Katharine Hepburn liked her trousers about three sizes too wide, so that they billowed like ship's sails when she walked. Whenever Lakey dared object, she blamed her taste on the likelihood of shrinkage by 'those damn dry-cleaners in America'. After one particularly contentious fitting Hepburn lingered over some cashmere jumpers on display in the front shop. Striding back to the cutting room with one in her hands, she said, 'Mr Lakey, would you please come here and try this on? I am thinking of buying one for my cousin and you are about the same size.'

Lakey obliged — the jumper fit well enough — and then returned to his cutting board while Hepburn swanned forth to make her payments and leave. A few minutes later, Brian, on front shop duty, came back and laid the jumper on Lakey's board.

'Miss Hepburn has just asked me to give this to you,' Brian said, 'from 'Katie'.'

Gregory Peck once came in with one of his stunt doubles for a pair of identical white mohair lounge suits. But whereas Peck was among Huntsman's no-fuss customers — delighted with everything, rarely asked for adjustments, always let you know in advance if he were going to be early or late — his stunt double was a right pain in the arse. He required three times the number of fittings Peck did for his suit, asking for this sleeve to come up a bit, this button over a smidge, the collar a bit higher, a little more room in the seat . . . and of course you will remember from the Tommy Jermyn trousers saga that white material is murder to alter; every pinhole and thumbprint shows up plain as day. This farce would have gone on ad infinitum if Peck had not finally pulled Packer aside and spoken up: 'I don't know what all this fuss is about,' Peck said. 'All he's going to do in that thing is fall off the back of a lorry and roll around in the street oil.'

As for Rex Harrison: well, he could be very nice, very appreciative, Lakey would graciously say, but God bless you if you rubbed Henry Higgins up the wrong way; he would blow out your eardrums taking you down. He had come to Huntsman in the fifties, having been referred by another customer — a man also affiliated with the entertainment industry and who had a penchant for especially tight-fitting clothes. Assuming Harrison had come in for a style similar to his friend's, Lakey cut him a pair of snugger-than-usual trousers and was treated to a condemnation

153

of such theatrical volume it would have easily reached the nosebleeds of the largest theatre in the West End. 'No, I do NOT want the same style!' Harrison bellowed. 'These are the most abysmal pair of trousers I have ever seen!' But for whatever reason — Lakey swears the changes he made were virtually imperceptible — when Harrison came back for his second fitting he was so chuffed with the new baste he pulled Packer aside and said, tipping his chin in Lakey's direction: 'That man's the best thing since cut bread.'

Lakey claimed never to have had any trouble with Harrison after that — and, in fact, it is common for a customer, rightly or wrongly, to challenge his cutter's work at the outset, to set the tone and let you know who is in charge. But Rex Harrison's temperament was often on display, if not with Lakey then whoever else was on hand. Huntsman made many of Harrison's clothes for stage shows, for which quick changes are common, of course — much of what Huntsman made for him had Velcro in lieu of buttons — and Harrison would often practise his changes in Huntsman's fitting rooms, with his costume dresser in dutiful attendance. One day the challenge was to change out of an ordinary two-piece lounge suit into a full dinner ensemble — white dress shirt, white bow tie, white waistcoat, black tailcoat, black dress trousers and black patent leather shoes — in fewer than five minutes. When the dresser assisting Harrison with this switcheroo made some little mistake that took two or three precious seconds to put right, Harrison wiped the floor with him. 'WHO *ARE* YOU!?' he roared. 'Bloody useless!' The dresser was used to it, evidently. Out of earshot, Lakey remarked that Harrison seemed 'a bit hot', but the dresser just shook his head and said, 'That was nothing.'

Another day Harrison came in with his dresser to order a smoking jacket he would be wearing onstage at the Haymarket with Claudette Colbert in *Aren't We All?* The dresser said it should be green, but Harrison piped up, 'No, no, I don't think we'll have a green one. We'll have a plum-coloured one.'

'But the producers want green,' the dresser said.

'I don't care,' said Harrison. 'We'll have a plum-coloured one.'

The dresser acceded. When he had stepped away for a recuperative moment, Hammick sidled up and said to Harrison, diplomatically:

'The green's quite nice, Mr Harrison.'

'Of course it is, but I have already got a green one.'

Following Sir Rex Harrison's knighthood, he came in and received a round of congratulations from the front shop and cutting staff. 'Yes,' he grumbled to no one in particular. 'About bloody time, too.'

In a tailoring workshop, one hears as much bad language as in a locker room. But in front shops and cutting and fitting areas, anywhere a Milord might appear at any moment, efforts are made to maintain a certain level of gentility. Packer Senior was particularly sensitive to the importance of such decorum and implored staff and customers alike to keep it clean. Then Stewart Grainger swaggered in one day unannounced and went straight down the long front shop to the cutting room, catching Hammick on the hop. Hammick apologised profusely — he had not known Mr Grainger was coming in and so unfortunately was not ready to fit him — in response to which Grainger puffed up his chest and began effing and blinding at the top of his lungs. 'Sir!' Packer hastened to shush down the commotion. 'We are indeed very sorry, but Mr Hammick is an artist, you know, and in any case we cannot abide the use of such language in Huntsman.'

Chastened, Grainger apologised, and was good as pie until he left. Then, from barely across the threshold, he popped his head back into the shop and called sweetly down its length to Hammick:

'Oh, Colin?'

'Yes, Mr Grainger?'

'Just one more thing.'

'Yes, Sir?'

'BOLLOCKS!'

★ ★ ★

The youngest of three boys from North London, Colin Hammick was evacuated during his early teens to Huntingdon, Cambridgeshire, and billeted with the local tailor there. He wore his first bespoke suit to an interview for assistant in lighting design at the notorious Windmill Theatre, home of Mrs Henderson's rousing *tableaux vivants* — but the director took one look at him and proposed an onstage role instead. Hammick declined — on the basis that backstage would have been the better vantage point from which to see the girls — and with this brief flirtation with show business out of his system wandered over to the other side of Regent Street, where Huntsman granted him a trial period as apprentice to its head cutter, Charles Borland. It was 1942; Hammick was fourteen.

Borland was a severe disciplinarian who

ruled his staff with an iron rod, literally beating them when they failed to meet his exacting requirements. He gave Hammick a dog's life. But Hammick, a keen observer and natural autodidact, stuck with it to work his way up from rock bottom, where his primary responsibility had been polishing the brass plates outside the shop's door. As Borland's senior apprentice, Hammick altered patterns, dispensed trimmings and ensured garments were ready when customers came in. He became self-conscious of his North London accent and paid for his own English and elocution lessons in order that the aristocrats with whom he was now rubbing shoulders might more readily regard him as one of their own. And when Borland died of cancer in his early sixties, Packer appointed 24-year-old Hammick a cutter in his own right, overseeing each of Hammick's fittings and reviewing Hammick's workload at the end of every day — 'making good progress,' Packer would say, or 'careful of that right shoulder' — just as Hammick would do for Hall and, thirty years later, Hall for me.

Brian Hall joined Huntsman seven years after Hammick, in 1949, when he was seventeen. Whereas Hammick had been an apprentice cutter from the beginning, Hall started up in the Heddon Street workshop as

158

an apprentice tailor. And whereas the norm at other houses was to outsource jobs and pay tailors by piecework, Huntsman had sufficient business to be able to afford its own multiple workrooms and to pay the tailors who worked in them livable wages year-round. In Hall's day, the Heddon Street workroom as I knew it was called the Clifford Street shop, for Huntsman also maintained another, smaller shop already named for its abuttal of Heddon Street — and which operated without electric lighting until 1973. Hall's tailoring days would not have been as trying as Lakey's — and yet, after five years of padding shoulders and pitching sleeves, followed by two years' National Service training in radar, Hall too forswore assembly to resume his Huntsman career in the cutting room, where he began to apply his practice to the more artistic phase.

He trained under Cecil Pressland, like Borland an excellent cutter, one of the few on Savile Row who really knew how to cut for ladies as well as men — a skill still rare today. Huntsman was Pressland's life: he worked half a century there and even managed to marry his daughter off to poor misshapen Cummings. And like Robert Packer and Fred Lintott, Pressland was kind, fatherly, supremely cheerful and gracious. Ironically, he owed this disposition, he claimed, to a congenital back defect that had rendered him bedridden for the first four years of his life. In the mornings he would wake up and through the little window above his hospital bed see the sun, or the rain and birds, basking or splashing around in the droplets — and these memories of his budding consciousness served always to remind him how lucky he was to have been healed and liberated from his cell.

Our rather less sanguine Hall opened his own book when he was twenty-six. Having to report to Hammick, only three years his senior, set the tone for many years to come: Hammick as Hall's superior, a romantic idealist forever a rung or two above his nearest colleague, who almost by default had to play the more reliable and rational practitioner. Every six months for forty years this dynamic was epitomised by a routine virtually irrelevant to the business at hand: Hammick was useless at anything mechanical — at anything other than cutting a coat pattern, really — so whenever it came time to change clocks each autumn and spring he would bring in all of his clocks — alarm clocks, radio clocks, pocketwatches, wristwatches, and anything else involving a timepiece — and on the way to his own board dump them on Hall's so Hall could change them for him before the end of the day.

The very first decade Hammick, Hall and Lakey spent all together in Huntsman's cutting room presented Savile Row with one of its greatest challenges: the swinging sixties. London became a buzzing locus of popular musical and artistic talent and the frenzy inspired wild new slants on sartorial style. Now in their late teens or early twenties and widely employed, the older baby boomers had money to spend and were lavishing it on records and clothes. The city's coolest shopping destination was Carnaby Street, to which nearby underground music venues like the Roaring Twenties and the legendary Marquee (where The Rolling Stones had their first formal gig in 1962) were attracting rockers and the fans who emulated them. To capitalise on this market, designer boutiques multiplied along the narrow streets now being trafficked by the likes of Mick Jagger, Jimi Hendrix, The Who and David Bowie. These clothing shops included Mr Fish, as in Michael Fish, inventor of the kipper tie; Mary Quant, a leading populariser of the mini-skirt and brightly patterned tights; and I Was Lord Kitchener's Valet, which recycled antique military dress as hip civilian wear — 'uniforms of the past to affront the uniformity of the present'.[1] Women's hemlines rose, but possibly the greater fashion revelation of the sixties was in menswear, which for 150 years had been generally sedate and tailor-made. Due in part to the 1950s Teddy Boy craze, which bred a generation of men comfortable with dressing in a way that attracted attention, and in part to a burgeoning anti-establishment culture whose hotbed lay provocatively just the other side of Regent Street from Savile Row, menswear was now reflecting wilder, more modish and psychedelic tastes.

For much of the first half of the twentieth century, the demand for regimental uniforms together with the Golden Age of Hollywood had kept major tailoring firms like Huntsman too busy simply filling orders to have much time for experimentation. But by the late fifties, Savile Row's client profile was

---

[1] This was according to a television reporter of the time. Jimi Hendrix allegedly found his iconic braided coat at Lord Kitchener's Valet, and Peter Blake, who designed the album cover for *Sergeant Pepper*, said it was inspired by the shop's window — although the suits The Beatles wore for the cover were designed by Manuel Cuevas, a Los Angeles-based tailor for rockers and country and western singers who also made the lips-logo prototype for the Rolling Stones.

changing. On the whole, soldiers no longer wore bespoke equestrian clothing and films were being shot all over the world, which meant the Hollywood sets saw less traffic and consequently the tailors loitering there fewer clients to solicit. Savile Row's reputation was mouldering, and while the refusal of some of its houses to modernise might have been in the admirable defence of tradition, the Row was also in danger of becoming a dinosaur.

Enter Nutters. On Valentine's Day 1969, Mayfair tailoring contenders Tommy Nutter and Edward Sexton opened a new shop directly across from Huntsman at Savile Row 35A, backed by Cilla Black and Peter Brown of The Beatles' company Apple — which less than a year earlier had moved its headquarters into no. 3 down the street. Nutters opened just two weeks after The Beatles played what would be their last ever concert together, on Apple's roof (dozens of tailors, several of Huntsman's among them, climbed out of their top-floor workshop windows to watch) — an event that for an hour or so, as the street swarmed with bemused policemen and ecstatic fans, made Savile Row feel like the centre of the world. Following a short plumbing career, Tommy Nutter's tailoring tenure had begun much like mine: he answered a 'Boy Wanted' advertisement and

163

became an errand-trotter. Then, as a front shop junior salesman at Donaldson, Williams & Ward in the Burlington Arcade, he fell in with mods and rockers and had dramatic style ideas he would be able to realise by teaming up with Sexton, a bona-fide bespoke cutter who had trained at Kilgour and who, like Lakey, had paid for his own tailoring lessons. Upon throwing open its doors, Nutters outraged much of the rest of the Row with its unconventionally direct window displays and flashy parade of celebrity clients, which would include Mick and Bianca Jagger, Elton John, Eric Clapton, Joan Collins and Twiggy — but it also gave the rest of Savile Row just the prod towards modernity it so desperately needed.

Brian Epstein was one of Hall's clients, and in the early sixties he said to Packer, 'You know, I've got four boys who might be interested in Savile Row.' Then he died and The Beatles went to Nutters — where they bought three of the suits on the cover of *Abbey Road*. Long-time customers started coming into Huntsman asking for a slightly more exaggerated look — brighter colours, a slimmer line, flared hems, wider lapels. So the company was obliged to keep up; experimentation was crucial to staying in the game. Sir Paul Chambers, a Huntsman client who also headed up ICI, the chemical lab perhaps most famous for inventing polyethylene, brought round the first length of Crimplene, which he asked Hammick, Hall and Lakey to use in cutting some suit models for a fashion show promoting the synthetic fabric's versatility. (ICI gave the workshop tailors 'instructions' as to how to handle and press the polyester knit, whose reaction to an iron was nothing like that of mohair or tweed — but, in fact, the best techniques were ultimately devised by the tailors and pressers themselves.) Times were palpably changing, and if what a customer wanted was a collarless jacket belted with PVC, or a velvet suit to go with a brocade waistcoat, nylon cuff-frills and a lavender cravat, the prevailing opinion at Huntsman was that it should endeavour to comply . . . within reason. By all means its cutters should be receptive to the evolution of taste, but it was imperative that they should do this within the Huntsman framework, while still adhering to its brand: without defying its principles of figuration and standards of quality, without diluting the famous Huntsman line so much as to make it unrecognisable, and without becoming commercially reliant upon any fly-by-night fads.

By this time Hammick had become joint managing director with Lintott. Like Lakey and Brian Lishak, Lintott was an enthusiastic champion of these developments, which they considered not only critical to remaining at the fore of the sartorial trade but also a welcome breath of fresh air. Hammick and Hall were somewhat less keen, embracing experimentation just enough to keep Huntsman afloat during a difficult time. As well as the Crimplene-and-kipper-tie craze, the sixties saddled Savile Row with increases in labour expenses, purchase tax and the cost of raw materials from abroad. Within a span of just five years the cost of a Huntsman suit went up 50 per cent. Robert Packer had always said he dreaded the day when he would have to charge three figures. At a board meeting in the late sixties the debate over whether to start charging £100 swung back and forth between the production directors (Hammick and Hall), who were against hitting the sound barrier, and the sales and administration directors (Brian and Lintott), who insisted it was imperative if Huntsman were to remain in business. The impasse was finally broken by Packer himself, who sighed, 'It's all about value for money. If your suit costs a hundred pounds and is good value you will sell it. If you charge ninety-five quid and it isn't you won't.' That concluded the issue and prices were increased accordingly.

And, of course, once the price tag crossed the three-figure threshold, it never stopped climbing: a genuine bespoke suit from Savile Row typically costs thirty-five times the sound barrier today.

In 1971 Hammick famously beat his own client Rex Harrison as well as the Duke of Windsor and the Earl of Snowdon to be named *Tailor & Cutter's* Best Dressed Man of the Year. Then the Clothing Institute named him Best Designer of the Year as well — 'sealing', as *The Times* would put it, 'his sartorial reputation'. (The same year, the Americans put Tommy Nutter on a Best Dressed list of their own.) For Hammick these honours were a publicity boon — suddenly he was a celebrity, and received numerous offers to engage in flashier, higher-profile work — but being an understated man who truly loved his work he stayed right where he was because he did not want to disappoint his customers. In the coming years it was his clean, classic, unfussy look — the one-button lounge jacket, cut with high armholes, a natural shoulder and two deep vents, coupled with trousers with a single front pleat — that would come to define the world-famous Huntsman line.

And yet while Hammick's quixotic perfectionism was certainly quaint and admirable, from a business standpoint it was not always ideal. His insularity could be at the expense of proactive salesmanship and keeping orders ticking over. He was royally stubborn about the weight of the material with which he would work — he preferred the heavier fabrics of yesteryear for being easier to make up and better at retaining the aspired silhouette over time — which all but forced many clients to look elsewhere for half their wardrobe. And twice, once in the seventies and again shortly after I arrived in 1982, the company maintained a waiting list. For six months at a time Hammick would insist that he was under too much pressure to cut patterns and so we would take on no new customers until the load had lightened. In one respect, the tactic backfired: extant customers heard this and, fearing a clientele-wide ban, hurried in to place new orders. To outsiders it must have looked like a publicity stunt, for no other Savile Row firm had ever had a waiting list and as a result Huntsman acquired an even clubbier, exclusive aura. Long-time clients would come in just to sit in the front shop, have a chat, browse through the handkerchiefs and ties, and smoke — and then leave without even having had a fitting. Some customers had as many as thirty orders on the go at once and waited two or three years for a finished suit. After a period of time some divine sign or supreme sense of calm would stir Hammick to say: 'OK. Let's write to the first six', referring to punters relegated to the list — which at one point had as many as 200 names, many of them world-renowned. Of course, by the time some of them were finally invited into Huntsman's hallowed fitting rooms they would have already gone elsewhere.

Hammick's fiercest opponent regarding business decisions was Brian, twelve years Hammick's junior but whose nose for business was twice as strong. Whereas Hammick and Hall were focused intently on what was happening on their cutting boards, in the fitting rooms and in the workshops upstairs, Brian's front shop experience and extensive travels, long ocean crossings and late dinners sharing stories with older members of the trade ('What else is there to do in Cleveland?' he used to point out) gave him a broad and valuable perspective on long-term business viability. Brian understood why houses including those reputed as the very best could suddenly disappear: the demand for tailored regimental attire waned. Postwar prices rose and customers re-prioritised their luxuries. Cutters failed to change with the times and accommodate the fashions. Expansion to New York exposed a house to the poaching away of its skilled tailors by clothiers in America. Some firms put too many eggs into international trade — to South America, say, and then faltered when it became too difficult to extract money from Argentina and Brazil. Others lost their Mayfair leases, prompting clients to defect to houses with more prestigiously or, indeed, more conveniently situated premises. Perhaps the most commonly heard death knell on Savile Row was the demise or retirement of a particular house's master cutter, for cutters grow up with their clients over the course of a generation; they develop relationships with each other, and once that irreproducible personality is gone, many tailoring houses must all but start over from scratch.

So Brian, by now familiar with such horror stories, was ever on the lookout for potential weaknesses in Huntsman's business workings in order that they might be preventatively reinforced. With Lintott, his mentor on the sales and marketing side, he sought to shore up the company's profit stream by establishing wholesale partnerships both at home and abroad. These included arrangements with Saxon Hawk of England, Caesar of Italy, Rowes of Bond Street (maker of the 'Jon-Jon' pea coat JFK Jr wore to his father's funeral), a shirt-making business based in Tyne and Wear, Barneys, Louis of Boston, Burberry (who sold the Newcastle shirts in France, Switzerland and Belgium), the premier bespoke bootmaker Maxwell's, and Kindwear, a manufacturer of high-quality ready-to-wear suits in Japan. With so many irons in the fire, Huntsman was able to continue making true bespoke clothes of the finest quality — an increasingly expensive and precarious tradition, but still the firm's prevailing pride and joy.

Despite these various expansions, Huntsman remained a family-run enterprise, in deed and at heart. As I have said, Robert Packer worked until four weeks before he died, at ninety. His son Edward was already chairman and had been for some years. During that time Packer Senior had no company title but still provided the benefit of his knowledge, common sense and seven decades of practical experience. Edward Packer's accomplishments both on behalf of Huntsman and, indeed, the whole of the tailoring trade would be no less notable: for several years he served as chairman of the Federation of Merchant Tailors, the Tailors Benevolent Institute and the Master Tailors, Benevolent Association. He believed strongly in the training and cultivation of young talent, developing curricula for the conveyance of technique from masters to apprentices and coordinating government-backed tutorials. It was under his aegis that I came aboard. But when Lintott died and Hammick's directorship was allowed to favour the bespoke side of the business over everything else, Huntsman's on-the-ground momentum began to lag. Brian left for Wells. Without him or Lintott to tend to them, Rowes was sold and the running of the bespoke shoemaker fell to Edward Packer's wife. The Newcastle shirt factory closed and, except for the Japanese and Barney's licences, all the other non-bespoke overseas ventures were wound down. The first eight decades of the twentieth century had dealt Savile Row many blows: war, economic depression, another war, mods, rent increases and unfavourable zoning laws — and the last two decades would bring more. Huntsman had bounced back from each of these trials to repopulate its fitting rooms again and again. But even I, at barely twenty years old, could see that the eighties were shaping up into an especially challenging period of doom and gloom. The company's bespoke output had fallen from a peak of 2500 coat units to 600 or 700 annually, which meant the cutting and tailoring teams had to be downsized accordingly — and there were even one or two midsummer days when walking into 11 Savile Row you could hear your footsteps reverberate.

Revelations

A man cannot make love with any kind of conviction unless he is wearing a coat cut within half a mile of Piccadilly.

Tailor & Cutter, c. 1860

In 1987, shortly after his second trip to America, Toby jumped ship.

I had not seen it coming, though it makes perfect sense to me today. Toby's experience epitomises that of many apprentice tailors who graduate from college with a degree in fashion design. They go on to do some work experience and then take a salaried position already knowing the difference between a single- and double-breasted suit (whereas I, as we know, pitched up unwise to the difference between a buttonhole and a spot of air), but soon conclude the non-academic trade is not for them. Although he had only three years on me, Toby was miles ahead in terms of experience; but he was jaded, and just that little bit too proud to put up with Hammick and Hall's near-implacable reticence, so by the time he had seen America

174

twice and was poised to become a cutter in his own right he had just lost steam. As his interest and concentration crumbled so did his relationships with Hammick and Hall, until finally he began to look around and extracted an offer to sell ties for Holliday & Brown. This would prove merely a brief thematic transition, for ultimately he left the trade altogether, to start a new life working with his brother making television commercials in Australia.

On one hand, I was gutted to see Toby go. He had become a true friend and I would miss our brotherly rapport. Yet in direct opposition to Toby's growing disinterest and lassitude, I had been chomping at the bit to learn more. Despite a bumpy start, which I now knew was the norm for new apprentices at Huntsman, I had made great strides in the five years since my trial period and was eager to progress. Quiet moments were rare, but during one I had asked Hammick to show me how to cut a morning suit. He waved me away, grumbling that he did not have the time and that I should ask Hall. Right. I was supremely frustrated by being held back and nearly every evening complained to my now-official girlfriend Fran and asked myself what the hell I was doing, running in circles, playing a patience game for which the reward was beginning to look like a mirage. But Toby's leaving lifted the brakes. Not a day later I pulled Hall into the boardroom and asked for more money. He said yes, and I was off running.

Of course what I also wanted just as much (if not more) than a pay rise was the chance to start measuring and fitting customers with an eye towards opening my own book. But by now I knew well enough this was not something you were granted with mere words. I had to demonstrate my readiness, and not once but several times over. I began to stand in on Hall's measurings and to observe more closely the pattern-cutting process, not just cutting brown paper with heavy shears but actually conceiving a successful design and translating it into the five basic parts of a template — a trick I practised countless times, measuring and creating mock patterns for every last obliging member of Huntsman's staff, my father, my brother, my friends, even Fran.

When a customer had chosen his cloth and told Hall what kind of suit he wanted, Hall would usher him into one of our fitting rooms and proceed to take, on average, fourteen coat measurements, calling them out one by one while I, standing off to the side, repeated each back to him and jotted the numbers down. The first seven measurements would be taken of the customer with a coat on — his own coat or one of our model coats in his approximate size — and the remaining seven with the coat off. The final bespoke product would be an amalgamation of these two sets of figures.

'Natural waist sixteen and three-quarters,' Hall would call out. This was the distance from the customer's neck down to the small of his back.

'Sixteen and three-quarters,' I would echo, scribbling away.

'Coat length thirty and three-quarters.'

'Thirty and three-quarters.'

'Half cross back nine.'

'Nine.'

'Centre seam to elbow twenty and three-quarters . . . Centre seam to cuff thirty-one and a half . . . Front button to side seam thirteen . . . Side seam to centre back nineteen and five-eighths . . . '

Encouraging a customer to stand naturally could sometimes be tricky, especially under a glare so disapproving as Hall's. Short of thumping your punter on the shoulder with the side of your hand (as I'm certain Hall would have liked to do), there is no remedy for what we call 'over-erectness', except to

177

note it down and adjust your measurements accordingly.

Now, with our noble patron in just his shirtsleeves:

'Scye depth back ten.' (The distance from the customer's left underarm round to his back, measured by a small metal square.)

'Ten!'

'Scye to centre front eight.'

'Eight!'

'Front shoulder fifteen and a quarter.'

'Fifteen and a quarter!'

'Over shoulder twenty-one and three-quarters . . . Chest thirty-eight . . . Coat waist thirty-two and a half . . . Coat seat thirty-nine and a quarter . . . '

In due course Lakey would join us, for his part to measure the customer five times over in his trousers: outside seam, inside seam, waist, seat and width of bottoms. Throughout the measuring process, both cutters would also be making mental notes as to the customer's figuration — his natural carriage and anatomical particularities, from the subtle to the severe. Is one shoulder higher than the other? (Ninety-nine per cent of us are slightly lower on the right.) Do they slope or are they square? Is one hip more prominent? Does he have a bulky chest? A paunch? Is his back rounded or flat? This evaluative phase was a bit like the lunchtime practising Toby and I had done with Hall to ready Toby for his trip to New York — except, of course, that now with an actual customer in the room Hall kept verdicts like 'crippled' to himself. More importantly, whereas our lunchtime tutorials had been about how to evaluate a figure wearing an already basted suit, I was now learning how to assess a body in order to create a pattern from scratch.

The ability to visualise a body even when its owner is no longer standing right in front of you — to convert his two-dimensional pattern into a three-dimensional image in one's mind — is called Rock of Eye. A reliable mind's eye puts a cutter one step ahead of the game, for it allows him to envision how the body in question will interact with its pattern even before the customer returns for his next fitting. Of course, it does not hurt to get started on your pattern as soon as possible after sizing your specimen up — in Hammick's case, this was often not until a good long spell of procrastinatory smoking had subsided, whereas Hall would be sharpening his chalk before the customer had paid his deposit and was out the door.

They both used the antiquated Thornton System, passed down in turn from their masters Borland and Pressland and immortalised in a book published in 1893 entitled *The Sectional System of Gentlemen's Garment Cutting (comprising coats, vests, breeches, and trousers, &c.)* by J. P. Thornton. Editor of the *Minister's Gazette of Fashion* and founder of the London Alliance of West End Cutters, Thornton was as much a philosopher as a practitioner of his trade. Accordingly, *The Sectional System* reads in places something like a Sartrean proof:

The difficulties of trouser cutting may be concisely summed up as follows:

If a trouser is cut to fit a man whose legs and body are in a straight position, thus
How can it fit the same individual when his legs and body are in a crooked position? thus
How can the two cloth cylinders suitable for the straight legs, fit without forming folds in the laps and under the knees when the wearer is seated? thus
I will myself supply the answer and say, in no possible way can it be done, and yet this is the demand that the tailor time after time is called upon to meet . . . But it must not be assumed that

180

because absolute perfection, or impossibility is not attainable, that we can afford to disregard the problems presented, and depend for our success in trouser cutting (for mankind will still wear them and tailors must still make them) upon the mercy of our customers. This would be a policy that only need be mentioned to be condemned. No trousers are in all positions perfect, but it is almost unnecessary to add that some are greatly superior to the majority, while just a few in their adaptable fitting qualities and general style or 'hang' are worthy of the trade and a credit to those constituting it.

Thus:

To cut a piece of clothing according to the Thornton System was not merely to follow a series of objective instructional diagrams, but to appeal to a kind of philosophical calling wherein the bespoke cutters of the world evoke a religious tribe forever baying at the unreachable moon of 'perfection'. The good cutter must design a garment in which his customer will look his best while standing, sitting, striking a contraposto, running, eating, playing the trombone, even furthering his prospects for 'making love'. Impossible.

181

And yet the good cutter must try. It is his trade; perfectionism is his duty. To remain sane he must ultimately acknowledge that there is no such thing as perfection, only gradations of imperfection — indeed that perfection is an abstraction; and yet he must pursue it nevertheless.

The first time I watched Hall cut a pattern from start to finish he took up his square, his tailoring scale and his freshly sharpened chalk, and began grandly by drawing what we were to envision as the coat's shoulder-line and spine: a massive T.

This is where he lost me.

'*Now*. Mark your crucial reference points, which are the natural waist measurement, sixteen and three-quarters, and the coat length, which is thirty and three-quarters. Now mark your depth of scye, which is ten, and square across all three. At the waist point, come in one and three-eighths and from here square down from the neck point; this is your centre back. Come in three-eighths at your natural waist to one-quarter at bottom and again square down to achieve your run into the small of the back. Note your half cross back measurement, which is nine, and halve your depth of scye and from five draw your half cross back line from the back's midpoint to the scye and square up.'

To ensure I was staying apace, Hall would raise his eyes — without moving his head — and stare at me sceptically until I nodded.

'Now look to the bottom of the coat and visualise where the customer's hip point should be. Mark it. Halve the coat-off seat measurement, which is thirty-nine and a quarter, and mark this point on your thirds scale, plus half an inch. Now angle the line slightly into the waist, and with your square connect the length of the coat to the waist. Mark your over shoulder, which is nineteen, adding one inch. Then, using your eighth, quarter and half scales, mark three points and connect them with a crescent — this is your armhole. Now shape the neck. Halve your chest measure, which is thirty-eight, so mark nineteen plus an extra eighth on the sixth scale. Square up and also come up one inch for the collar, then round it out to connect to the shoulder point. Now add some shape to the sides: bring it in a little at the waistline and out around the seat, so it kicks out a little at the hips. Put some life to it. Got that old fruit?'

And this was only the back. *Half* of the back. Which Hall would then cut out and, using his chalk sharpener and square as paperweights, spread over a fresh piece of paper for reference in making the forepart.

At which point round two of this arcane and frenzied demonstration would commence.

'Halve your chest measurement, which gives you nineteen, measure from the centre back and mark it — then add two inches, and another two. Mark the quarter chest, nine and a half, and from the centre back: three and a half. Pull your tape to your first two-inch mark — from scye to centre front, the measure should equal from here to here within a whisper. Mark halfway, square up and down, and here you have your front edge . . . ' As Hall worked, my eyes skated frantically over the results, searching for recognisable features of something, *anything*, resembling an aspect of human apparel. When I did it was a magical moment. Having inserted a pencil tip through the reinforced hole at the end of his measuring tape and holding its fulcrum at the pattern's neckpoint, Hall would swing this makeshift pendulum across the paper's surface and — *voilà!*: the coat's convex bottom edge. With a similarly Da Vincian move: *voilà!*: its waist. Then he would sketch in one or two buttons, the deep curve of the neck and lapel, the armhole and one or more darts, and finally a sleeve, each emerging feature bringing our life-sized gingerbread man closer to life.

The first dozen or so times I watched Hammick, Hall or Lakey cut a coat or trousers pattern, it would seem utterly ungraspable, a cipher bordering on witch-craft.

The process would begin rationally enough: with the plugging of objective numbers into a scaled algorithm followed by a bit of join-the-dots. To practise I would borrow Coombes or Reina from upstairs, or my mate Andy after a bit of Saturday morning football, and take set after set of the key nineteen measurements. Then, careful as you please, I would plug the numbers into the Thornto-nian algorithm that would become my mantra: 'halve your depth of scye . . . come up two inches to account for the inlay . . . add three-eighths here for your waist seam . . . '

And all this would go well enough — but then it is only half the job. One's figuration notes, Rock of Eye, and even a character assessment of your wearer must also be summoned to transform the draft pattern into one that will 'bestow', as the 1804 *Dictionary of English Trades* defines the bespoke cutter's task, 'a good shape where nature has not granted one'. Indeed, because they influence posture, carriage and one's personal style, even a customer's temperament and sense of humour can go some way to dictate the lines of his ideal suit.

So Hall would show me how to accommodate, say, a 'corpulent figure' — and yet, because not every paunchy, flat-seated punter who walks in the door is exactly alike, there is unsettlingly little objectivity in exactly how best to elongate his trunk and boost his backside, never mind that we have not yet accounted for his relative jocularity. As carefully as I would watch each pattern marked out, hoping to spot the legerdemain responsible for its ultimate success, developing a fluent 'magic' of my own to this effect would require years of practice, trial and error, and visions of brown paper patterns marching through my dreams.

When a customer's pattern had been established — or when an extant customer would reorder, in which case Pepper would fetch the customer's previous pattern and measurements list and the cutter would run a tape around the customer's every relevant dimension all over again, to check whether any shrinkage or expansion had occurred — the cutter would then detail the requested style features on the new order's ticket, which in the case of a suit would specify: the catalogue number and weight of the selected

186

cloth, whether the coat was to be single- or double-breasted, how many buttons, how many pockets (inbreast, outbreast, or ticket right- or left-cross), how many vents, whether the trousers should be straight-top or scalloped for braces, whether they would have straight or slanted side pockets and an extra pocket for keyfobs; whether they would have pleats or plain legs and turn-ups or straight hems — et cetera. The permutations with which a customer could assert his personal sartorial requirements and style seemed infinite, and the more I practised my patterns, their fruition as yet a blur of rich colours and sleek silhouettes in my head, the more desperate I became for the day when I would wear a true bespoke suit myself.

★ ★ ★

If you worked at Huntsman and had an eye in your head you could not help but feel self-conscious about what you wore. Hammick was the most formidably classy, down in part to his long lean figure and Best Dressed mantle. As though they were doctor's scrubs, he used to change his suits at lunchtime, and sometimes even mid-morning and mid-afternoon as well, 'to stay fresh'. After almost each wearing, his suits would be re-pressed and sponged as necessary, for as any good tailor will tell you: a suit should only sparingly be dry-cleaned. The chemicals dry-cleaners use strip fabric of its natural oils, just as shampoo can overdry hair. So Huntsman always urged its customers to bring any stained, musty or limp garments back to the shop for forwarding to a specialist cleaner — situated in the Scottish Highlands and whose mysterious methods involved the application of water and very mild soap only — then the garments would be sent back to Number 11 for hand-pressing and returned to the customer, fresh and supple as new.[1]

Hammick had only one lung. The other collapsed when he was twenty-nine and in Athens for a tailoring convention from which he had to return early for retrieval by Brian and Lintott at Heathrow. Still, he inhaled three packs of Piccadillies a day, but because of his suit-changing habit never smelled of smoke. (Everyone smoked then. A permanent fog hung over our heads as we worked. Toby

---

[1] At a pinch, as Brian Lishak would advise the many business and leisure travellers among Huntsman's clientele, a tired-looking garment may be hung up in a steamy bathroom for twenty minutes and then allowed to dry naturally. But only at a pinch.

188

nailed a pack a day. Hall three, at least. Friday afternoons Hall would send me over to a little kiosk on Regent Street to get him a hundred Embassy Number 1s . . . and the first thing he would ask me to do when I got in on Monday morning was to go round to the kiosk for another hundred.) Dress-wise, Hammick would begin the morning in a blue spot, at lunch switch to a grey stripe, and by teatime be lighting up in a blue stripe. If there were no customers around and he were working he would take off his coat and lay it behind him, on my board. When he went to the loo, Toby or I used to take the coat he had been wearing and switch it with another one (and, for good measure, fluff the outbreast pocket handkerchief up to a ridiculous height), so when he came back he would absentmindedly put the blue spot coat over the grey stripe trousers, or a blue stripe coat over grey spot trousers — how wicked we were! — and not until his next scrubdown notice the difference.

I would later learn that Dorothy Cumpsty, Hammick's partner of thirty-seven years, once took him to a Tina Turner concert at Wembley Stadium, for which he dressed as though for tea with the Queen. Turned out in a single-breasted mohair cable-stripe, a cashmere tie and customary silk handkerchief in the left breast, Hammick was the only person in the stadium who remained seated throughout — a hand on each thigh, not even a finger twitch to the music. He did later concede that Ms Turner 'gave a fine performance', though I suspect it vexed him slightly not to have been able to change his suit during the interval.

By contrast, Hall wore the same suit all day and never removed his coat, not even when there were no customers in sight. His coat was his armour, his security. I think he probably went home and watched telly in it, right up till it was time for bed.

Lakey was a bit more relaxed, although so conscientious about the always-wear-a-coat-with-a-customer rule that when a story about Huntsman ran in *Forbes* accompanied by a cartoon unmistakably depicting him crouched in just his shirtsleeves, trousers and waistcoat to inspect the writer's knees, Lakey was so mortified to have been represented unclad as such that we half-expected him to sue the cartoonist for libel.

So what with Hammick, Hall and Lakey's impeccable dress, and our eternally smart-looking front shop team, I, of course, was ever at pains to improve my own sartorial repertoire. But with a pittance for a salary and given Hammick and Hall's stinginess with the Pork Rail, it was not easy. It certainly occurred to me to try to pinch a model or discard for myself. The Pork Rail was a veritable period piece, stuffed with coats some of which were a decade old; you would think a single garment gone missing would go unnoticed. But Hammick had an uncanny sixth sense of whether you had just done something wrong or were about to, and plundering the Pork Rail without permission was on a par with felony. He once gave Toby a right scare. A beautiful double-breasted Prince of Wales check Hammick once cut for a model had hung untouched in the back for at least ten years. One Friday Toby 'borrowed' it for a party over the weekend. At five past nine the following Monday morning Hammick lit a cigarette and, with supreme calmness, said, 'Toby, would you please pass me the Prince of Wales check?'

He knew exactly where it was, of course — in Toby's bedroom, back in Chelmsford — but nevertheless let Toby run around the firm for the best part of an hour 'looking for it' until finally the search was tacitly abandoned, allowing Toby to 'find' the coat the next day.

Toby's horn buttons still an irksome memory, I was not about to waive my own right to some free new gear in honour of my own first trip to America — which Hammick and Hall informed me would take place in January 1988. By this time I already owned one Huntsman suit and an overcoat, but they were not true bespoke and I had paid dearly for both. A year or two earlier one of Hammick's customers, an art dealer with an infallible eye, had ordered a tweed overcoat and three-quarters of the way through the process said, 'Hold on now. This isn't the material I ordered.' Indeed, we had received two bolts of the 'same' tweed, and the sample the customer had chosen turned out to be a near-imperceptible shade lighter than the length Hammick had used to make the order up. Hammick duly acceded to starting over from scratch and the darker overcoat went onto the Pork Rail. I fancied it and hinted as much. Bloody weeks of hinting went by until finally Hammick called me into the board-room and said, with great panache: 'Mmm, yes, Young Richard. We'd like you to have the coat, and what we've decided is that we'll charge you two hundred pounds for it. And what we thought we would do is take fifty out of your wages a month for the next four months.'

Christ! I was only making a hundred quid a week! Being docked two weeks' worth would absolutely kill me. And yet, of course, Hammick had said it as though he were offering me the keys to the kingdom. I could not say no.

My first Huntsman suit was a grey worsted. Among the partnerships forged by Brian and Lintott to fortify Huntsman during the difficult seventies and eighties was one with Chester Barrie, the cloth supplier for our relatively new ready-to-wear line, made of slightly less expensive material than that reserved for bespoke. Hammick had got hold of a length of this fabric to make up a model coat for a promotional brochure. When he had basted the sample together and fitted the model and the photo shoot was done he brought the coat over to me and said (again, very grandly: more keys), 'Mmmm, yes, Young Richard. You may have this.' The model was about my size, so the coat needed only a bit of additional adjustment, and there was enough material left over for some trousers, too. But I had to pay a couple of tailors £300 to finish the job, and when I asked Hall one Friday evening if he would not mind fitting me in it I had to endure an extra dose of the usual grumbling.

It was not until my inaugural trip to America that Huntsman finally afforded me one of its suits at no cost, and still it was not quite the real deal: a heavy, dark-grey diagonal off-the-peg in which Hall again reluctantly fitted me for adjustments. Not for another fifteen months and what seemed like miles of brown paper worth of pattern practice would I finally wear a truly bespoke suit — cut by yours truly. One of our very wealthiest customers, a dynastic patriarch whose multiple homes included sprawling castles in Scottish glens and a luxury hotel suite on permanent let, placed an order for a dozen trousers made of exceptionally fine, light-grey flannel with a handle like velvet. Sir Osmund was a massive chap with a waist twice as many inches around as his legs were long, and just to get sufficient width in we had to order so much flannel there was more than a suit's worth in just the excess. I went about salvaging it quietly, for although Hammick and Hall sanctioned personal work for the learning curve they did so reservedly, there being some stigma attached to it in the trade. The first time I floated into Huntsman wearing this double-breasted grey beauty with royal blue lining Hall took one look at it and rightly observed, 'Are you wearing Sir Osmund's *leftovers*?'

Indeed, I was. I still do today. And as soon as I could afford the material I made myself another suit from my new pattern: a navy cable stripe with pillarbox-red lining. I had the flavour. To put a true and properly made bespoke suit on for the first time is a revelation: immediately you take to its positive influence on your posture, the comfortable snugness about the arms; you stand up straighter and feel at once more comfortable and confident — that you are a better person, or at least that you have it in you to be a better person, a person of unique capacity, sensibility and class. And for me this was like a drug.

★ ★ ★

Everything at Huntsman came at a high price. Mine for the honour of my first transatlantic adventure was that I, too, would be accompanied by laugh-a-minute Hall.

I was twenty-three and had never been to America before, so could not help but be excited. I knew, of course, that business travel does not typically afford much sightseeing time, so there would be little disappointment in missing the Statue of Liberty or even the Metropolitan Museum, the latter which was a mere quarter mile from our Upper East Side hotel. What I had not known to expect before touching down in Brooklyn was that Hall's crankiness, liberated from Hammick's gentility and watchful judgement, would reach a new peak.

The very first day we opened our suite at the elegant Carlyle for business, a dapper little chap came by on the referral of a long-time Huntsman customer and said he had heard wonderful things about the firm and wished to be measured up for a simple, single-breasted navy worsted. The catch was that he wanted slightly wider shoulders and a roomier waist than are germane to the Huntsman line — fairly significant but not necessarily egregious deviations. (And as we know: if your name happens to be Katharine Hepburn you can have whatever line you want.) But Hall, who I suppose thought he could talk the fellow down, declared with chilling disdain: '*You*, Sir, are *not* my idea of a Huntsman customer.'

A mortifying blow-up ensued and we never saw the fellow — or his friend — again.

Another day we had been working flat out all morning with a few fittings running overtime and a couple of customers pitching up unannounced. By noon six of them were waiting in the sitting room of our suite — all politely enough, but the sheer number threw Hall into such a flap he told them all to go away.

'Go away!' he shouted, clapping and making shooing motions with his hands. 'Go downstairs! Wait in the bar, and we'll call for you when we're ready!'

Each looking more bemused than the last, our six wouldbe punters stood up and filed out quietly while I stood in the corner feeling like an extra in a Marx Brothers film.

And Hall would get really wound up about his food. He had heart problems, so understandably he had become sensitive about his diet, but some of his aversions had no discernible basis in the laws of nutrition. At lunchtime every day I would cross the street from the Carlyle to Three Guys Sandwich Shop, where with your sandwich they gave you a gherkin on the side. The first day I came back with Hall's ham-and-tomato and when Hall unwrapped it he pulled a revolted face.

'Next time, old fruit, no pickle. I don't like the pickle.'

The next day I went back to Three Guys and ordered one sausage sandwich and one ham-and-tomato, no pickle with the ham-and-tomato. They put one in anyway, and when Hall saw it he tore his hair out.

'*Aarrgghh* you berk. I said *no pickle*.'

The next day I went round to Three Guys again and with God as my witness I ordered a sausage sandwich for myself and a ham-and-tomato WITH NO PICKLE. 'Please,' I begged the guys behind the counter. '*Please.* NO PICKLE.' 'Is there a pickle in there?!' I asked when they handed me Hall's sandwich. 'Nope!' I was assured confidently. 'Absolutely not. No pickle.'

Needless to say, when I had couriered Hall's ham-and-tomato across the Carlyle's black marble lobby and up six flights in the lift, Hall unwrapped it to find, snuggled between the sandwich's two halves: a pickle.

Which he threw at me.

By the end of each day we would be so knackered from back-to-back fittings and *Dam Busters*-style manoeuvres that we could do nothing other than shuffle to a restaurant in the immediate vicinity, take our sustenance quietly, and go to bed. Early on I hinted once or twice at dining further afield, to see a new neighbourhood or two in our limited downtime, but this was met with such an appalled look you would have thought I had suggested we take the subway out to Coney Island. I feared our time together in Washington and Boston would be much the same. We were due to share a hotel suite every night for two weeks. I knew this was my big chance, it being just the two of us and my performance being critical to the ramping up (or snuffing out) of my Huntsman career — but Hall was such an oddity, also more than twice my age and so immutably determined not to enjoy himself, that I was beginning to hold little hope for our ever relaxing out of our Odd Couple routine.

The unlikely angel of our rapprochement came in the form of Frederick Seidel.

A customer since the early eighties, when he pitched up in hot pursuit of what he would call the 'swervy suave severity' of Huntsman's cut, Mr Seidel is your consummate bon vivant: epicure, oenophile, Ducati aficionado, global itinerant, and a prize-winning poet of terrifically arch verse; according to at least one prominent critic he is the best American poet writing today. Curiously, he is also an avid fan of our very own Brian Hall. It was an affection bordering on the perverse. When in London, Mr Seidel would come into Huntsman for a fitting or indeed just to soak up the atmosphere and while sitting on the front shop sofa grin hugely in anticipation of seeing his far-and-away favourite member of the staff, whom he teased much in the way a garrulous Don Juan woos a shy maiden. Mr Seidel would have none of Hall's cantankerousness — indeed, the grumpier Hall became, the more ribald Mr Seidel's rejoinders — and at the end of an hour or more of this great jolly, the charm and hilarity of which ultimately registered even in the tinily upturned corners of Hall's mouth, Mr Seidel would insist upon the pleasure of 'the Reverend's' company over lunch.

So when Mister New York, as Hall referred in turn to Fred Seidel, invited us to dine at Café Luxembourg on the Upper West Side before we would depart Manhattan for Washington, I was rather relieved. We arrived to find Mr Seidel already seated at what was indisputably the best-positioned table in the house — and from which, over the course of the evening, he would conduct an amused, proprietary surveillance of the rest of the room's patrons as though they were extended family members gathered in his own home. Chablis for three was summoned and drunk down before Hall and I could even open our menus — Mr Seidel knew his by heart — and when we did get around to the question of ordering and I had made my decisions and laid my menu back on the table I was confounded to observe Hall meaningfully look up and down his options for what felt like a full five minutes more. Every night for the last week I had watched Hall perfunctorily order and eat exactly the same meal: the soup of the day, whatever that was; a steak, medium-rare; and a dish of ice cream (vanilla). But now, with Mr Seidel looking expectantly on, and the Chablis already raising some pinkness in Hall's cheeks, some gastronomic switch was thrown — and within twenty minutes Hall was eating, and seeming immensely to enjoy, asparagus beignets, salmon tartare and roasted Long Island duck breast washed down with a 1978 Pommard Premier Cru. A parade of pretty hostesses, chummy waiters and the sommelier came by to say hello and ask how everything was, and to each of these solicitations Hall, mouth full, enthusiastically nodded in the customary manner of pleasure and contentment. In fact, as he devoured his meal like a man unfed for days, I actually saw on Hall's face what looked like genuine flickers of *joie de vivre*, buoyed perhaps by a relief at having escaped, if only for a couple of hours, his cage of order. Mr Seidel spotted a friend across the room, ordered a bottle sent over, and the favour was returned, so pop went a third cork and Hall began kicking my leg under the table such that I might understand he was overdoing it and I should drink his share — but even now, sober as a rock, I can palpably recall the immense gratitude I felt that night: to Fred Seidel, for occasioning the revelation of Hall's capacity for something akin to fun, and to Hall, for permitting its revelation in my presence. The honeymoon would not last long, for the wine made Hall sleepy and then our cab driver rubbed him up the wrong way by taking off before Hall could pull the full length of his herringbone overcoat through the door — and yet the old sulking would resume too late to erase what had preceded it. I had seen Hall happy. *Happy.* Hall! And tacitly, the experience effected just the subtle tonal shift in our rapport that would convert our first shared journey abroad into a success — as well as the additional three we would make together over the next two years.

Sebiro

Nineteen eighty-nine marked the seventh anniversary of my togetherness with Fran — who, while I forged a career bestowing good shapes and dodging pickles, had earned a degree in art at Leicester and then landed a job at a home furnishings retailer as a tile designer. Between us we had saved enough money to get married or make a down payment on a house, but not both. To the dismay of Fran's Irish-Catholic parents, we chose the latter — in the form of a two-bedroom railway cottage on Bedford Street in Watford valued at £65,500 — and promised to make good on our sins in due course.

Housing was of economic concern on Savile Row as well. The late eighties had seen a serious drop in sales Row-wide, and when it came time this same year to renew the Heddon Street workshop lease its rent skyrocketed by nearly 250 per cent. It was the foreign markets that kept many companies afloat, accounting for more than 60 per cent of their income. Thanks in part to the trips Hall and I were making, Huntsman's

American sales remained strong, and halfway around the world resided our second-largest market abroad: Japan.

Savile Row's popularity and significance among the Japanese are such that the very word for 'business suit' in Japanese is *sebiro* — a homonym of 'Savile Row'. The country's vast population of corporate professionals with a strict sense of office decorum certainly goes a long way to account for this, but the national consciousness of Savile Row is an even broader cultural phenomenon. In the main, the Japanese have long been in awe of Western styles (it is common to flip through a Japanese fashion magazine or catalogue and not see a single Asian model); moreover, they love a brand. In the late seventies, Brian and Lintott had sought to capitalise on this interest by arranging the aforementioned brand-licensing agreement with Kindwear, a menswear manufacturer based in Tokyo and which at the time was presided over by a man with the imperial-sounding surname Watanabe. One of only two Lishak-and-Lintott-forged foreign partnerships that had survived Lintott's death and Brian's reluctant departure, the Kindwear licence was still going strong, enabling Huntsman to retain its prized sunlit production room and remain on Savile Row when many other houses could not.

In January 1991, when I was twenty-six, I represented Huntsman in America for the first time on my own.

It did not begin well. I had booked all the flights and hotels myself and was due to be in Boston for an early fitting on the first Monday of my journey, but after arriving at Heathrow, checking four large suitcases of dozens of model coats, bastes, forward fittings, swatches, handkerchiefs, cufflinks, belts, braces and ties, and sinking with relief into my seat — the plane sat on the tarmac for three hours. There was a problem with the fuselage, we were finally told; the flight would have to be cancelled. Chaos erupted in the terminal, irate passengers hollered implacably, no one could tell us whether and when our bags were coming off. It being a Sunday afternoon in the pre-mobile age, I could reach none of my superiors to report the glitch. Finally, I was offered a late flight to New York, where I would then have to arrange my own internal flight to Boston — in between collecting and rechecking my four massive suitcases, loaded up with thousands of pounds worth of silk, silver, mohair, leather, and of course months upon months' worth of scrupulous labour.

Eighteen hours later I paced nervously around the baggage claim at Logan for the best part of yet another hour before spotting my four orphans lined up neatly at the far end, being circled by a sweeper. I made it to the Ritz Carlton, unpacked, splashed some water on my face, and with fifteen minutes to spare rang Hammick and Hall to deliver a breathless account of my tribulations and fortitude, expecting a medal. On the contrary, what with all the harrumphing on the other end of the line you would have thought I had mis-wired the fuselage myself.

And, of course, handling all of our scheduled clients on my own I had even less time than with Hall to catch my breath over the next two weeks.

Contrary to his spittoon-toting forebear, your typical modern American customer of Savile Row knows what he wants and will be perfectly forthright in expressing it to you. I once had a fitting with an American billionaire; we will call him Wells. When I had put a basted coat on his back and was standing behind him to inspect his reflection in the mirror, Wells abruptly spun aside so that *he* was standing behind *me*, the two of us now looking at my reflection, eclipsing his. Almost certainly I was wearing the smart grey flannel number I had cut from Sir Osmund's overage (I wore it virtually every day for two years), but suddenly I felt about as confident as I had nine years earlier, in my St Michael's school blazer on interview day.

Wells gripped my shoulders tightly.

'Look,' he said, pointing at my reflection. 'Look at *your* shoulders, and look at *my* shoulders. I want *mine* to look like *yours*.'

He was not rude, not in the slightest, and when I assured him this was my goal — we were, after all, only at the very first fitting stage — he was perfectly respectful and genial. But our momentary reversal of position was a brilliant power play on his part; it put me right onto my back foot and set the tone for our relationship. I would not, in fact, be seeing Wells on my first solo trip to the States — he had little use for scheduled visits, his resources being such that every couple of years he would elect instead to fly one of us over for a weekend to fit him exclusively — and yet his assertive certitude is exemplary of many of his compatriots, billionaires or no, so much so that fielding a dozen in one day while also contending with jet lag was bloody exhausting.

The measure of a trip's success is in part the number of new orders it generates — and on the flight over I had made up my mind to aim for twice what Hall and I had accomplished on the last of our four sessions stateside. But America was at war now; oil prices had spiked and Bush Senior was deploying troops to Kuwait, with no end to the economic malaise in sight. Meanwhile, I was still feeling out which customers would appreciate or take umbrage at being told by a 26-year-old that they should go in for an extra corduroy sport coat. Still, in the end I think I just about broke even, which seemed to impress Hammick and Hall but disappointed me for being a less than spectacular début. When I got home, Fran asked about all I had seen and heard in my off-duty time, but in truth most nights I was too knackered to do anything but eat a Hall-style meal at one of our local haunts and then fall asleep to CNN footage of Operation Desert Storm.

Back on Savile Row, the good results of my assiduous cutting practice were duly acknowledged and it was declared time I should be granted a first bespoke customer of my own. I had been at Huntsman nine years, longer than it takes some people to graduate from medical school, but the milestone itself turned out to be something of a non-event.

Huntsman's house style was so distinct that if two unacquainted men were walking down the street, or sharing the lift in Claridge's

— or indeed in a hotel halfway around the world — and happened both to be wearing a suit of Huntsman provenance, they would almost always recognise as much and very often speak up. Customers told us stories of this happening all the time. And yet, within the house line, an individual cutter's hands will make their own tiny indelible stamp — an ever-so-slightly rounder or straighter front edge, for example — much as handwriting bears minute self-distinguishing propensities within an alphabet.

So, mindful of our very minutely different cutting styles and, of course, our relative experience and temperaments, the front shop salesmen would decide which cutter would best suit a new customer (subject to the occasional veto, usually by Hammick). Rightly, the first customer assigned to me was none too famous, none too disfigured, and as amenable as they come. I cut a suit that required only three fittings to finish satisfactorily all around and the customer took it home delighted as you please.

Whew.

It was another early customer who would cause me sleepless nights: a well-known actor who previously would have been assigned to Hammick but at my request was given to me. With one of the front shop salesmen on hand to take down my measurements, I ran my sartorial stethoscope up and down and all around the customer fourteen times, calling out numbers that would prove far too big: an 'easy measure' rather than a 'true' one — a common mistake among young cutters, owing, I suppose, to the subconscious knowledge that it is easier to salvage a suit cut too big than one having too little cloth to begin with. When this man returned for his baste fitting I followed him into the fitting room and did my nipping here, tucking there, thoroughly chalking him up, and then Hall came in to check my work and sneak disparaging faces in my direction, for the coat was quite obviously too big in many places — although, it has to be said, if the customer noticed anything awry he did not let on. Many of Savile Row's stage and screen clients would come by just before they were due in a nearby studio or West End theatre, and in order to warm up for the imminent rehearsal or performance they would hum while you did your bit around them. So my new actor-client was doing this, absent-mindedly humming scales or 'The Owl and the Pussycat' while I proceeded to stick three dozen pins in his surplus, seemingly oblivious that the coat we had basted up for him looked as though it had been cut for Coco the Clown.

But this was a rare hiccup. Moreover, at the baste stage very little is irredeemable, especially (paradoxically) at Huntsman, where on average you faced at least two more fittings in which to identify a garment's correctable imperfections and put them right. Not that I afforded myself any laxity down to this excuse. For a former exam truant, I was developing a rather ironic obsession with gradable achievement — with getting a coat right in my teachers' eyes as soon as possible, preferably in the first go, reserving only minor adjustments for the follow-up stages. It would never be so easy; it is a new and unchartered path to 'perfection' every time a customer places an order, and yet I suspect that in pushing myself nevertheless I did gain a crucial advantage, namely a foundation for the day when I would eventually have to answer to my own standards: no less strict or lofty than my mentors' and yet indisputably mine.

Within a year of opening my customer book I had got all easy measures out of my system and was on to expanding my repertoire of figuration solutions: how to counterbalance uneven shoulders, short

211

arms, thick necks, pigeon chests, bow legs, humpbacks, Charlie Chaplin feet — each new punter through the door having his own unique combination of improvable features. I cut suits for bankers, barristers, professors, property investors, journalists, musicians, mafiosi, clergymen and royals. Furthermore, I was not only measuring, cutting and fitting for my growing clientele of Huntsman bespoke; it had also been decided that to compound my experience I should be solely responsible for fitting every customer coming in for our adjustable ready-to-wear line as well. Hammick and Hall were no less stringent with their requirements now that I was working more independently; the spotlight of their circumspection was no less unforgiving than back in my bodkin-fumbling, 'get a haircut' days; and yet the frequency and nature of their critiques of my work undoubtedly had a more subdued, collegiate quality. It was decided that I should make a second solo trip to the States, on the strength of which the company would consider sending me twice annually. My customer book swelled to include dozens of persons of extraordinary accomplishments and stern demands. I had a promising future at one of the most grand and formidable of Savile Row's institutions, regarded by many as bespoke tailoring's standard-bearer.

And then Edward Packer did exactly as Brian Lishak predicted: he sold Huntsman lock, stock and barrel — to the Japanese.

Con Men

Let us take a moment to widen the lens and discuss an unfortunate feature of most industries, even the genteel art and business of bespoke tailoring:

The confidence man.

Savile Row knows two basic categories.

The Inside Man

Every Savile Row house has been hit by at least one, working in some capacity — even Huntsman, where between Hammick's brain and Hall's cards you would have thought they knew every last bloody coat in their purview.

When a coat appears to be finished, a good cutter does not allow it to be dispatched until he has personally 'passed' it, which he does by putting the coat on himself (or a fellow employee, if the coat is too small for his own frame) and scrutinising its reflection in a mirror to confirm that in every last respect it meets his standards. Taking into account the customer's relative height, does the collar sit well — or is it too round and rises up in the back? Do the sleeves hang smoothly in a neutral position? Does the front edge fall to the right point against the thigh? Very good cutters do this not only before dispatching a coat, but at each fitting juncture along the way — after the coat has been basted, forward fitted *and* finished — always to remain one step ahead of the game. So at Huntsman, every afternoon at two, with an almost religious regularity, all of the company coats being made upstairs would be brought down by a tailor or yours truly and Hammick and Hall would drop whatever else they were doing to pass each of them personally — and send those below par back up to the drawing board.

Conducted primarily as a quality-control tactic, this ritual was also thought to keep its participants fully informed of what was happening upstairs at all times. But one day in the seventies the audit figures came round and the trimmings orders failed to match up with the number of units sold. The workshop tailors finished early on Fridays, so one Friday when they had all gone, Hammick and Hall went themselves up to the Heddon Street shop, which at that time was run by a man named Fagle and his right-hand mate, Pease. What Hammick and Hall found hanging up there were dozens and dozens of ticketless coats they had never seen. Fagle had been on a right roll, orchestrating the production of as many as a hundred coats using company-bought trimmings and almost certainly on company time but which were going out the back door. In other words: he was selling suits to friends and private customers — suits made with Huntsman trimmings, overheads and labour — and pocketing what it would have cost to pay for the same himself. The only ingredient he paid for was the basic cloth, probably from Holland & Sherry, next door.

Hammick and Hall confronted Fagle, who confessed and was duly sacked, while Pease, who had known about the scam but pleaded his hands were tied, was chastised yet retained. Some of the other tailors had probably also been in on it and given a little backhander, but Pease would not squeal. Hammick declared that from then on no private work whatsoever on the premises would be tolerated, and Hall engineered a more rigorous safeguards campaign of more frequent auditing and premises checks for unticketed and otherwise unaccounted-for goods.

Being done by one of your own cutters or tailors remains a common problem among tailoring houses. Many are wide-open operations managed by head cutters who are indisposed — if even they have the time — to be involved on every level, and so internal robbery of goods and labour can become the normal run of things. A junior cutter works with a customer for a couple of years and then, if he is so inclined, may say, in the privacy of the fitting room: 'Look. You're paying three thousand through the front door when you could pay me fifteen hundred cash-in-hand for the same thing. Come to my house or I'll come to your office and let me give you a deal.' Oldest trick in the book. Many customers would recognise the crookedness of this and rightly guess that in going in for 'a deal' they will get exactly what they paid for (and sometimes less), but still there are some whom the Confidence Cutter comes to recognise as price grumblers potentially deficient in the integrity department. In this way, the proprietor of one prominent Savile Row house was fleeced for half a million pounds by his own managers. For years his bespoke-division heads took orders that instead of putting through the company they billed out the back door then split the proceeds with the house's cutters, with whom they had struck a deal. Their owner's office was at the top of the building, and on occasion he would descend for a front shop pass-through, to run his hand over the fabrics and have a chat to the cutting staff — but before he could possibly penetrate their faithful veneer and see what they were really up to he would return to his ivory tower, none the wiser.

The Customer

In this case, a new customer comes in, orders a suit, pays you, everything's fine. Then he comes in again, for the same deal: orders a suit, pays you, fine. Gets your trust up; very chummy. Then he comes in and this time swells up to something quite grand, placing an order for, say, half a dozen suits and putting a deposit down for half the amount due. Then the suits are cut, basted, fitted and finished, all according to the now-perfected pattern; dispatched; the balance invoiced for — and the customer is nowhere to be found.

The Confidence Customer actually has something of a basis in tradition. Traditionally, a gentleman's tailor was always the last man to be paid. No one paid his tailor until he had to. The grocer, the butcher, the baker, the barber — all of these purveyors and servicemen would be paid before one's tailor, which meant in turn that tailors waited as long as possible to pay their cloth suppliers. The cloth supplier would become irate and want the money the tailor owed him — meanwhile the tailor had kitted Lord So-and-So out with five suits three years ago, still had not received a penny, and, according to the quaint logic that a tailor should never give his customers the impression of being in economic need, would be too averse to ask for the outstanding amount to extract it.[1] It was a cycle of pandering, stalling tactics and debts — often stemming, ironically, from the unwillingness or absent-mindedness of perfectly solvent customers to pay their bills. Huntsman eventually offered a 10 per cent discount to customers willing to pay in full up front — and in some cases, by the time the garment was done the interest earned on the

---

[1] For years, tailors have been aided in this cultivation of flush appearances by the famous first line of the original Assimil English-language instruction course. 'My tailor is rich,' begins *L'Anglais sans peine*, or 'Painless English', written by Alphonse Chérel and first published in 1929, 'but my English is poor.' Maybe Chérel's tailor did have a fortune, but if so I dare say it did not come from tailoring. Generally speaking, 'My English is not bad, but my tailor has a cash-flow problem' would have landed closer to the mark.

already banked 90 per cent would have exceeded the 10 knocked off. Conversely, but also advantageously, once a customer pays, he wants his garment, which helps maintain shop momentum and keeps orders ticking over. (By the same token, if money were tight, a client who had not paid up front would delay his fitting because he knew then that he would not yet have to pay.) Another Huntsman tactic was to ask new customers for multiple credit references confirming the patron had a history of paying promptly and in full.

So there is a fine line between the customer who, consciously or not, seeks to foster Savile Row's time-honoured tradition of tardy imbursements and he who has no intention whatsoever of paying up at all. One telltale sign of the latter is that leading up to the big order he gets out a massive wad of money and starts counting out his bills right under your nose. Very impressive. You can chase these guys down, of course, but it is not always easy. You could establish a policy by which you hold your finished garments hostage until the balance due has been received, but there are so many customers with whom this lack of trust is simply not called for — and whose loyalty would be undermined as a result — that enforcing such a policy would do more harm than good. So how to collect remains a dilemma for many houses, because while there is certainly a wish to honour tradition and cultivate amity we cannot afford to swallow a ten grand shortfall on a regular basis.

★ ★ ★

Designers: a subsection, arguably less egregious. Flush fashion designers who like the look and make of a bespoke suit will occasionally order one — or dozens — as a way of trying out different prospective designs. In the eighties, one famous couturier placed an order with nearly every tailor on Savile Row. From Huntsman he ordered a suit and two pairs of trousers, one with one pleat and the other with two. And halfway through his fittings, well beyond the point where such alterations could be made, he decided he wanted deeper pleats. There was not enough material for deeper pleats, and poor Lakey had to scrap it all and start again. This happened two or three times, until finally Hammick said to the designer: 'Sir, I'm sorry, but if you ask for something significantly different each time, you'll have to pay.' The designer did, no problem, but he never took the suit and trousers — they are probably still hanging on Huntsman's Pork Rail today. He was just trying out different styles, and for some cutters being a party to this kind of experimentation is no problem — or flattering, even — if you are alive to it, which I endeavour to be. It is all about clarity. There are plenty of cutters and tailors for whom being manipulated into aiding designers is an insult to their work ethic. If the customer's intentions have not been made clear, a worthy cutter or tailor aspires to create something truly personal, something that will be worn and appreciated by an actual living and breathing body for years to come, not a template destined for this season's fashion racks — if it is even going to leave the tailoring shop at all.

★ ★ ★

So, indeed, the Golden Square Mile is a national treasure right down to its Dickensian villains — disingenuous at best, at worst out-and-out criminal. My first taste of it was back when I was on trimmings duty as a teenager — when Markus Berkovic, the smart-looking trousers alteration tailor from Mauritius, offered me a fiver for some company coat lining. Unfortunately, it would not be my last. Even being aware, inasmuch as I was, of the tricksters and traitors potentially afoot on Savile Row, I was unable to see what was coming at Huntsman from a mere cutting board away.

Not Memorable

By the time Fran and I finally married, our sinful cohabitation had gone on for so long that her family had already given up on its redemption and at toast-time my mate Andy Hayes thanked everyone for coming to celebrate 'Richard and Fran's Twenty-Fifth Anniversary'. I elected not to invite my Huntsman patriarchs, so as not to blur the clinically strict boundaries I try to delineate between my home life and my work — but I did cut my own frock coat, waistcoat and trousers for the occasion, as well as suits for my dad and wise guy of a best man. Given the stigma attached to private work, I hired some non-Huntsman tailors to put my suit together, and to my horror they made a hash of the sleeves, which puffed up at the shoulders to look more like something the flower girl might wear. In a panic, for the wedding was just a couple of days away, I asked Hammick for help — and valiantly he summoned not just any tailor but the supreme and unflappable Reno Inglima from upstairs to put everything else aside and right the job. Which Inglima did.

Fran, too, had her own sartorial emergency: inexplicably, the 'custom-made' dress that arrived just before the ceremony fitted about as well as a potato sack and had to be adjusted substantially at the eleventh hour, giving rise to even more gratuitous high drama. It occurred to me to intervene, of course, but I had not seen the dress in question, and in the name of tradition (and so as not to disrupt some long-laid stag-do plans) I elected to stay out of it. An emergency team of tailoresses was brought in and Fran turned out beautifully — I rather less so, as the photos attest. The frock coat was a success, but it would have taken a ski mask to hide the residual effects of a rather late night and my nuptial nerves.

Meanwhile, much to the relief of those of us holding down the fort, Huntsman Sebiro would prove not all that different from Huntsman Savile Row. The profitability of Kindwear's licensing arrangement with Huntsman in Asia had inspired its overseers to offer to buy the company from childless Edward Packer, bringing to an end six decades of family dynasty. But for many years Huntsman's new ownership by Kindwear would feel largely symbolic. There were no abrupt staffing overhauls, no new protocol decrees affecting the bespoke division, no heavy-handedness from afar. Every once in a while Yoshio Watanabe would fly over accompanied by his glamorous interpreter Noriko Suzuki — visits in anticipation of which we would spend a week executing a manic shop-wide tidy-up — and for Noriko's benefit Hammick would become the very picture of debonair. But these meetings of awkward bows and smiling silences bore little influence on life as I knew it. The Kindwear takeover drove home the point that not even national treasures are impenetrable to globalisation — and yet, day-to-day, the Japanese largely left us alone to get on with business as we saw fit.

By now I was making two solo trips each year to the States, where I was well on my way to establishing a warm and mutually respectful rapport with even our hardest-nosed American clients — all except one, an exceedingly pernickety businessman who no matter my efforts, and indeed no matter the quality of his coats, simply could not be satisfied. I had seen enough punters by now to be able to distinguish between legitimate, constructive critique and the sort of non-specific grief a client gives you when he merely wants you to know your place. This man's fittings were routinely soured by the latter, until one day I was fitting him at the Carlyle and the suite doorbell buzzed and when I went to open the door in walked my next customer: Henry Kissinger. 'Good afternoon, Mr Anderson,' Kissinger said courteously. Détente. The first customer's jaw dropped — then he gathered up his things, shook my hand timidly, nodded at Kissinger, and left. I have not had a single complaint from him since.

Shortly after I returned from one of these American trips, Hall had a heart attack. He had taken a rare holiday abroad, in the south of France, and three days into it collapsed. He was taken to a hospital in St-Tropez, then to Marseilles, where a specialised unit saved his life — though he would not return to work for six or seven more weeks, during which time Hammick and I had to do all the coat cutting on our own.

While I would not wish a heart attack on anyone, even someone known once upon a time to have launched a gherkin at my face, I am grateful today for the hectic spell Hall's recuperation occasioned, for it forced ever-more dramatic evolutions in my technical capacity and tested my mettle. As I have said, in the late eighties and early nineties sales slumped all along Savile Row — nevertheless, if a coat-cutting team of three unexpectedly finds itself one man down, especially an ultra-organised workhorse like Hall, it can suddenly feel to those still standing that all of London wants a bespoke suit finished yesterday. Indeed, we were so busy that when the cutting room's telephone rang Hammick would try to answer it without actually having picked it up. 'Hello? Hello! *Hello!*' he would shout, bent low, all ten fingers still minutely adjusting the positions of his chalk and square. When no one responded, he would become annoyed — and by the time he realised he had not actually picked up the receiver he would have missed the call, irritating him all the more.

Beleaguered as such, Hammick had no choice but to share out many of his more illustrious clients — including Gregory Peck, Gianni Agnelli and the Duke of Aspremont. The last two would come in together after lunch and it was as if lunch were still going on, what with all their chattering, laughing, practising golf swings in the fitting rooms and taking turns posing in the old britches saddle. Fitting Agnelli was like playing pin-the-tail-on-the-donkey, the man found it so hard to stand still; no sooner would I have put a coat on his back than he would begin wandering around — and by the time I caught up with him he and the Duke would be tutting at their watches, reminding each other that they were due elsewhere, and then singsong 'Bye now!,' giving a cheerful little wave as they left me holding my chalk in a daze. (Lakey tells me that Peter Sellars and Peter Ustinov once did the same thing. Having happened in at the same time, they were so chuffed to have run into each other they spent the best part of an hour standing together at the end of Lakey's board, trading impersonations and sampling stand-up routines that had the entire cutting room on its knees — and then walked out, all smiles and locked shoulders, without having tried a single thing on.)

Shortly after Hall returned, early on a Friday morning in October 1993, Fran gave birth to our first child, Tom.

I had been at hospital all night and rang Huntsman at half-eight in the morning with the news and to say that I would not be in. Hall, whose brush with death in the sunny south of France had done little to lighten his disposition, suggested that I make up my one day of 'paternity leave' over the weekend.

Which I did.

Not long after Tom was born, Hammick announced he wanted to retire.

For all the news's enormity, I felt conflicted. I would miss Hammick terribly — not just his extraordinary talent but the whole gamut of eccentricities as well: his moody procrastination, his imperious sense of humour, his obsessive suit-changing, his handless phone-answering, the ubiquitous Piccadillies, every third of them lit from the wrong end. I also felt not a little trepidation at the idea of being left alone with Hall, who I think had not cracked a smile since our last visit from Fred Seidel.

On the other hand, this inevitable development was freshly inspiring. Not one to wallow in nostalgia for yesteryear, I saw yet a new opportunity to prove myself up to the challenge: to do everything in my power to ensure Huntsman's reputation would survive Hammick's departure — indeed that the conclusion of his stellar career could also be seen to mark the beginning of a newly productive and well-regarded era that some-day would be just as celebrated in its own right.

Reasonably — yet nevertheless to my chagrin, for it meant no immediate call-up for me — Hall decided that in order to stay apace we would need to recruit a new senior cutter from the outside. We hired Fred Pugh, a man who approximately twenty years earlier had apprenticed Lakey before amicably leaving Huntsman for a junior cutter position elsewhere on the Row. Hammick agreed to stay on long enough to oversee Pugh's re-entry and training up — but, of course, as we know, Hammick was not terribly effectual in the training department, and Pugh promptly put Hammick off with his rather unusually loud sartorial style. One morning Pugh showed up in a royal blue suit, a shirt striped broadly in every colour of the rainbow, a pink tie and an oversized white collar. As he passed Hammick on his way to his board, Hammick raised an eyebrow and said quietly: 'All you need are some flashing lights on there, Mr Pugh.'

Pugh had a laugh exactly like Muttley's in *Wacky Races*. Once he got going, he could not stop — which would get me going, too, and then Lakey and the front shop salesmen, all of us completely losing it while Hammick and Hall looked on in bafflement. One day shortly after one of these contagious laughing fits, Hugh Laurie rang up to make an appointment for his first Huntsman suit and I asked Hammick if I could cut for him.

'Who is Hugh Laurie?' Hammick asked.

'A comedian!' I blurted out, incredulously.

'Well then,' Hammick replied, 'why don't we have you cut the coat, Young Richard, Mr Pugh the trousers, and then we'll have all the comedians in one room together.'

Pugh's cutting was perfectly serviceable, but his harlequin ensembles and high-pitched giggling made Hammick suspicious, and Hall even more truculent, and in the end Pugh stayed less than a year before defecting of his own accord for a smaller house around the corner on New Burlington Street. Hammick agreed again to stay on a bit longer in order to 'help' get yet another someone new up and running; by this point Lakey, too, was due to retire, but Hall asked him to stay on for an additional six months while the company looked for a new trousers cutter as well.

Next up: Ray Jordan. A tall, elegant, neatly moustachioed man, Ray blessedly had the right attitude, sense of decorum and a promisingly instinctual cutting technique. To my delight he also had a glimmer of old Toby's mischief about him: at the end of an especially ugly week during which every last one of Hall's gripes seemed bound for our new recruit, Ray spotted a newspaper advertisement for Hamley's annual Santa in the Grotto attraction and with his pattern shears snipped it out and inserted it among Hall's ticket clips.

But within six months of joining us, just as he was beginning to have some success achieving the Huntsman silhouette, Ray was diagnosed with Hodgkin's lymphoma. He was only fifty and insisted on working through his chemotherapy but it was obviously wearing him down and Hall, who seemed not to grasp the severity of Ray's condition, afforded him not even a modicum of special treatment. When Ray died in February 1996 — having worked with us for only two years, eighteen months of which were haunted by illness — it was as though Huntsman had poisoned him to death, and the experience left a bad taste in everyone's mouth.

The same week Ray Jordan died, my first daughter, Molly, was born.

By way of congratulations, Hall summoned me into the boardroom.

'Now, Richard,' he said gravely. 'What I want you to do when you are planning your nights of passion, is think about your business.'

Say again?

To this day I remain unsure whether Hall actually meant to suggest that when Fran and I next opened our diaries to schedule a 'night of passion' I was to take sufficient pause to conclude that the attendant possibility of impregnating my wife was too risky for my career — or indeed that in the midst of a 'night of passion' I should try to bring my mind round to 'my business' (and Hall, inevitably) in order that said passion should wane. In any case, I was gobsmacked. Looking a trifle embarrassed, Hall left the room without a further word. I half expected he would pop back in just long enough to suggest that I also get a haircut.

Our next trial cutter was Harold Toomey, a thick-set chain-smoker who had worked for a time with Jordan at the same high-profile house down the street. Hammick's departure having finally taken official effect (he spent the afternoon prior to his retirement party seated regally at his board, smoking and eyeing the caterers as they laid out wine-glasses and sausage rolls in his honour), we continued the process of juggling his long-time clients. These included a posh old chestnut whose name I knew from my interview nearly fifteen years earlier: Zohrabian. Zohrabian had lopsided hips, a bulging belly, feet splayed at ten to two, and he liked his pleatless trousers so tight they looked sprayed on. He drove Lakey mad. Often Zohrabian would bring in his own cloth, and it was beautiful enough, but he wanted so many fittings and adjustments in his trousers that by the time he took the bloody things home (*if* he took them home) it was a miracle they were not threadbare. Anyway, Hall and I were overseeing a fitting between Zohrabian and Toomey and where Zohrabian's old chap resided there was a bulge that Toomey, bless him, trying to make the skin-tight trousers look good, cupped with his palm and started *moving around*. We all tried our best to pretend nothing was amiss but as soon as Zohrabian left Hall pulled Toomey aside and said, 'We don't fondle the customers, old boy. They don't like it.'

Another one doomed.

It has to be said that, as our new managing director, Hall was finding himself under more pressure than ever before. He was now solely in charge not only of the cutting room but also the entire tailoring staff, workshop repairs, sales, lease negotiations and marketing, and whereas Hammick used to contend with stress by lighting a cigarette and slowing everything within his reach down to a glacial pace. Hall's anxieties expressed themselves in a different way. Hall was always wanting to tell you that he came from Kent; I think because he fancied the implied association with villainous East End spillover. And now that Hammick was out of the picture, Hall seemed to go out of his way to bully, or at least antagonise, all the unsuspecting customers Hammick had indulged for decades. Sir Ashley Devalcourt was the worst case in point. He was an extremely demanding and impatient man, always shouting for you if you were not there, and he had little use for our appointment cards; he came in exactly when he pleased and instead of allowing a salesman to install him in one of the fitting rooms would stand just outside them and glare down the shop until his cutter took notice and jumped-to. Whereas Hammick always did his best to accommodate such visits — in fact, Hammick used to keep all of Sir Ashley's coats on the rail right next to his board, in order that they should always be immediately on hand — Hall would have none of this. So one day Sir Ashley came in and Hall let him boil outside the fitting rooms for twenty minutes before deigning to receive him, at which point a crimson-faced Sir Ashley exploded: 'HOW *DARE* YOU MAKE ME WAIT?!'

Hall shrugged. 'We sent you a card.'

'WHO do you THINK you *ARE*?!' Sir Ashley roared, jabbing his finger into Hall's chest. 'You're owned by the Japanese, aren't you!'

'No.'

'Yes! You are!'

'Correct! We are.'

We never saw Sir Ashley again.

★ ★ ★

Brian Lishak had been with Wells of Mayfair for about eight years when Wells was beset by a fate common among residents of the

236

Golden Square Mile: it lost its lease.

Hall set about wooing Brian back to Huntsman to help with the firm's director- ship and stimulate falling sales. The company is in a bit of a state, Hall said to Brian; come back and we'll make it worth your while. (Hammick had also tried to lure Brian back over a drink a few years earlier, but Brian had demurred.) Brian would still have to worry about our ownership, of course, for just as Packer Junior had sold Huntsman to the Japanese, the Japanese could sell the company on to yet another entity. But, as Hall assured Brian, the Japanese were largely hands-off proprietors; what's more, Brian had an already established friendship with the Watanabes, for years earlier he had arranged for Yoshio Watanabe to stay with one of Huntsman's clients in America while Yoshio, then a boy, learned English. Brian also had an unusually good relationship with Hall, whom he had his own quiet way of defusing, and with whom he also spent time in the Royal Air Force and lived near in Kent. So the offer now seemed fortuitous, and Brian persuaded his partner to buy Brian's share of Wells so he could return to Huntsman as managing director of development and business abroad.

I was thrilled. Due in part to Hammick's conservatism and then, paradoxically, his retirement, business and morale had slumped, and I could think of no person better than Brian to reverse this trend. As I have said, Hammick's background was in cutting, not marketing, so under his direction sales had not been top priority. Moreover, in the tailoring business one's clientele is fluid: it is common for your customers to grow older with you, as Hammick's did until they died or he retired. (Robert Packer used to say that a company must acquire at least two new customers a day just to make up for the ones falling off the other end.) So we needed Brian's sales expertise — we also needed his perspective on the operating finances. Thanks to Robert Maxwell we had a pension-fund problem, as well: theoretically we were all in favour of the government safeguards established in his honour, but implementing them was proving bloody expensive. Our debts were guaranteed by the Japanese, but on any additional money we wanted to borrow we had to pay a premium. And, except for the sale of one of our little auxiliary companies — Allan's, a tiny shop just the other side of Oxford Street that made shoetrees for a vast percentage of the trade — Huntsman had not made a profit in almost ten years.

As Brian rolled up his sleeves to tackle these affairs, Hall and I refocused our attention on the cutting department.

Wandering hands aside, Toomey's patterns were too militaristic for Hall's taste. Moreover, Toomey was an ambler: no matter how bustling or urgent things were in the rest of the cutting room, Toomey moved around it at the only speed he knew — molasses — which drove Hall wild.

So Toomey was sacked and replaced with Giuseppe Grasso, a diminutive Italian we prised away from yet another large house on the Row. As with Ray Jordan, I had high hopes for Grasso, who was an absolutely lovely man and an elegant and sensible cutter — but then the atmosphere at Huntsman seemed too much of a jungle for him. He was too gentlemanly to bear Hall's raucous bollockings and the consistency of his work would occasionally be sabotaged by his nerves. He did stay on for two and a half years or so — and then we arrived at work one morning to learn that Grasso had had a stroke in his bathtub at home and died. It was horrifying. I dare say I was not alone in wondering whether there was something in the air at Huntsman and sooner or later we would all be done for.

It was not just the cutting team that struggled in the human resources department. In the front shop we had a new salesman, Trevor Maynard — a fantastic salesman, one of the best I have ever seen, but he could do nothing else. Could not put something into the diary, could not book up an order, could not take a phone call, nothing. All he could do was sell, and ice to Eskimos, so we kept him. One day shortly before his retirement Hammick had been fitting one of his customers, Charles Tabor, when one of my customers, John Taber, rang up wanting to arrange a fitting with me. Maynard had taken the call and came bounding over to Hammick and Tabor and said, 'Mr Taber! I've got your father on the phone.'

The elderly Tabor looked aghast.

'Your father! He's on the phone!'

'My father? My *father*?' Tabor said. 'My father has been dead for years.'

'No!' Maynard said — insisted! — 'I've got him on the phone! He wants to speak with you.'

All Hammick and Tabor could do was stand there and gape at the madman.

Hammick had some great put-downs. When he met someone he did not rate, he handled it with old-school discretion. He would not say outright exactly how he felt, opting instead to sum up the offending character as 'not memorable'. Which in my book is worse than being called useless or incompetent. And which, fairly or not, is what I suspect Hammick (if pressed) would have said about many of our recent hires who did not die prematurely — perhaps even about the two who did as well. Certainly something particular to Huntsman was missing in many of them, something personal and instinctive I dare say no amount of technical proficiency could have eclipsed. But, to be fair, Hammick and Hall did not make it easy. They expected men who had taken years of training elsewhere to discern, as if by magic, how to cut a suit plainly and purely of the Huntsman line. These guys were accustomed to finishing something on the first go and being told it is lovely, brilliant, right, on to the next job, whereas at Huntsman they were being sent back to the drawing board three, four, five times before their efforts would be accepted — and then only begrudgingly. It is a bit much to expect that a cutter in his forties or fifties and who has been in charge of his own customer book for twenty-odd years should suddenly revert to being scolded like a child. Of course, all these men falling around me was good for my own career, for I had grown up in the Huntsman mould and it was not long before Hall decreed that despite being ten-to-twenty years older and paid three times as much, our candidates could not do the job as well as I. So my sixteen years of determined practice and endurance finally paid off: I was crowned a Huntsman senior cutter — and yet arrival was bittersweet. Hammick was gone. Lakey was gone. Hall was counting down the seconds to his own retirement, and, as much as I would have liked to, I was not going to be able to handle cutting for the entire company on my own. What was the answer? Was there someone out there who would be a perfect addition to the team? Or could it be that as Huntsman approached its 150th anniversary and a new millennium, its standards were so lofty as to be unviable?

★　★　★

In January 1998 my third child, George, was born.

The following spring, having cut his last masterpiece — a blood-red melton motorcycle coat for Fred Seidel — Hall turned sixty-five and summarily retired.

Kindwear appointed Brian managing director and the following autumn I was assigned to the directorial board as well — as director of production and head cutter, the youngest in Huntsman's history.

Together, Brian and I sat down to assess our bequest. Within an hour it was decided that we needed urgently to do two things: increase Huntsman's prices by 20 per cent (Hall had not raised prices in five years — not even a 3 per cent nod to inflation) and increase sales and production by 20 per cent as well. To the latter end, we brainstormed marketing events in commemoration of the company's anniversary. As a rule, Savile Row's established bespoke houses generally do not go in for paid advertising, so this was not a consideration; but by the same token for years Huntsman had done little more in the way of marketing than to send out a card with all its Royal Warrants on it and then sit back and wait for the orders to come in. Seven decades earlier, when Robert Packer took over a company whose success had been built up on military britches that were soon to become obsolete, he set his mind first to increasing trade with Huntsman's existing customers and resolved to sell every man who came in for britches a coat as well. Likewise, Brian and I came up with new ways to re-engage our existing clientele. We commissioned the Perfumers Guild to design an exclusive Huntsman cologne that would be given complimentary to bespoke customers and sold at the shop. We announced a lottery whereby any customer who placed an order worth £2500 or more before the end of the millennium would be eligible to win: four new suits, a blazer and a topcoat (first prize); three suits (second prize); or one suit (third prize). And we designed new anniversary tweeds and Super 150 worsteds in six different designs and colourways, including a new version of Huntsman's famous window-pane check — and presented these worldwide in customer mailings, a campaign that effectively tacked an extra sale onto almost every bespoke order that came in.

Within just a few weeks, business began rapidly to pick up, and I found myself cutting around the clock, which meant we now had to light a fire under the workshop tailors, as well. We assessed production and offered bonuses if they could ratchet up their pace. This would have to be done without compromising the garments' quality, of course, and no doubt bearing this in mind Reina and Inglima said the numbers we wanted were unrealistic. Brian and I dis-agreed — or at least we were curious to see what the promise of a reward would bring. The workers were doubtful, but within two months production surged, the promised bonuses were paid, and morale continued to climb.

The shop was in desperate need of a sprucing up. The *Evening Standard* had recently published a story on Huntsman in which the writer extolled our ongoing sartorial stature, declaring that a 'single-button Huntsman suit, with its suppressed waist and tapered trousers, is one of the most quintessentially English of status symbols,' while in the same breath taking the mick out of our stomping ground: 'In 1919 Huntsman set up shop at 11 Savile Row, and to look at the place it was last given a lick of paint about then. It is Savile Row's riposte to Miss Havisham's house.' But we had already borrowed as much money as the Japanese were willing to lend us and could not afford to get redecorators in to do the job. So a couple of weeks before Easter Brian went down to Tottenham Court Road and bought a load of paint, brushes, buckets and Polyfilla and said to the workshop tailors: 'Come on, guys, the place needs tarting up. Let's all come in over the holiday, I'll pay you, and we'll do it ourselves.'

Fourteen guys pitched up, Brian's wife provided refreshments, and the job was done by Saturday afternoon. While the team stood on the pavement, admiring their work through the shop's window, a passer-by stopped to ask whether they wouldn't come round to his house and give him a quote.

Indeed, we were rekindling Huntsman's spirit: sales and production were mushrooming and the staff was regaining momentum. Garment sales and output increased by 50 per cent — from 600 to 900 units annually. We were able to begin clearing our debts, bringing the pension fund up to where it needed to be, and attracting more and more business in the States, where Brian had resumed visiting the West Coast in addition to the East. For the first time in a long while, it was all going well.

Too well.

In 1999, the Japanese announced they wanted to sell.

The Japanese economy had been struggling for years and many Japanese companies were electing to withdraw from businesses abroad — Aquascutum being a case in point. Yoshio Watanabe, the same man Brian had ambassadored to America when Yoshio was a boy, had decided Huntsman Savile Row was no longer of interest. The Huntsman product in Japan remained successful, but all Kindwear needed to keep this iron in the fire was its label licence. Anticipating further economic decline, they no longer wanted the responsibility of sustaining a tangible operation halfway around the globe.

Brian rang up Watanabe to say that he himself would be interested in buying the company.

Watanabe was taciturn, and stalled. Eventually he disclosed that Holland & Sherry, Huntsman's long-time cloth supplier next door, had expressed interest in buying the company and so Kindwear wished first to open our accounts to them in due diligence. Brian showed Holland & Sherry's owners around the shop and then sat down with them to review the books, but because the fruits of our renaissance had not yet hit the accounts, all Holland & Sherry saw was how bad the numbers had been — how the last profit Savile Row's premier bespoke tailoring house had made was through the sale of a shoetree shop. They withdrew their interest, and Brian reiterated his own — but, again, Watanabe was non-committal.

Meanwhile, we desperately needed another cutter. Brian enquired among his various trade contacts and was told the man with the talent was one Trevor Swift. We met Swift at Brown's Hotel for an interview and learned that like Brian and I, and Hammick, Hall and Lakey before us, Swift had worked in the trade since he was a teenager, and this had some appeal. Huntsman would be his first post on Savile Row proper, but his CV listed recent experience in a large clothiers' nascent bespoke division and we were so snowed under with orders we decided to give him a chance. And . . . he was fine. A Route One cutter who worked off the blocks but genially complied with my requests for a wider shoulder here, a svelter waist there. His personality was a bit bland, which was not good, because to an extent customers *like* character; character breeds loyalty. (Even a good number of Hall's customers liked *his* character, for they were a little bit like him — it is something like people coming to look like their dogs.) But in contrast to a couple of his predecessors, Swift was a relief, and to some degree *because* he was inconspicuous. Certainly we hoped that in time his cutting would more closely approach the Huntsman line and a winning personality would reveal itself, but in the meantime we were satisfied enough, for with his unassumingly diligent assistance we were poised to make the company's first bespoke-driven profit in almost a decade.

★   ★   ★

The night before Brian was due to make one of his journeys to America his solicitor rang to say that the Japanese had an offer.

Brian called Watanabe to ask whom it was from and how things could have possibly progressed to this point without him being aware of it.

True to form, Watanabe was reticent.

'Well,' said Brian, 'tell me what the offer is, and Richard and I'll top it.'

'We don't work that way,' said Watanabe.

'But we have a special relationship,' Brian said.

Watanabe said he would discuss the suggestion with his team and they hung up. Brian went off to America as planned and a day or two later rang Watanabe in the middle of the night New York time for the figure. It was not prohibitive. Watanabe agreed that if Brian could raise the amount plus a small topping percentage within a week of his return the Japanese would sell us the company. When Brian got back he went straight to his bank to ask for the money. No problem, the bank replied. We'll have it to you in two days. We held a retirement party for Trevor Maynard, our sales-man-cum-séance conductor, and during the party Brian was summoned to a conference call with Watanabe's Japan-based analysts, who were looking at the latest figures and wanted him to defend the purchase of a modest company car.

Meanwhile the bank's two days stretched to three, then four, then five — and finally Watanabe rang to say he had accepted the other offer.

Again, Brian asked who the buyer was. Was it someone we knew?

'Yes,' Watanabe said. 'It is someone you know.'

But he would not say who.

A few days later, a despondent Brian, our company secretary and I followed orders to turn up at a solicitors' office where we knew no one. Watanabe was conferenced in by phone, along with a man who introduced himself as Don Bargeman, in virtual attendance on behalf of Huntsman's new owners-to-be. As managing director, Brian was required to authorise the liquid buyout of a company he had served for forty-three years. He will tell you that holding the pen, staring down at his signature, remains the worst moment of his life.

★ ★ ★

It was a sweltering July afternoon and I was working at my cutting board when a murmur came down from the front shop that our new owners had arrived. Despite the heat, intensified by the sun streaming through the skylight directly above my board, I instinctively reached for my coat, for I had got it into my head that 'Don Bargeman' was a front for a customer and I wanted to make a good impression.

In fact, I recognised none of the four men whom Brian led down the shop and up the stairs to the boardroom on the second floor. Swift and I had mountains of work, so I tried to remain focused on my cutting, but waiting was murder.

About half an hour later, Brian finally came down alone and, without a word to me, went back to his desk at the front of the shop. His face looked ashen.

After another fifteen minutes or so had elapsed, one of the four men came down — a large man, with a lively and voluminous presence — and, also without a word in my direction, crossed the cutting room straight for Swift's board, where, wearing a broad, comradely smile, he clapped his hand on Swift's shoulder.

'Hello, Trevor,' the man said.

'Hiya, Don.'

It was then that I realised we had been done. Done by our third category of con man: the plant.

Inconspicuous. Unassuming. Not memorable.

That was Swift. Not memorable. Doing us from three feet away.

Hook, line and sinker.

He played it well.

We were done like kippers.

The End

Huntsman is an acquired taste. It is the grandest, stuffiest, priciest tailor on Savile Row. Quite how its eminence came about is a mystery. Henry Poole is older. Anderson & Sheppard makes suits for the Prince of Wales. Kilgour French Stanbury retains the services of that legendary cutter, Ian Fallan. But Huntsman has a mystique that others cannot match.

Financial Times, 5 June 1999

The above appeared almost a month to the day before Huntsman was officially sold to a consortium of sixteen investors headed up by Don Bargeman and Trevor Swift.

In the six months between our hiring him and the consortium's takeover, Swift had been a very quiet, diligent and agreeable worker.

Now we knew why.

A team of prospective backers keen to buy a tailoring house had tapped Swift with the role of getting a job in one and relaying the information they would need to assess the company's prospects and make a competitive offer. When Swift landed at the most prestigious firm on Savile Row — and it was up for sale — they must not have been able to believe their luck.

Earlier that spring, Brian had taken Swift to Paris, with an eye towards getting Swift up and running on the overseas sales side. During the days, Swift enquired eagerly about Huntsman's foreign reach, client base, staffing decisions and internal finances — but then, in the evenings, when Brian would propose a working dinner, Swift excused himself repeatedly to retire early, one night saying he had a migraine, another that he had to ring his wife about his son, who was having trouble of some unspecified nature. It was not until after the consortium bought Huntsman and we found ourselves in the boardroom with Don Bargeman — who expressed his knowledge of the company in terms nearly identical to those revealed by Brian to Swift in Paris — that we thought to suspect Swift of having made reconnaissance calls from the inside.

Don Bargeman's background was in marine insurance. He also told us that he was a lawyer, but presumably not practising, as our accountant was unable to find any trace of him among the published lists of practising professionals. His wife's family was supremely wealthy — indeed, our impression was that family money comprised much of the consortium's capital. (As far as we could tell, none of the investors except for Swift had any practical experience in making or selling clothes.) Bargeman's boisterous way of bounding around the shop as he familiarised himself with his new acquisition made me think of Tigger from *Winnie-the-Pooh*; indeed, there was something warm and likable about his enthusiasm — that is, until it bore its first consequence.

Bargeman appointed himself Huntsman's chairman and made Brian 'deputy chairman'. Brian urged Bargeman that the company would do best not to undergo any dramatic changes right off the bat because sales and marketing were finally back on track and on Savile Row the consistency, quality and integrity of a brand are everything.

'Of course,' Bargeman agreed. 'We won't change a thing.'

Then he sold the Heddon Street workshop.

Brian had only just recently concluded renegotiations for a new and favourable lease. Several tailors were sacked and the remainder displaced downstairs to the basement, considerably dimmer and one-third the size. The sectionalised system of coat-making that had distinguished Huntsman from the rest of the tailoring establishment for over a century was dismantled step by step until finally it had been wholly replaced with a system whereby non-specialist tailors were individually responsible for assembling coats from baste to finish.

A team of 'marketing specialists' was brought in to propose that we replace our traditional Huntsman cream-and-burgundy wrap with solid-black gift boxes and matching tissue paper. They also suggested that we emboss our packaging and engrave our cufflinks with an H.

Brian was incredulous. 'We cannot use H,' he said, pointing in the direction of New Bond Street, two blocks away. 'H is for Hermès.'

Funereal wrapping and the H were scrapped, but Bargeman was insistent that Huntsman needed a new jewellery range, which he put his wife in charge of designing. Shortly after it went on display, Joan Rivers came into the shop to browse for some gifts. Hearing that she was on the premises, Bargeman came forth from his office in the back to introduce himself as Huntsman's new owner — but he had made it only to my board when Ms Rivers spotted our new cufflinks and recoiled, shouting:

'Oh my *God!* These are the most dis*gusting* things I have ever seen in my *life*!'

Bargeman did an about-face and returned to his room.

Time-and-motion consultants came in to pore over our books. Decades earlier, Edward Packer had secured a special, government-sanctioned VAT dispensation whereby even if customers had paid cash up front, a deposit or the entire amount due for an order, Huntsman was allowed to defer payment of VAT on these receipts until the garments in question had been completed and dispatched. For more than thirty years the VAT lords had sanctioned this exception and came by regularly, every two years or so, to examine the company's books and extend the allowance. But, for no reason we could fathom, the time-and-motion consultants determined this arrangement was 'not right' and had to be changed. Brian went blue in the face trying to dissuade them — it was a wholly pointless adjustment that would ultimately cost the company half a million pounds — but in response the consultants reasoned that 'the owners have invested all this money and it has to be spent'. Nay, squandered.

Bargeman attended board meetings in his cycling shorts. Hammick would have fainted.

Bare limbs outstretched, he swore like a trooper and quickly grew bored with following the agenda. We would jump from point one to point eight to point three, then Bargeman would halt the proceedings in favour of a coffee run. Just to get some cutting done I had to arrange in advance for one of the salesmen to ring up the inter-company phone pretending that one of my customers had come in for a fitting. Bargeman had decided that all of our buying should be done on a consensus basis, and this included any additional consortium members who also happened to be in attendance, so whereas previously Brian and I alone had done the monthly ordering in fewer than thirty minutes we now had eight people in a room, one of them half-naked and one or two others giving the impression of having just set foot on Savile Row for the first time in their lives, congregating for two hours to choose what ties we were going to sell in the front shop.

The tie salesman proposed an order of two hundred.

'Not enough,' Bargeman said. 'Double it.'

'Don,' Brian said. 'Do you know how many ties we sell a year? Customers are going to tire of seeing these before we can possibly sell four hundred of them. It's too many to take all at once.'

'No, no,' Bargeman said. 'You can't sell the stock if you haven't got it. Triple the order!'

The tie salesman could not believe his luck — and by the end of the week we had ties coming out of our ears.

When not in his cycling shorts, Bargeman was partial to navy trousers. Huntsman had never sold casual, ready-to-wear navy trousers. Beige, cavalry twill, corduroy, yes — because these are less common on the high street and go well with a large range of sport coats — but men simply do not come in droves to a Savile Row bespoke tailoring house to buy off-the-peg navy trousers.

And yet, because Bargeman wore navy trousers, we ordered two hundred pairs of them.

'And let's get rid of these horrible hairy tweeds,' he said to me once, wrinkling his nose at one of the company's most popular commissions, lugged up from the stock room. 'No one wears tweed any more.'

In September 1999, about four months after the consortium took over, my fourth child was born — another girl, Mai — and Bargeman promoted Swift to the position of managing director. Never mind that it was a post definitively above mine; it was an honour formerly held by the likes of Colin Hammick, Brian Hall and Brian Lishak, whose cumulative service to Huntsman amounted to 140 years. Swift had not yet been at the company for one. Moreover, he had no group management experience to speak of — prior to working for Hackett's new bespoke division, he had been a one-man band — and suddenly he was going to oversee a production team of sixty tailors. When he showed up to work the day after his promotion carrying a book on 'how to manage people', I could not help myself from going to Bargeman and questioning the logic of this appointment with as much politesse as I could muster.

Bargeman became exasperated.

'Richard,' he sighed. 'We're very clever people. We're going to get this right.'

To his crossover customers, the majority unaccustomed to Huntsman's prices, Swift offered discounts. One day a new customer came in, placed an order with the front shop sales staff, and, perhaps having heard that Huntsman's prices were now negotiable, requested a reduction. The salesman went back to the office to consult Brian, who declined. Aside from the customary discount of 10 per cent for anyone paying up front in full, Brian

260

explained, we could not accommodate markdowns on an individual basis.

The salesman went back to the customer with this news and the customer said he would take his business elsewhere. The salesman returned to Brian to register the threat, but Brian held firm.

'Tell him we're very sorry, but we have a policy here. Our prices are our prices.'

When the salesman returned once again to relay Brian's final word, Swift was already there — agreeing to the lower price.

I have made the point that the customer who is unwilling to pay the full asking price for a proper bespoke suit will very often get what he pays for — and in some cases less. In order to afford indiscriminate 'discounts', the dishonest cutter will show a customer the finest, most expensive samples on hand (a black mohair priced at £120 a yard, for example) and then 'sub it down', which is to make up the order with a visually similar but vastly inferior fabric (priced, say, at £30 a yard) — and charge for the former. Houses and customers alike must remain vigilant for this kind of craft debasement, and while Brian and I never observed Swift try his hand at anything quite so audacious at Huntsman, he did go in for other questionable tactics that had us in a constant state of alarm. His manner with customers became bolder, but not winningly so: in the presence of aristocrats Swift assumed an incongruous Cockney barrow boy persona and cracked off-colour jokes, one of them about the exceptional height of a certain envoy's wife — in her presence. He raised the prices on a category of garment, like sport coats or our unshiftable hoard of ready-to-wear suits and navy trousers, by a considerable percentage, then brought them back down again and called the occasion a 'sale'. He took an order from a customer for two vicuña overcoats, priced at £30,000 apiece, and paired them — these coats made of one of the most precious materials on earth — with one of the cheapest linings a pittance can buy. (Brian happened to see the coats before they were dispatched and insisted that Swift replace the lining — which he did.) Swift rarely actually passed a coat before dispatching it, and, unbeknownst to anyone else until after the fact, one weekend he let himself into the shop in order to arrange for the sale of Huntsman's entire collection of specially commissioned tweeds, some of them antiques of consider-able historical and indeed monetary value, to a wholesaler. He told us he had received only £500 for the lot.

Every day felt like another nail in the

coffin. Brian and I made impassioned pro-
tests, of course; the hallowed boardroom saw
some terrible rows. But just as often, when
Brian or I questioned yet another grievously
unsound decision or oversight, Bargeman, incred-
ibly, would just shut down, as though our
objections on behalf of his company's reputation and solvency were the antics of wanton
troublemakers. I cannot explain it — for as I
say Bargeman's energy had its appealing moments
and often his heart did seem in the right place
— except perhaps to suppose he was out
of his depth and too embarrassed to admit
having jumped without knowing how to swim
in the first place. All but denied a voice, Brian
and I endeavoured to put our heads down
and focus on the little areas over which we
still had some control — in my case, cutting
and overseeing production for my clients, while
Brian concentrated his efforts on development and marketing abroad — but it was a
gruelling trial. We were plagued by the sinking
suspicion that Bargeman and his co-financiers
thought of Huntsman as a mere plaything
— that they liked the idea of owning a Savile
Row tailoring house but had mistaken the
combination of high price tags and quaint
history for unassailable durability and guaranteed returns. They could not have been more
wrong.

Staying was untenable — but then the logistics of leaving could not be taken lightly. I had a steep mortgage. Four years earlier, to accommodate our growing brood, Fran and I had sold our cottage at a £9,000 loss and bought a semi-detached three-bedroom for £90,000 on St Albans's Folly Lane. Already we needed even more space, now that Mai had come along — and, of course, I had to think of all the additional expenses involved in raising four children, the oldest seven, the youngest not yet even a year.

And yet about needing to start afresh I was as certain as night follows day. I wanted Brian to be involved — but initially Brian was tentative, understandably; nearing retirement age, he was contemplating closing his chapter on Savile Row and moving to Spain. Still, I was so unhappy and eager to begin anew that even with Brian's precious consultation from afar I would have taken the leap alone.

In the end I would not have to. About nine months after the consortium had taken over — forty-three years after Brian made his first trip to America on Huntsman's behalf — Brian returned from a sales trip to the States and said he had made up his mind: he could not carry on any longer. He felt like a fraud. Except for what I was cutting and overseeing down to the button, Huntsman's products were no longer something he could represent with any modicum of sincerity or pride. He was having trouble even looking clients in the eye.

But he was not ready to call it quits.

'Look,' Brian said, 'I'm sixty-one. I don't want to go on like this. I used to love coming to work. Now it's agony. I'm either going to retire, which I don't really want to do, or — if you're still interested, because I admire and respect your talent and feel that with my experience and contacts I can take care of the business side . . . let's do it. Let's go out on our own.'

That clinched it. Every weekday morning for nearly a year I had approached our beloved Huntsman with dread. Hammick and Hall phoned from time to time and Lakey, sometimes wearing his Katharine Hepburn jumper, often dropped by to say hello and see how I was getting on, and the only thing worse than my own anguish over what was happening to Huntsman were the heartbreaking reactions in the voices and faces of these three men, my emeritus mentors and mainstays in a tradition of quality, integrity, honest hard work and superior standards, when they saw just how blithely and irrevocably their life's pride was being run into the ground by a cutter of dubious principles and a skipper from Steamship Mutual. It was unbearable. Whatever the risks, Brian and I had to get out. And so, on the second Friday of November 2000, two days after my thirty-sixth birthday and nearly nineteen years after I arrived at 11 Savile Row for the first time in slushy turn-ups, I resigned.

Huntsman indeed is gone from Savile
    Row,
And Mr Hall, the head cutter.
The red hunt coat Hall cut for me was
    utter
Red melton cloth thick as a carpet, cut
    just so.
One time I wore it riding my red
    Ducati race — what a show! —
Matched exotics like a pair of lovely red
    egrets.
London once seemed the epitome of no
    regrets
And the old excellence one used to
    know
Of the chased-down fox bleeding its
    stink across the snow.

from 'Kill Poem', by Frederick Seidel

267

Lucky Number Thirteen

Garage Leave

Once again in need of more space, Fran and I moved house — this time from our three-bedroom on the now disquietingly named Folly Lane to a semi-detached five-bedroom with the luxury of its own double garage in St Albans's Marshalswick.

The latter was no dream abode. It had not been renovated in years and needed considerable work. But at £290,000 it was just within our financial reach (Folly Lane had gone for £169,950), and it was a space generously accommodating of the six of us. Equally in its favour was that I had been able to hasten its sellers to close the transaction prior to my giving notice at Huntsman — in other words: before I became an unemployed father of four, at which point winning a mortgage from any level-headed lender would have been nigh on impossible. We moved in the early autumn, I resigned in November, and by Christmas I was well into my three-month gardening leave, a penance coinciding neatly with the dead of winter.

Brian, too, was serving out three months of workless indenture at home, for it was together that we had confronted Swift in the boardroom to announce our resignations from Huntsman — causing Swift to blanch and Bargeman to ring Brian at home the following Sunday evening with a curt order not to bother coming back to the shop at all. Bemused, Brian rang me to ask whether I, too, had received a call issuing my immediate dismissal, but I had not, and none came.

The following morning I returned perfunctorily to my board, where I had to endure a public address by Bargeman to the rest of the staff about my 'very sad' decision to move on. Whereas Brian's input had been deemed directly dispensable, the relatively esoteric services of a head cutter must have seemed to warrant a more gradual relinquishing, for it was indicated that I should remain on hand for a while to help effect a smooth transition. But the company's general decline and Brian's ludicrous banishment had so direly poisoned the place that in the end I could not stay out the week before packing up my shears and bidding Huntsman farewell for good.

In theory, gardening leave obliges one to remain professionally idle for its duration, but — just as the grounded schoolboy plots the vindicating adventures to commence upon his release — my and Brian's minds raced with plans for our new future. We first discussed the obvious: what to call ourselves. Brian's managing director contract with Huntsman was no longer in comprehensive effect, but it did still bear some legal ramifications, one of which was that he could not grace a new company with his own name. Thus, 'Anderson and Lishak' was out of the question — and yet Brian was perfectly sanguine about this point, for, contractual shackles aside, we arrived at the mutual opinion that 'Richard Anderson Ltd' was the better choice. It foretold longevity, it emphasised my cutting faculties as the centrepiece of our services, and, according to an informal poll of friends and family members over the age of four, it had the more resonant ring.

With matters of nomenclature out of the way, we then focused our strategy on three objectives to be pursued as soon as our gardening leave expired: identifying willing investors, cultivating a new clientele, and securing an attractive and central premises for our trade.

Ironically, the first prospective investor I would eventually approach was the most daunting customer I had ever known: an Iraqi entrepreneur who had built up his own extraordinarily successful business from humble beginnings and whom I respected equally for his seemingly innate sartorial circumspection. Having dismissed the disappointing services of another prominent house, Ahmed Agassi first came to Huntsman just a couple of months before Hall was due to retire. He ordered eight suits — all of which Hall cut beautifully and had seen through to the forward-fitting stage, but which had not yet been dispatched by the time Hall left. So Agassi came in and with me, Johnny New Boy, presiding, donned each coat, one after the other until all eight had been tried, and as he did it became clear he was not 100 per cent satisfied by their appearance. If anything, I thought, perhaps — and just perhaps — the coats looked the very tiniest bit too small on the front edge, but given the consistently excellent quality of Hall's work and my unfamiliarity with this customer's natural stance and figuration, I could not be certain.

Agassi, cool as ice, said nothing.

Instead, he just eyed himself dubiously in the mirror — which was worse.

The coats went home, but he sent them all back a couple of days later for being too tight when the inside pockets were filled with wallets and pens. They arrived on the arm of an unapologetic chauffeur, and I redid all eight, letting out the side seams a good quarter each side. When they went home a second time they stayed there, but coming just a month or so into my working independently of Hammick and Hall, and being not an eardrum-blowing tirade but rather the perfect composure of a self-made man determined to get exactly what he came for — the best coats money can buy — it was an unforgettable lesson in the power of tacit shrewdness. Thirty months later, I wanted Agassi on my side.

He took my call from his yacht. We spoke for about fifteen minutes, during which he advised me that what Brian and I needed were two tiers of investors — one of financiers who would put in £100,000 pounds each, and the other for contributors of £10,000 each. He hardly had to think about this — it was as though I had asked him what he had eaten for lunch — and against a tranquil aural backdrop of squawking seagulls and lapping waves, he readily offered to put in some money of his own.

As word spread of my and Brian's plans, several other of our former customers offered to invest as well, all of them disenchanted with the new Huntsman and eager that we should land on our feet so they could start ordering bespoke clothing again. In February

2001, we placed a notice in *The Wall Street Journal* and sent a letter to prospective American clients announcing that in just a few weeks' time Richard Anderson Ltd would be making its inaugural journey to the States, receiving clients in Boston, New York, Washington, Naples, Marco Island, Tampa, Palm Beach, Houston, Chicago, San Francisco and Beverly Hills. In most of these cities, Brian had known people for donkeys' years, and when we went out a good number of them made a point of placing orders just to further our cause. In San Francisco, an Episcopalian reverend, Olympian athlete and Chinese-art collector who had been a client of Brian's at Wells, said, 'I know how difficult it can be, starting up a business, and I want to help you out.' He ordered ten suits all at once. The journey overall was tremendously reassuring: by the time it was over we had collected approximately £75,000 worth of orders and, no less inspiring, countless words of encouragement and confidence in the eventual positive outcome of our leap of faith.

And yet, for all our orders in hand, we still had no shop.

Ideally, naturally, we wanted to be right back on Savile Row. Moreover, we wanted a ground-floor showroom, for we had seen many businesses struggle in first-floor or basement spaces because they had little visible presence with which to pull people in off the street. We engaged Keith Wilson, of the Mayfair estate firm Wilson and McHardy, to monitor the possibilities, but months passed with no turnover to speak of and holding our breath for a choice opening on the Golden Mile (which is actually only about 300 yards) began to feel like waiting for Buckingham Palace to appear in Hampton's listings. With the estate agents we spent hours upon hours scoping out suitable prospects, enquiring as discreetly as possible about lease terms and trying to gauge the commercial health of companies loitering in the addresses we coveted most. At the top of our list was Number 13, a Grade II-listed Georgian townhouse whose ground floor was inhabited, ironically, by Hackett, the fledgling bespoke operation Trevor Swift had worked for prior to accepting a job offer from us. The company had been on Savile Row for barely a year (Swift had worked at their Sloane Square operation), and even from the street we could see they were not doing well. However talented, Hackett's cutters were the new kids on the block; they had no readymade bespoke following and, judging from the little traffic we saw pass through its doors, we guessed it was not a question of whether Hackett would vacate its prestigious premises, but when.

Meanwhile, to centralise our bookkeeping and remain close to the action, Brian rented a modest desk space a block away on Old Burlington Street, while I tackled my cutting back in St Albans — in my new garage.

Never mind the strangeness of no longer suiting up each morning and making the forty-five-minute commute into town as I had for years (I now dressed for breakfast in jeans and a T-shirt and within seconds of depositing my juice glass in the dishwasher was unrolling a length of brown paper on my makeshift board), the havoc wreaked on the Anderson homestead by this improvised set-up had all the trappings of a farce. My tweeds and mohair and tailoring tools — my scale, my scye square, my chalk plectrums, my chalk sharpener and, of course, my precious shears — made for a comically demure still life surrounded by hammers, wrenches, shovels, rakes, tyre pumps, grease rags, tricycles, bicycles and my scooter, a Hexagon 125. Our Episcopalian angel out in San Francisco had requested that one of his coats feature some slanted patch pockets, my template for which was a coat Hammick himself had worn once for a photo shoot. For the sake of getting the pockets right I had dug this picture out of my maudlin box of

Huntsman souvenirs and taped it to the breezeblock over my board — but it might as well have been there for the mordant Mona Lisa expression on Hammick's face, which seemed to keep an eye on my every slice while also registering a bit of disdain for my jeans. Spring arrived, and as the days grew milder I began to work with the garage door open, a spectacle arousing the curiosity of our new neighbours as they walked their children to the bus or drove by to rubberneck from their cars. After a week or so of eyeing me suspiciously from the other side of the street, an acquaintance of Fran's got up the nerve to cross over and ask from the edge of the driveway what I was doing. Her tone suggested a collective neighbourhood impression that I had gone off the deep end and, in the manner of a mad scientist, was fashioning myself a time machine — or maybe a bomb. And as for Fran herself: there had been something of a honeymoon feel to the first month or so of my working from home — in all our years together we had never spent so many consecutive days in such close proximity — but when business began to pick up following my and Brian's return from the States, the arrangement's sweet novelty gave way to a stormy war of wills over the home phone line. Our sole landline was being rung up with increasing frequency by Lord This or Sir That, enquiring about the status of a dinner jacket or to make an appointment to meet me in town. (To conduct fittings, I used a small room in Holland & Sherry, the cloth supplier formerly interested in buying Huntsman and which still resided next door.) From morning till dinnertime and sometimes beyond, Fran struggled to keep her cool taking down a message from, say, the Bulgarian envoy while baby Mai screamed blue murder on her hip — or, when a friend or relative called to speak with her, enduring a show of impatient eye-popping and frantic gestures as I implored her to wrap it up pronto. Several months earlier, when Brian and I first discussed striking out on our own, he had said: 'Partnerships are difficult. You share everything. Whenever you've got something on your chest, you have to say it. Sometimes it's even harder than being married, because you spend more time with your business partner than with your wife.' Indeed — unless one of you is working out of his garage, in which case your wife is counting down the days until you and your business partner ride off into the sunset so she can have a chat to her mother in peace.

To assemble all the garments I was cutting, I had tracked down some old contacts, the majority of them Huntsman retirees — including one who happily returned to the force to become my new baster: Horace Goddard. I also hired two coatmakers: Billy Heaton, another Huntsman alumnus, and Roly Bowditch, a younger tailor who had once given an impressive interview at Huntsman but for some reason had been passed over for someone else. To make up trousers I tapped George Kellatte and Nick Demetriou, Huntsman trousers tailors both; to implement alterations I hired George Antoni, Huntsman's premier machinist and top tailor of the younger guard; and to fell lining, add topstitching, cut buttonholes and affix buttons, I enlisted Dorothy Alvarez, a colleague from my baste-ripping days up in Heddon Street.

By late spring, a growing number of disillusioned Huntsman customers supplemented by long-time contacts of Brian's in London and abroad had ordered upwards of eighty units from Richard Anderson Ltd — which was still without a home. In Marshalswick, I tried to keep regular hours, starting around eight in the morning, breaking for a sandwich at lunchtime, and quitting at five, but with the orders mounting, and all my work and cutting paraphernalia just a wall away from where I bathed, took my meals, bid my beloveds good morning and good night, and slept, I was finding it nearly impossible to switch off. Also taking its toll was all the toing and froing I was doing between St Albans and London — usually on the Hexagon, with my half-made coats, overcoats and trousers neatly folded and sealed in the scooter's external boot — in order to fit customers and trade goods with my assembly team, who were scattered all over town. Coordinating all this activity with no central hub, storage or workspace ate into valuable cutting time, which, because so many daytime hours were given over to scooter-riding and street-corner assignations, stretched later and later into the evenings. Cutting suit after suit in my garage, alone but for the occasional visit from Fran or a teacup-bearing child and, of course, my goading Colin Hammick totem, had a curiously purifying effect on the work at hand, for it distilled the craft down to its very essence, without all the trappings of a well-appointed showroom and smartly dressed salesmen — which, after all, and though they can be a critical part of the bespoke experience, are not what the customer ultimately takes home. What he takes home is an item of clothing that must achieve the closet tangible thing to perfection no matter the coordinates and circumstances of its creation. For all its transcendent value, however, there was no getting around that this was a bloody inconvenient operation that if we continued pulling new orders would soon be unsustainable. So by spring's end I had been ready for months to get back to the centre of the storm . . . and then it happened.

Hackett caved.

The Sunny Side of the Street

On 12 March 1733, the *Daily Post* reported that 'a new pile of buildings is going to be carry'd on near Swallow Street by a Plan drawn up by the Right Hon. the Earl of Burlington, and which is to be called Savile Street.' This is the first published reference to Savile Row. Like all the other streets in the estate, it was given a Burlington family name, in this case that of the Earl's wife.

Richard Walker,
The Savile Row Story, 1988

The street named after Lady Dorothy Savile began primarily as a residential lane, lined with grand townhouses whose stables were hidden away on Heddon Street, the H-shaped alley abutting Regent Street and which would later give way to tailoring workshops and a Ziggy Stardust shrine. By the mid-nineteenth century, Savile Row's inhabitants included nobility, military officers, some tailors and several doctors as well, but as the number of

284

tailors grew, the doctors defected to surgeries in Marylebone — a detail that springs to mind whenever I am struggling to fit an especially corpulent or misshapen customer and wonder whether he would not do better to seek the services of Harley Street instead.

During the Second World War, three bombs fell on Savile Row, causing 'damage beyond repair' (according to the London County Council) in three areas: where The Beatles' company would later be, at Number 3; at the north-west corner of Savile Row and Clifford Street; and at both the north-east and south-east corners of Savile Row and New Burlington Street. While many other old buildings along the Row survived the bombs themselves, the street's western foundation was so weakened that many more townhouses on this side — including Henry Poole's former premises, a beautiful building with chandeliers, a sunken showroom, and a wooden pulpit in which a man presided over an enormous ledger as if he were St Peter at the Gate — had to be razed. Erected in their place were several modern office buildings with dark boxy façades characteristic of so much of London's postwar construction; by contrast, the architecture on the sunnier, east side of Savile Row remains largely as it was before the attacks, and (whether by happenstance or trends of affordability and preference, I do not know) it is the side where one finds the vast majority of older and established tailoring houses based on Savile Row proper today.

When Brian started working on the Row eleven years after the end of the war, two of its three bombsites still had not been rehabilitated and England was a very poor country, still on rationing — which until 1948 included coupons even for clothing. By this time the Row was filled with tailors, as many as seventy or eighty little operations, and not just in the ground-floor shops but in several of the upper- and lower-ground-level spaces as well. Some of these tailors had been on Savile Row for decades, and, being too old or disabled to serve in the military, remained throughout the war to make its uniforms instead. They shared the street with cloth suppliers, who at that time were known to specialise in a particular kind of cloth — in tweeds, say, or lightweights — and it was easy for a cutter or salesman to toddle two doors down to a supplier and bring back some samples for a customer's immediate consideration. Like many of the tailors, however, most of these suppliers were run not by hard-nosed businessmen but by artisans, and in time a good number were compelled to move out to a less expensive neighbourhood, declare bankruptcy or join forces with a larger firm.

One such merger involved Collard Parsons, a cloth merchant who had occupied 13 Savile Row for approximately forty years. Formerly based on the corner of Savile Row and New Burlington Street, Collard Parsons was forced to move when its premises were destroyed by one of the three aforementioned bombs. In 1945 it took over the entire townhouse at Number 13, where it remained until the mid-1980s — by which time the number of Savile Row cloth merchants had dwindled down to just the big international guns. Collard Parsons relinquished its own house to move next door and become incorporated by Scabal, a Brussels-originated supplier-cum-suitmaker that had moved into 12 Savile Row in the sixties, and Number 13's ground floor was rented out to the incongruous Indonesian Trade Centre.

It was not until the end of the millennium that the Indonesian Trade Centre moved out and Hackett took over Number 13 — spending half a million pounds refurbishing its aloof ground-floor façade and 1,600 square feet of commercial space into a beautiful, bright, off-white air-conditioned gallery with a broad front window, a crystal chandelier, glazed skylights and two spacious fitting rooms at the back. Within a year, Hackett had decided Savile Row was not for them. By this time Brian and I had all our investors on board and a log of eighty-odd units in production after having been cut in my garage. We had made some inroads into leasing a smaller space on the darker, more modern side of the Row — directly across from Huntsman, incidentally — but when we learned that Hackett was jacking it in for a more suitable site on Regent Street, Brian and I jumped to take its place. With no history or figures to speak of, it took us weeks of haranguing various contractors and agents to take our hatchling of a venture seriously — and during which time Number 13 stood vacant with a TO LET sign in its window — but finally, in June 2001, we arrived at an agreement for a sublease from Hackett, to whom we agreed to pay a guaranteed deposit of £100,000 plus £60,000 a year for seven years.

When the TO LET sign came down, we were confronted with our first unanticipated deliberation: what to put in the window in its place.

On the glass itself, RICHARD ANDERSON LTD soon appeared in handsome gold lettering, but this was progress of only fleeting satisfaction, for the wide white sill underneath remained empty, looking rather more suggestive of a dentist's office than a tailoring house. We had no coats to display, for those already finished had been dispatched and everything I had cut for myself was still being worn regularly by me or Fran, who had taken an inspired liking to my Sir Osmund coat. What we *did* have was an antique sofa and oak writing desk, both of which we had bartered from an antique dealer named Chris Howe over on Pimlico Road in exchange for three suits; we also had our first bolt of exclusive Richard Anderson Ltd fabric: a large-check fawn-and-burgundy tweed from P. J. Haggart. So we recovered the sofa with our tweed and fished some nude female dummies out of a skip that had pulled up across the street in front of Hardy Amies, where some spring housecleaning was under way, and with these — our scavenged dummies and bespoke sofa — fashioned a little window tableau that, if not precisely to the point, at least turned heads.

Richard Walker's beautiful book *Savile Row Story: An Illustrated History*, first published in 1988, contains several photographs of traditional shop interiors as they have looked for generations: clubbish dens laden with chandeliers, marble fireplaces, leather-bound ledgers, cloth bolts, long wooden floorboards and Oriental rugs that seem to fray right before the eyes. And in *The Art of Sewing: Basic Tailoring*, published in the mid-seventies, one sees two priceless pictures of Huntsman in its Hammick-and-Hall heyday: the first of Hall fitting a ginger-bearded man on the old britches saddle (Hall's cufflinks reflect the scarlet hunt coat like tiny mirrors) and the second of the front shop as it was when I arrived: Hammick and Cummings can be seen entertaining Mr and Mrs Milords amidst the cloth bolts while from over the fireplace the massive stag heads look on. Behind them Huntsman's front window rises in all its austerity: no dummies, no ties, no coats; not even a modest length of cashmere on display — just the formidable montage of Royal Warrants that shared the glass with a bunched green curtain, denying any curious pavement riff-raff even a peek at the gabardine and gentry within.

Much as we loved the Huntsman of yore, this funeral parlour aesthetic was not what Brian and I deemed best for our own, new-millennium foray. For Richard Anderson Ltd, we wanted an atmosphere of refinement, certainly, but one that was also warm, youthful and welcoming. Rather than hide the cutting and tailoring area away at the back of the shop, we elected to move this vital workspace forward, so that customers could actually see their clothing being worked on. And from Simon Chalk, an old Watford schoolmate who had become a successful oil painter of landscapes and street scenes, I commissioned some artwork for our walls: a pastoral fox hunt and a picture of our new shop's exterior with a dark-clad dandy striding by.

At Huntsman, music had always been forbidden; not even the tailors were permitted to listen to earphones while working upstairs. There were practical reasons for this, defended by Hammick: if there were a radio in the well-populated workshop upstairs there would undoubtedly be fights over which stations to which it would be tuned; but nor could individual headphones be condoned, for they were viewed as isolating distractions. One day one of Hall's alteration tailors, a little Italian chap called Pastori, came down and walked past Hammick's board in order to ask Hall a question. Hall answered, the tailor went back upstairs, and after standing there for a moment, Hammick turned to Hall and said, 'Brian, was Mr Pastori . . . Did he have *earphones* on?'

Hall said he had not noticed, though one wonders how this could have been possible

— when Pastori came down again with another question he was indeed wearing what passed for earphones in 1983 and they were bigger than ear-muffs. Not that we ever saw them again.

Brian and I agreed that a firmwide ban on music was yet another custom we need not retain, on the basis that while it was just the two of us and our new trial tailor Vito Calo knocking around, a quiet and tasteful soundtrack would have a positive influence on our working environment as well as go some way to make new customers feel less self-conscious upon walking in. We had to be sensitive, of course, as to whether the coincidence of even something as tame as Bob Dylan with the arrival of a nonagenarian Lord might provoke irrevocable alienation — a discussion which gave rise to some half-serious jokes about whether to install a concealed switch under my board, so that depending on who pitched up I could toggle between Celtic rock and Chopin. Ultimately we elected to take our chances and perhaps even broaden one or two aesthetic sensibilities along the way.

To help Brian in our new shop, we employed Clive Gilkes, a salesman of peerless patience and good nature who had been at Huntsman for thirteen years — and before that at Gieves & Hawkes, down the Row at Number 1. Clive, who had been no less distraught than we by Huntsman's devolution, informed us that following my and Brian's resignation a string of long-time clients had called up demanding to know where we had gone — and that Bargeman and Swift would not tell them. One day a customer came in and, after several attempts to extract a clue to our whereabouts, said,

'All right then. What time do you close?'

'About half past five,' said Clive.

'Right,' the man sighed, sinking resolutely into Huntsman's front shop sofa. 'Unless you tell me where they've gone, I'm going to sit here until half past five.'

It was eleven in the morning.

Clive, no fan of antagonistic resistance, threw up his hands and sang like a bird, confirming that we had gone out on our own and would soon be opening up a new shop just two doors away. Swift gave him an earful in the board-room, but Clive could not have cared less. We had already promised him a job, to commence as soon as we had a shop to put him in, and shortly after we got it Clive joined our growing alliance of Huntsman deserters, now nine strong.

By September, the shop was fully up and running and Brian and I were due to make our second journey as Richard Anderson Ltd to the States. I had approximately fifty units to fit on Americans who had placed orders the previous winter during our maiden voyage, and, thanks to some handsome brochures we had made up and sent west in advance — promoting our windowpane tweed, diagonal pinstripes, and certificated blazers and overcoats made with Guanashina, a rare blend of Andean guanaco, pashmina and yearling cashmere, the three finest fibres on earth — we had received several enquiries auguring new orders as well. That the journey should be fruitful felt critical to the extreme, for we now had a steep lease and three full-time wage packets to clear, as well as an ambitious three-year business plan whose resources demanded considerable shoring up. We booked flights, hotels, fittings and introductions in New York, Boston, Washington, Chicago, San Francisco, Los Angeles and Houston. The plan was for Brian to fly over a few days in advance to visit his sister at her home in Bethlehem, Pennsylvania, and then drive to New York, where I would be arriving later in the week — and from whence we would launch our epic journey towards greater solvency and success.

On the morning in question Brian left his sister's and had got no further than a gas station up the road when the attendant on duty asked where he was headed.

'Manhattan,' Brian said.

'I don't think so,' the attendant said, shaking his head.

It was 11 September.

While Brian tried to get a handle on what was happening stateside, I was sitting on a plane taxiing along the tarmac at Heathrow when its pilot hit the brakes so suddenly that I nearly hit my head on the seat in front of me. The flight's scheduled departure time came and went and still we sat for another hour with no sign of resuming movement — and yet, recalling my first solo journey to America ten years earlier, I suspected no worse than faulty fuselage and maybe a minor delay. When we were finally told the reason for our abrupt halt, the horrific news gave rise to great agitation — people demanding additional information and clamouring anxiously to be released — and it was not for several more hours, after taxiing back to the terminal and locating my luggage bursting vainly with bastes, that I managed to reach Brian, who was back in Bethlehem, where he would spend another week awaiting the limited resumption of commercial flights so that he, too, could return home.

Six weeks later we tried again, having

whittled our grand American tour down to just a few days in New York, in order to follow through with existing customers there and defer the rest of the country till spring. Manhattan was eerily quiet, and the general mood very sad, of course. New Yorkers went to work, then straight home; very few were bothering with restaurants or plays. Everyone concentrated simply on living, getting by. Whether and when another shoe might drop was obviously a very frightening contingency; the city's vitality, its dynamism, had been tamped down into a contagious apprehension.

If you know one market is under stress, you must focus your efforts elsewhere, so as the autumn progressed we marketed the company relentlessly in Europe and held our production team to a consistent pace in order not to lose momentum even as orders lagged. We were fortunate to have already accumulated a small but loyal clientele, which in times of depression or recession is what sustains purveyors of luxury goods and services. We heard news of many houses' struggles to weather the sharp decline in American orders — among them Huntsman, which we would hear was in need of a cash injection — but with our considerably smaller staff and lean overheads, we managed to pull through with figures that were respectable enough. By January the markets began to show small signs of economic and emotional recovery and Brian and I even began to discuss taking on someone new to assist in the errand-running and cloth-striking departments — the same capacity in which I started out at Huntsman. But before we could even get around to placing our own version of the 'Boy Wanted' advertisement that drew the likes of Brian Hall, Colin Hammick, Tommy Nutter and, of course, myself to Savile Row, our new apprentice pitched up unsolicited on our doorstep — wearing a skirt.

Cherchez la femme

Careful readers, perhaps especially the feminists among them, may have noticed the overwhelming prevalence in these pages of the male pronoun. This is not because I am against the egalitarian merits of using 'he or she' or 's/he' (although the former is unwieldy and the latter inelegant), but rather because referring to the general customer of Savile Row as 'he' nineteen times out of twenty actually fairly approximates the male-to-female ratio of its patrons.

For that matter, it may fairly approximate the ratio of male-to-female cutters as well.

There are two prominent reasons why more women do not come to Savile Row for their clothing, and to an extent they are mutually reinforcing. Women do not wear suits (or suit-style coats) as frequently as men; consequently the ambience in most bespoke tailoring houses has long had a masculine tenor, sometimes one sufficiently intimidating to put prospective female clients off.

As I have said, the atmosphere at Huntsman was palpably tense and electric:

there was no mucking about, no personal chit-chat; indeed, the closest any cutter came to asking about a colleague's weekend was when Hammick alluded to the whereabouts of the Prince of Wales check coat Toby swiped for a party. What one *did* see was merciless ribbing, subtle (and not-so-subtle) assertions of one-upmanship and bollockings galore. All this bluster and bravado seemed to add up to an essentially masculine vibe — certainly not because I am of the opinion all women chatter on about their weekends and tiptoe around each other's feelings, but rather simply that the presence of a female in the cutting room's midst would have inspired dramatically different conduct. Female customers were welcome, needless to say. The wives, girlfriends and daughters of male clients on the whole were abided amiably. And, of course, we had our crucial female office staff: June Glasspool, on reception; Pearl Taylor and Christine Dennison, who oversaw the bookkeeping; and the many excellent tailoresses upstairs — whose presence gave little pause to one elderly coatmaker who used to change out of his dress trousers into his tailoring clothes right in front of them every day. ('Oh, put it away!' the girls used to cry, shielding their eyes.)

But aside from these all-but-inevitable

cameos, visits from the fairer sex were so discouraged at Huntsman, where their presence drew askance glares and meaningful throat-clearing, that pending emergencies I advised Fran against setting foot in the cutting room — for that matter, the front shop as well. If we had plans to meet for lunch, or to spend the evening in town, it was arranged that she would wait around the corner, outside the Heddon Street exit, in the manner of trysts far tawdrier than a man enjoying a ploughman's at half-one in the company of his own girlfriend. Of course, I knew Hall and Lakey had wives and that Hammick had a partner named Dorothy Cumpsty, but it would be many years before I would actually meet these women — in lovely Dorothy's case, at Hammick's retirement party. Fran was admirably sporting in her countenance of this convention; she understood, I think, that failing to honour a tradition going back 150 years would have dealt a swift conclusion to my tailoring career. Some of the customers were no better, coming in with wives one day and mistresses the next; although at least one such philanderer was found out thanks to the ever-clueless Trevor Maynard. A married customer — we'll call him Dunn — brought his girlfriend round to have her measured up for a cashmere coat, and when the coat was ready for a baste fitting Maynard rang up the Dunn residence and said, 'Mrs Dunn! Your overcoat is ready! . . . Your cashmere overcoat! . . . You remember! The one Mr Hall measured you for a fortnight ago!' Try to get out of that one. And it certainly did not help the feminist cause when the driver who used to come round every Friday to collect our dry-cleaning entered the shop one afternoon trailed by two heavily made-up women who helped him carry our suits out to the van on the street. A few weeks later he stopped showing up and we learned that he had been done by the police for running a prostitution ring over on Clapham Common — out of his van.

Of course, there is an arguably valid and practical reason to exclude women from the cutting room, and that is that many men regard all matters of their dress (and related undress) a sensitive affair. While they are happy to share it with male cutters and male apprentices, the very notion of a woman within ten yards of the fitting room can be profoundly unnerving. This attitude is by no means unilateral, but it is common enough that many tailoring houses play it safe by endeavouring to preserve a virtually female-free zone.

You will remember Mr Wells, the hard-nosed American businessman who demanded shoulders like mine and flies me out to New York to fit him exclusively. A few years ago, Mr Wells rang up to arrange one of these visits, and I invited Fran along. She had never been to America — every one of my past journeys had taken place with Hall or, once I began travelling alone, when one of four pregnancies deemed her unfit to travel — but now I was my own employer and our children were old enough to be entrusted to their grandparents for a spell, so it seemed time. Mr Wells being an early riser, however, and my having been instilled with the notion that the presence of 'superfluous' women unnerves some clientele, I hastened Fran out of the Carlyle shortly after dawn the very first morning in order that Mr Wells should not arrive in our suite to detect anything more feminine than the faint aroma of her perfume. To make matters worse, the day was one of torrential rain — but then Fran was heroically good-humoured about it all, for a concierge equipped her with an umbrella of gargantuan diameter and she soon found Bloomingdales, from where she rang me at lunchtime with the mischievous news that she had passed her morning of damp exile 'spending all that money you've been making'.

As for Huntsman's female customers, who comprised less than 5 per cent of its business: they were always cut for by Hall, who had been expertly trained in the specifics of how to measure and accommodate the female figure from his own excellent teacher, Cecil Pressland. A woman is measured just as a man, except that in lieu of just one chest-circumference measurement, with a female customer the cutter must take four — one above the bust; one at the bust's widest point; one just below the bust, around the lower ribs; and one vertically from the nape of the neck down to the bust's front. With regard to measuring a woman for trousers: to avoid running one's hand up to a potentially impolite altitude on the inside thigh, male cutters are advised instead to calculate the inside-leg measurement by subtracting the length of the woman's hip from her outside leg while she sits in a chair. And the basic principles of cutting a woman's coat pattern are also quite similar to those for a man's — especially within the Huntsman line, which naturally has a relatively 'feminine' tapered waist — with two significant differences. The first is that women's coats overlap right over left, rather than left over right,[1] and the second, perhaps more obviously, is that a woman's pattern must account for her chest.

In this regard, the traditional Huntsman line might have seemed less easily adaptable for the female figure, for its coats tended to lie close to the chest, a style one might find somewhat trickier to modify in the presence of spherical appendages there. Adding extra fabric to one area of a coat will significantly affect its overall balance: whether it is sufficiently snug in other areas and how

---

[1] There are at least two supposed historical reasons for this, both related to the fact that approximately 90 per cent of people are right-handed. When buttons came into use in the seventeenth century, they were largely reserved for the clothes of wealthy people, and while aristocratic men dressed themselves, women tended to be dressed by their servants — the majority of whom would have found it easier to do so from the right, i.e., the woman's left. Furthermore, while the average man would choose to pull his coat back with his left hand and reach for his sword with his right, women traditionally rode horses swordless and side-saddle, with both legs on the left — in which case wearing a coat that overlapped on the left was better protection against a head-on wind.

smoothly and evenly it hangs. But for Hall, achieving the perfect balance in a coat, *especially* one for an atypical figure, was perhaps the most gratifying part of the job. Like Pressland before him, Hall mastered feminising the Huntsman line to become, arguably, the best women's cutter of his generation — creating patterns for Irene Worth, Virginia McKenna, Sarah Ferguson, Baby Jane Holzer, Jeanette Winterson and Margot Fonteyn. In fact, it was precisely his renowned supremacy as a ladies' coat-maker that made it all the more dramatic when, in one instance — and to my knowledge the only such instance in Hall's career — Mother Nature prevailed. A new customer came in for a suit, Hall took her coat-on and coat-off measurements, and all of this went very well; the lady left and Hall set about cutting a pattern for which I struck the cloth and the basting team pieced it together beautifully. But when the woman, who as it happened was rather exceptionally endowed, returned for her first fitting, her bust strained against the coat's lapels. So Hall went back to his board, re-cut the forepart and bust panel to give more roundedness to the area in question, and when the woman came back for a second fitting the coat's chest was now adequate but would not come in close

305

enough underneath to lie flat against her stomach and hips. Hall tried yet again to re-cut the pattern such that it might both supply sufficient room up top and a flattering snugness below, but the woman's third and fourth baste fittings achieved no more than additional tutting and embarrassment. Utterly flummoxed, Hall spent a good portion of every day for the best part of six weeks drafting and redrafting the coat, whose balance began to seem unachievable. One afternoon about three months after the woman had first been measured up and put down her deposit, we all heard a dejected sigh and looked up from our cutting boards to see Hall crouched over his latest iteration of the pattern, his elbows on his board and his head in his hands.

'Something wrong, Brian?' Hammick asked.

'*Yes!*' Hall cried. 'I can get *over* them, but I can't get *under* them!'

This singularly defeating episode took place in the pre-email era, when all of Huntsman's correspondence was by hand- or typewritten mail, and all of it concluded with the words: 'assuring you at all times our very best care and attention we are Dear Sir your obedient servants, pp H. Huntsman & Sons'. (One short-lived secretary refused to sign off as such, on the argument that he was 'no

306

one's obedient servant', and Brian Lishak advised him that in that case he had better find alternative employment.) Hall's uncharacteristic capitulation was a subject of such mortification that he could not bear to explain the reason to the woman face-to-face, and it fell to Brian to write her a letter — which, in essence, informed the poor lady that down to her exceptionally curvilinear physique Huntsman was ultimately, regrettably, and only after full exhaustion of perseverance and resources towards the cause, unable to provide her with a coat up to its standards, 'assuring you at all times our very best care and attention we are Dear Madam your obedient servants'.

It was Hall, of course, who in turn taught me how to cut for the female form, and in the years since his superlative tutelage I have cut coats, suits and overcoats for several women whose figures have never been thwarting, but rather always refreshing variations on the more common assignment. In one remarkable case a woman came to me for a coat when she was newly pregnant, which meant, naturally, that over the course of her fittings critical ratios in her measurements would change — but the challenge posed by her example transcends the bounds of gender. Customers of both sexes frequently mention at the measuring stage that they have just started a diet and intend to be as much as a stone lighter by the time the garment in question is finished — the implication being that the cutter should account for this anticipated shrinkage at the pattern-cutting stage. Well, you cannot hit a moving target. Of course, with a pregnant woman you can generally trust that the predicted weight fluctuation will actually occur and estimate expansion accordingly. But still: as a rule, cutters must measure and fit their customers' bodies as they are right there and then, and if a client gains or loses weight, his (or her!) cutter can almost always find a way to let garments out or take them in accordingly at the time. (When the Atkins diet first became popular in the States, a spate of American customers lost as much as two stone and proudly returned their coats and trousers to us for adjustments — and six months later every last one of them came back to have them let out again.) So when my client told me she was pregnant, I advised her in turn that unless we deferred her fittings until after the baby was born, what she was going to get was a bespoke maternity coat — which, as it turned out, was exactly what she wanted, for soon after having her

308

first baby she became pregnant again.

As for customers' wives: I once heard an anecdote concerning a cutter who worked years ago for another one of Savile Row's oldest and most esteemed houses. He was fitting a customer whose wife was in attendance, and the woman so riled the cutter with complaint after complaint and even a bit of imperious advice as to how he might improve his technique that finally the cutter stormed out of the fitting room hollering: 'Get *rid* of her! GET RID OF THE WIFE!' I myself have never observed or met with such extreme provocation — on the contrary, the female spouses and companions of my clientele are a supremely gracious, constructive and appreciative sample — but, indeed, bespoke tailoring seems to have had such a significantly contentious history of wifely interference that in *The Modern Tailor Outfitter and Clothier*, originally published in 1947, an entire subchapter on salesmanship was dedicated to 'The Wife Problem':

Tailors are frequently perplexed at the failure of an apparently perfect suit. The customer can find no real fault with it — he 'doesn't like the cut' or 'can't feel comfortable'. The answer, of course, is *cherchez la femme*. More and more of late years wives have been taking a great interest in their husbands' clothes — even to the extent of accompanying them to the tailor and dictating what they shall wear! Curiously enough this seems to be most frequent in military circles. Let the tailor and his salesman beware of this. The lady may be a useful ally to him, but she will prove a deadly foe. Should he annoy her, his customer is as good as lost.

Where husband and wife are agreed the going is fairly easy, and an occasional appeal to the lady's judgement will ensure her friendship and high opinion. But when a clash of wills appears the salesman must, like Agag, walk delicately. The 'difference' will often arise from an attempt on the part of the wife to dig her husband from a rut along which he has progressed placidly for years, and to force him into something smarter or 'younger'. Our salesman must use all his tact to avoid falling between the two stools. Whilst he may support the lady up to a point, particularly with regard to colour, he should not allow himself to be forced into taking an order for tight or waisted garments for a man who is used to a very easy fit and who habitually stuffs his pockets full of luggage of every description.

About six months after we opened, a young woman came into Richard Anderson Ltd to ask whether we would be willing to grant her six weeks' unpaid work experience. She had already been up and down the Row, asking various other houses if they could use her, but had not had any joy. Her education was relevant — she held a Bachelor's degree in Visual Arts and Textiles from Australian National University and was now in an exchange programme at the Winchester School of Fine Arts — but then, as I have said, and as Toby's experience illustrates, school does not always yield a lifer. Still, the request happened to come the day before Brian was due to be away on a sales trip for the best part of five weeks, so we would otherwise be one man down in the increasingly busy front shop — and as I say I had been in need of an apprentice for some time. So we agreed to take the young woman on to run errands, collect deliveries, assist with the paperwork, and perhaps even try her hand at striking mungo.

Seven years later, Rebecca is still with us — striking the majority of my jobs,

311

preparing their trimmings, and beginning to learn J. P. Thornton's near-extinct cutting system.

It is unusual to have a female apprentice on Savile Row, but certainly not unheard of; in fact, at least two of the larger houses have employed female cutters, one of them full-time. Undoubtedly this is a trend propelled in part by a desire to draw more female clients to bespoke tailoring, although I dare say the notion that female cutters attract female clients is of disputable logic. Long before Stella McCartney became Edward Sexton's protégée, Sexton and Tommy Nutter had little trouble drawing an extensive female clientele. And if there are women who would only go to a female cutter, I suspect there are just as many (or maybe more) whose preference would be to have their suits cut by a man. The only hitch is the very same practical disadvantage that female cutters must overcome, but with the genders reversed: when a male cutter serves a female customer, decorum dictates that he excuse himself so that she may change clothes, because while many people are unfazed by the intimate scrutiny of a doctor of the opposite gender, this would not seem to be the case in the non-clinical field of bespoke tailoring.

At first consideration it may not seem so very disadvantageous to have to vacate the room while a customer changes, but, in fact, it compromises a critical aspect of apprenticeship training. When I used to assist Hall and one of his male customers would come in for a fitting, it was customary that I should accompany the client into the fitting room and be on hand there to assist the change — to help the customer out of the coat he was already wearing, to hold it while he removed his trousers, to hang everything up, and then to help him into the new garments — and very often this process would occasion a little conversation. Nothing momentous, just a bit of chat about the weather or maybe some news item pertaining to business or sport (and only when the customer himself initiated it), but over time such encounters add up to a very valuable rapport. And when Hall would then join us for the fitting itself, I would remain present to note down the necessary adjustments, hang up or retrieve garments, and observe how best to behave in that particular customer's presence. So both technically and socially one's welcome presence in the fitting room is a vocational advantage — and given that men account for approximately 95 per cent of Savile Row's clientele, it is an advantage overwhelmingly skewed towards aspiring male cutters.

Perhaps a rise in the number of women coming to Savile Row for bespoke garments will increase the number of female cutters, rather than the other way around. But a gender-wide penchant for suits would probably take some encouragement from the female fashion industry at large. The kind of clothing that looks good on the icons of an era (such as Twiggy, Madonna or Kate Moss) inevitably becomes the iconic look of that era. In this respect, bespoke tailoring should have a leg-up on off-the-rack fashions, for its very mission is to flatter its wearer; in theory everyone, including Kate Moss, should look her best (when dressed) in high-quality bespoke. Indeed, perhaps female models and celebrities will come to Savile Row in greater numbers, and this will change the tide. Perhaps bespoke coats, trousers, overcoats and whatever other garments women have tailored to their dimensions will see a new renaissance of experimentation through partnerships forged by bespoke tailoring houses and fashion designers interested in our untapped potential. Meanwhile, and despite the occasional sight of an extremely smart women's suit or blazer in our shop windows, it does not seem likely that Savile Row's tailoring houses will be resounding anytime soon with the echoes of a new chorus — cutters decrying 'The Husband Problem' — though we all should be so lucky.

With the Band

Founder of Savile Row is a title long ascribed to Henry Poole, although this is down to something of a technicality. When Poole's tailoring house opened in 1849, its official street address was on Great Burlington Street, one block west, but according to Row lore the Prince of Wales complained about the shop's layout, which required that he pass among the workers whenever he wanted to join Poole for a sherry-drinking session. Rather than move his office, where the sherry bar would have been, Poole simply turned the whole shop around — so that its headquarters, which already overlooked Savile Row, would now be within a mere stride of Poole's new entrance at Number 32.

In fact, there were many tailoring enterprises already established within the Golden Square Mile prior to the opening of Beau Brummel and the Prince of Wales's favoured Poole, and one of these was Strickland & Sons. After starting up around the corner on Clifford Street in 1780, Strickland moved to Savile Row in the early nineteenth century and soon developed a significant international presence as a premier dresser of nobility, aristocrats and diplomats in Europe and North America. In the twentieth century, representing the firm abroad was the supremely genteel Bert Cracknell: an immaculate, bespectacled man with a bushy handlebar moustache who met Brian for the first time in 1958, in the middle of the Atlantic on the *Queen Mary*. Their paths would cross again many times over the next twenty-five years as they made their countless Savile Row sojourns abroad, but when Cracknell died in 1983, Strickland had no ready replacement, and Strickland's international voyages became shorter and more infrequent, their far-flung clientele less consistently served.

Twenty years later, Strickland & Sons would comprise only three employees: Eric Tricker, a 74-year-old cutter who still worked in the traditional striped trousers and black jacket of the Savile Row of yesteryear; Victor Dagley, his octogenarian partner, who oversaw Strickland's administration largely from home; and an office clerk who still did all of the company's bookkeeping in purchase and sales ledgers in pen and ink. Having already allotted to Richard Anderson Ltd their clientele's bespoke shirt-making orders, Dagley and Tricker approached Brian in late 2003 to inform him that owing to their great age they were compelled to retire, and wanted to sell the company — but not just to anyone; they wanted to know their beloved customers would be in good hands. We were greatly moved, of course, to have been tapped for this inheritance, especially by men Brian had known and admired for years as highly dedicated, honest and conscientious champions of the craft; moreover, the proposal seemed to have very few if indeed any logistical drawbacks. Strickland's figures were modest but in the black; the company's reputation could only reinforce the integrity of our own; and by incorporating Strickland's client list we stood to supplement ours with more than 4000 new names. So on the first of April 2004, Dagley and Tricker, the latter in his black coat and striped trousers for the last time, came round to Number 13 for champagne and the ceremonial transfer of Strickland's massive stash of paper patterns — *5000* of them, which Tricker insisted upon carrying gingerly downstairs to our storeroom all by himself, not wanting to lose sight of them until the very last second of his proprietorship.

And thus the Row's youngest bespoke tailoring house incorporated one of its oldest. Strickland's 4000 client names would eventually prove fewer in practical terms, for when Brian took the uncomputerised list with him on a reconnaissance journey to Halifax, St John's, Calgary, Toronto, Montreal, and then south to the States, he discovered that quite a few of our new patronage were long dead. Among the living, however, we discovered a good number of compensatory gold mines: customers who wanted to buy virtually everything Brian showed them. Pashmina sport coats, double-breasted overcoats with mink collars, the world's first bespoke hooded duffel, inspired by Paddington Bear — one man ordered one of each of these while another clotheshorse signed up for eight mohair suits in one go. Evidently, these long-latent enthusiasts had never encountered an active bespoke marketing campaign — Strickland had had neither the inclination nor the personnel — and now that Brian was pitching up on their doorsteps with swatches, models and brochures showcasing the great range of possibilities, their interest in Savile Row came flooding back.

Contemporaneous with the Strickland boom, we were also beginning to enjoy a renaissance of interest among a rather different category of clientele: media stars.

It is worth mentioning that disclosing the name of a client without permission is (or should be) anathema on Savile Row; if an extant customer of mine has been identified by real name in these pages it is only with express consent. But on occasion a celebrity client will enthusiastically disclose the provenance of his clothes, and provided his fame is not of the criminal or otherwise unsavory nature his tailoring house will generally welcome the publicity. (This is not to say Savile Row has not dressed its share of criminals; a Huntsman client once ordered and was duly fitted in a suit that then hung in the storeroom for ten years, and we only learned when he came to pick it up that he had spent the decade-long interim in jail for mob racketeering.) Certainly it was good for Richard Anderson Ltd when Sir Ian McKellen came to us for something to wear to the Oscars — a privilege dealt our way, ironically, by another fashion house whose own touting for the honour had backfired. Upon learning that he had been nominated Best Supporting Actor for playing Gandalf in *The Lord of the Rings*, Versace sent a bouquet to Sir Ian McKellen's home along with the suggestion that the actor wear Versace on ceremony night. But Sir Ian was not at home when the flowers arrived, so they were entrusted to his neighbour, a friend and customer of ours — who took the flowers round to the actor later in the day and, in response to the actor's apparent umbrage at the notion that his choice of attire could be so easily won, said:

'Why don't you go to my tailor, Richard Anderson?'

'Thank you,' Sir Ian McKellen replied, taking the flowers. 'I will.'

Weeks later, having driven three hours north to fit Sir Ian in his midnight-blue tuxedo at Wigan Little Theatre, I discovered a CNN crew already there to shoot my every nip and tuck for a televised profile — so much for confidentiality. But then I cannot complain, for the coverage that followed gave rise to the tuxedo's inclusion in an exhibition entitled *21st Century Dandy*, presented by the British Council, and seemed also to herald a renewed interest among performing artists in the potential of classical bespoke tailoring. Accordingly, by the time Richard Anderson Ltd reached its first birthday, we were in a position to purchase some additional tailoring boards and give a few of our outworkers their own stations under the glazed skylights; we also invested in our own in-house pressing machine — although we could not yet afford to hire a presser full-time, opting instead to smuggle Michael

Granger, who was still working for Number 11, in and out the front door of 13 to do our pressing during lunch.

Late one afternoon in July 2004 I was working at my board when the shop phone rang and I happened to be the one to pick up. 'Richard Anderson,' I said — immediately to be barraged by the words of someone sounding rather like a long-lost sister.

'*Richard!*' she said breathlessly. 'My name is Faye Sawyer and I'm a stylist from a record company and I'm outside right now! I'm outside right now and I'm coming in!'

I was still holding the receiver to my ear when an exceedingly energetic woman came through the door and bee-lined for my board, talking all the way.

'I'm a stylist for BMG,' she announced, 'and you've been recommended. I need four bespoke suits in two weeks.'

Still holding the phone, I stared at her.

'They're for a band,' she said. 'Whose new album is a jazzy, swingy sort of thing, a Rat Pack tribute, and we want them to wear suits. *Real* suits. Not ready-to-wear. Not 'bespoke-couture'. It has to be Savile Row.'

'Who's the band?' I asked.

'Westlife.'

I advised the woman that cutting, basting, fitting, forward fitting and finishing four bespoke suits within a fortnight was next to impossible. It would require measuring the boys immediately, cutting patterns and cloth within forty-eight hours and asking my entire team to set aside everything else on their boards for the duration.

'So?' she said. 'Will you do it?'

I would need some time to discuss the logistics with my staff, I advised the woman. Could I call her with an answer later that day? She left the shop (but not the neighbourhood, I guessed), and some time later I rang her with the news that provided the suits would not be photographed until they met with my approval and provided the boys could be measured up straight away, I would take the order.

'There's just one more thing,' she said.

'What's that?'

'They're in Sligo.'

★ ★ ★

Growing up twenty years ago in East London, Faye Sawyer used to sit on the Tube with her grandmother and whisper, pointing across the aisle: 'Nan, do you see Lady Number One? She'd look much better with Lady Number Three's handbag. And the man with the book should switch shoes with the one in the hat . . . ' Such fixations are not easily relegated to recreational indulgence, but even by the early 1990s, when Faye enrolled at the London Institute — whose alumni include Stella McCartney, John Galliano, Mike Leigh, Anish Kapoor and Jimmy Choo — the job title 'professional stylist' was still years away from becoming a rife ambition with an academic track all to itself. Today, by contrast, the London College of Fashion offers no fewer than five courses on professional styling, one of which accepts students as young as sixteen, and the vocation has accrued such glamour that a good number of professional celebrity stylists are celebrities in their own right. But all this came long after Faye made up her mind that it was a waste of money and time to be attending classes where notions of the perfectly designed garment prevailed over the perfectly personalised look — long after she forswore academia in favour of knocking on doors for an apprenticeship that would immerse her immediately in hands-on training.

It was a good move, for not too many doors later she got a prize one — with Richard Caring.

This was pre-restaurateur, pre-property mogul Caring, who got his start as a 'rag-trader' in the sixties, designing dresses with the help of a girlfriend in fashion school and peddling the priciest ones on the street for £2 each. When Faye Sawyer joined his company thirty years later, he had become one of the leading suppliers of inexpensive fashions to Marks & Spencer, Next and Topshop; he had also begun experimenting with haute couture modelled by the likes of Christy Turlington and Claudia Schiffer. Facilitating such photo shoots became Faye's responsibility, whether that meant fluffing chiffon skirts or fetching a pack of Benson & Hedges from the off-licence on the corner — although her errand-trotting was not always limited to the local or even greater-metropolitan scale. 'Bring your passport tomorrow,' Caring used to say, and the next morning Faye would find herself on a plane to Bombay with £3000 worth of taffeta to be dyed. There were also some stealthy recon-naissance aspects to the job, such as posing as a patron of upscale fashion boutiques with a pair of manicure scissors hidden up her sleeve and, when no one was looking, snipping minuscule samples of tulle or jacquard from the garments' inside hems. '*That* was *my* education,' Faye says of her taffeta-shuttling, artful dodger days.

My Mayfair neighbour Richard James has rightly pointed out that the Savile Row tradition is not about the ego of a designer;

325

it is about the ego of the customer. The point applies equally well to the business of professional styling, in which the emphasis is on how to make the customer look his or her personal best. So when Faye, whose can-do, whatever-it-takes work ethic I found extremely admirable and appealing, came to me about suits for a quartet of pop stars in their twenties, the prospective collaboration struck me as an unmissable opportunity — even if it did entail a bit of emergency travel into the Celtic crescent. After a bone-shaking connecting flight from Dublin, I wobbled off my twelve-seater to see, standing in the middle of Sligo airport's otherwise empty tarmac, a single man holding a piece of paper with my name on it. This man, who I suspect was not, in fact, a professional chauffeur but rather an old school mate of someone involved, ferried me round to my new patrons' off-duty retreats — at one house, having been told my client was still asleep, I settled into a sofa to drink tea and chew biscuits with his mum for the best part of an hour while straining to perceive some indication of consciousness upstairs — and then back to the tarmac for two choppy hops back to London, where Brian and Clive had already ordered the cloth and I spent an entire day cutting patterns to be struck and handed over to Horace for basting up within the week.

Rather miraculously, the four suits came together, requiring only one forward fitting each — it helped, of course, that everyone had young, generally lean and athletic figures — and there was even time for Faye and the boys to add some signature details to the suits: a wider lapel there, a constellation of sparklies down the front. The album cover was shot, everyone was happy; my tailors and I duly collapsed.

And then Faye came back the following December, this time for *twenty* suits, which she needed by early January, when the band would be going on tour.

Now I really had a problem. I had already established the patterns, but even so: producing twenty suits in four weeks would all but wipe out my staff, and one must always be careful to shift priorities in a way that will not upset other customers' time-tables — especially when it could be construed as reprioritising in favour of showbiz glamour. But once again we were able to marshal resources without undue disruption; once again the band members were unfailingly appreciative and charming throughout the process; no one had outgrown or developed some deformity beyond his existing pattern — in short, we pulled it off. When Westlife's No. 1s Tour came to Wembley the following February, Fran, Tom, Molly, George, Mai and I were generously invited along for a backstage hello and then to watch the show from front-row seats — ideal for appraising the pitch and balance of every last gyrating thread. About halfway through the concert, Kian Egan announced between songs that all the suits onstage had been made by Richard Anderson, and weren't they fabulous? Whereupon, while the audience stomped and applauded and screamed its assent, a massive spotlight swung round to illuminate my seat — which was empty, because I had taken 6-year-old George to the toilet.

Back at the shop, we began receiving emails along these lines:

Dear Mr Anderson,
My name is Bethany Wilkins and I am a huge Westlife fan.
I went to see the boys in Manchester on 26 February.
I just wanted to let you know that I think you did an excellent job on their suits.
Yours sincerely
Bethany Wilkins
Aged fifteen

Hi,
I hear you design clothes for the pop band Westlife. Well, I am a big fan of Westlife and if I ever win the lottery I will send my husband to you. My aunty loves Westlife, too, so if you ever see them again would you please say Renée is a big fan?
Thank you,
Bridget

Hello,
I recently attended Westlife's No. 1s Tour 2005 concert in Dublin, and noticed your name in the programme. My enquiry is about a certain outfit that a member of Westlife wore during the concert. It was a purple all-in-one suit, with matching silk tie and silk shirt; it was worn by Kian Egan, a member of Westlife. Would it be at all possible to have a replica of this suit and accessories recreated for myself?
Mr Gareth Wibberley

In addition to the oblique flurry of fan mail, we also began to receive orders from a new generation of men curious as to the potential of traditional bespoke — many of them via Faye Sawyer and the other stylists with whom we have come to work, most of whom now send our way every one of their clients in need of a suit. But some of them are also the Gareth Wibberleys of the world: people who had not known about Savile Row's potential prior to seeing it onstage and were intrigued by what could be accomplished by a marriage of classic tailoring technique and modern designs. Some dropped by to say they were not quite ready to order a bespoke suit, but were saving up for one — and meanwhile were curious to see the shop and ask a bit of advice, such as where I would suggest one go for bespoke hats (Lock & Co. or Herbert Johnson) or shoes (Cleverley, in the Royal Arcade). Already, in response to a growing interest in unconventional suit fabrics, we had begun to experiment with denim, velvet and sequinned coats in red, silver and black; now the media were taking notice and Bryan Ferry wanted a black sequinned dinner jacket for a concert in which *The Times* would later say he 'gleamed like the skin of an otter'. And yet it was not just twenty-somethings and rock stars going in for all this flash: Fred Weil, a retired doctor out in Chicago, ordered a black sequinned dinner jacket of his own — for his ninetieth birthday party.

Savile Row East

Richard Anderson Ltd had been in existence for about three years when another modern aspect of the business began to demand our time: exports to the East. In 2004, the Japanese luxury department store Isetan approached us about co-producing a small line of custom suits for sale in Japan. The line would bear the Richard Anderson label, but its suits would be produced by a factory run by the Ogha Corporation in Osaka, and then customers would meet me at Isetan's flagship store in Shinjuku to be fitted for adjustments. Rather than choose from the factory's established patterns, or even from block patterns already established for our European and American ready-to-wear clientele, I conceived a new template specifically for this new market, taking into consideration the particulars of Japanese men's figuration — which on the whole involves a slightly shorter coat than in Western styles. A couple of my new Japanese colleagues came to London so that I could measure them and perform a collective figuration analysis; then, when the resulting drafts approximated the pattern I wanted, I flew out to the factory in Osaka to approve each detail of the pattern's final iteration such that the template's quality and viability would be ensured.

As I would learn, my Japanese friends have some curious ways of testing the authenticity of one's acumen. In the days leading up to my first journey to Japan, where the Osaka factory was already experimenting with some draft patterns I had sent over, my Ogha contact Ryo Hayashi sent me an email with two photos attached, 'A' and 'B', requesting that I compare the two coats' shoulder widths and articulate my preference. I spent the better part of a day playing Spot the Difference with these photographs, zooming in on every last pixel, and — God help me — the two single-breasted navy pinstripe coats looked utterly identical. Finally, at half-eleven that evening, I responded saying that despite the assiduous application of all my faculties it was difficult to see any difference between the coats; to which Ryo replied:

Dear Richard-san:
Thank you very much for your quick response.
To tell you the truth, these two jackets photo-shooted are the same jacket.

Actually intentionally I didn't give you the detailed explanation because to avoid to give you bias.

Reckoning it would not be long after my arrival in Osaka before I would be bowled another googly, I did my best to dedicate the initial twelve-hour flight alternately to sleeping and collecting my wits. But flying halfway around the world is inevitably a knackering business, and by the time I had made my connecting flight from the eerily calm and spotless Narita airport to Osaka, I was a walking stupor. Waiting for me at the airport was my interpreter, Hironobu Uchida, an avid football fan and fluent multilinguist who, although he himself is fifty going on nineteen, is employed by Ogha not merely to ease communications between Western visitors and their Japanese interlocutors but also to babysit said visitors around the clock. Indeed, for the next four days Hiro would not leave my side except for when I slept or used the loo, and when I suggested on the first evening that we have sushi for dinner I was told that on the off-chance it might disagree with my digestive system I was forbidden to eat raw fish until the night before I was due to fly home.

The Ogha factory is the most sparkling and

efficient operation I have ever seen. Reminiscent of Chaplin's *Modern Times*, except of course absent the comic bumbling, every worker at every station is monitored by a meter that tallies how many foreparts he has struck, or how many buttons she has sewn on, and from the intensity of these workers' stone-faced determination one senses that falling short of the prescribed quota happens rarely and, when it does (if ever it does), occasions profound shame. It was this attention and dedication to quality that enabled the establishment of a workable model approved by me within just a few days — after which, beginning the following year, I began to make semi-annual trips to Tokyo to fit the model's customers at trunk shows held every March and September. These shows give Japanese fans of Western labels a chance to meet with representatives of the labels themselves: one Saturday Richard James might be there, then Nick Hart, then Timothy Everest, then Richard Anderson Ltd, and so on, the majority of us offering suits ranging from high quality off-the-peg to individually altered custom suits — because as much as the Japanese love *sebiro*, only the exceptionally rich have both the time and money to come all the way to London for the real thing. Many of the rest aspire to one day, and some are so enamoured by the institution that they regard those of us hailing from Savile Row itself as celebrities.

Once, after I had spent about an hour fitting a Japanese man in his suits, he sat down at my little provisional desk and momentously handed me a business card, while making a scribbling motion with his free hand. It was the first time I had ever been asked for my autograph, and writing my name alone seemed somehow inadequate. 'Best wishes,' I eventually eked out. 'Hope you enjoyed it!'

Later the same day I was trying my best to be patient and polite while fielding questions from a journalist bent on rehashing Huntsman's troubled times when I noticed that a potted poplar tree in the corner of the room had begun to sway. An earthquake! Everyone else seemed not to notice or was remarkably blasé. Hiro advised me that this little rumble would have registered no more than a one or two on the *shindo*, Japan's equivalent of the Richter scale; moreover, 'It is no problem if building sways side to side; it is when it goes up and down that we are in trouble.' However, it was yet another first for me, England being rather more seismically repressed. In a photograph taken ten minutes later for a promotional brochure I can still be seen eyeing the plant warily.

So much excitement on top of back-to-back fittings would have me ready for my pillow by the end of each day, but so as not to be left unchaperoned long enough to consume any toxic sushi, I would be all but required to tag along while Hiro did exactly what I suspect he does with the majority of his evenings when I am not in the picture, which is to watch Japanese Beatles tribute bands. The favoured venue was a restaurant-cum-music club called Abbey Road, where, just to get in, even accompanied by someone of Hiro's 'member' status, one must stand in a queue feeling something like an underage commoner trying to get into Chinawhite on a Saturday night. Down a flight of stairs, on a dais surrounded by screens playing videos of the originals, a rotation of Japanese Beatles impersonators perform — among them The Parrots, who (I am given to understand) are one of the two premier bootleg Beatles bands in Japan, a status warranting profound reverence, as apparently there is no shortage to the number of grown Japanese men whose profession it is to impersonate The Beatles on a nightly basis. Roppongi's Abbey Road offers three shows an evening, and from the look of it any fewer would not sate the crowds — a fanship largely comprised of young women dressed as if by Mary Quant herself and middle-aged businessmen swaying to 'Yesterday' with their neckties around their heads. In The Parrots, Mamori Yoshii (aka 'Chappy') plays John; Takeshi Noguchi, Akihiro Matsuyama and Teruyuki Matsuzaki play Paul, George and Ringo, respectively; and a man named Fumiya Matsuyama plays the keyboard à la Billy Preston, although he looks more like Yoko Ono. Appearances aside, the music and vocals are uncannily dead on, so much so that one suspects some secret Suzuki-esque method is behind their precision. On the walls, attesting to the club's allure, are several autographed photos of its celebrity fans, among them Liam Gallagher, the cast of *Friends* and the Arctic Monkeys. Whenever I have been there I have been the audience's sole Westerner, feeling very much the pasty giant, a condition that became all the more conspicuous when I made the mistake of telling Hiro that my mum is from Liverpool — and suddenly *I* was the man of the hour, bowing and being bowed to by each member of The Parrots while a sea of screaming girls seemed on the verge of crushing one another just to touch my Cleverley-shod feet.

Every year Isetan announces a new theme

according to which its Savile Row licensors create a new suit design, which I enlist Fran to sketch out on paper for my Japanese colleagues' review. The first year the theme was 'Icons', so I took my cues and made a 'John Lennon suit': navy mohair with bootcut trousers. The following year the theme was 'The Great Gatsby', and everyone involved put his own spin on the white lounge suit Robert Redford wore in the film. Presently, we sell approximately 250–300 custom suits in Japan annually, but as yet no true bespoke — except, as I say, to those customers who can make the trip to London. For whether you are trying to break into Japan, China, Russia or any other emerging market, you need half a dozen or so committed customers in the region before you can afford to set yourself up for a week in the local equivalent of the Carlyle or Four Seasons and conduct the requisite measuring sessions and fittings. And you cannot go out just once; you have to return, for follow-up fittings and ideally to pull additional customers through word-of-mouth, so until you have your reliable core clientele the venture simply is not cost-effective. I am optimistic that in time — within ten years, I should think — the custom market in Japan will support the addition of Tokyo to the list of international cities to which we bring true bespoke. And India and China are next. In fact, I gather China already has its own Beatles tribute band: The Broadwoods, who play at a club called Mr Moonlight in Hong Kong.

★   ★   ★

By the time Richard Anderson Ltd turned four years old, Brian and I had achieved more or less what we had expected from our three-year business plan — launched, as it was, on the ominous note of 9/11. In year one the company endured a considerable loss; in year two it endured a smaller loss, and in year three, we broke even. Sales and production were mounting such that we needed yet more tailors and office staff — niches we filled again without placing advertisements or recruiting, because in December 2004, four years after the company's sale to Don Bargeman and Trevor Swift's consortium, Henry Huntsman & Sons went into receivership.

Upon receiving news of his redundancy, Eugene Maccarone, a Huntsman coatmaker for fourteen years, walked out of 11 Savile Row and right into 13 to ask us for a job. We also hired Christine Dennison, Huntsman's consummate bookkeeper of twelve years, to help Brian with our mounting accounts — and Michael Granger, whom we could finally afford to make an honest man by employing full-time. Then there was the venerated Carmelo Reina, who in fact at sixty-six had already retired as Huntsman's workshop foreman of twenty-five years, but so disliked the idle life that after six months in Sicily returned to London to ask if I could not use him as an additional coatmaker three days a week — which I could. This brought us up to fifteen-strong — and still every day seemed busier than the last.

A Day in the Life

The alarm goes off at six fifteen. I shower, dress (today in a light-mauve poplin shirt, a navy double-breasted hopsack and a silver dogtooth-check tie), grab a piece of toast and — the weather is dry and warm — ride the Hexagon to St Albans station in time to catch the seven fifteen. For nine years I biked all the way into town, but I have been knocked off one too many times for a father of four, so Thameslink it is — and on the train the sartorial scrutiny begins. The blazer on the lady across the aisle is made of a handsome fabric but could do with a bit of surgery under the arms. The grey suit in front of her is too fair for its wearer's white hair. The navy pinstripes to my left are drowning a pair of milk-bottle shoulders. This goes on all the way to King's Cross, and on the Tube to Piccadilly Circus, past the underground fashion bills, film advertisements, and the window displays along Regent Street, down Vigo Street, behind a too-short overcoat just exiting Starbucks, and round Gieves at the top end of Savile Row — where even two hours before bare-chested musclemen will

341

station themselves at the emporium's doors one's nostrils fill with the smell of Abercrombie & Fitch perfume.

In the back of Number 13, I change out of my 10-year-old navy thirteen-ounce commuting suit into my second suit of the day — nine-ounce single-breasted candy-blue mohair cut eighteen months ago — and pour a coffee. Then I check that everyone else has arrived — Brian usually gets in around seven, Rebecca and the tailors by eight — and working on whatever he or she needs to be furthering along to stay apace. It is a Friday, so Mr Reina is in, raising and shortening a collar on a windowpane check. Eugene, at his left, is crookening the shoulder of a black cavalry twill dinner jacket. Antoni is bicycling some black cord through his Brother and Granger is pressing a red melton coat lined with black-and-white skull-print for the Episcopalian Reverend out in California. Clive, Rebecca and I review the log to identify what must go out via DDI before day's end: a black cashmere overcoat to Manhattan, two Prince of Wales check three-pieces to Cheshire, a green cord safari jacket with patch pockets to Singapore, and a single-breasted denim lounge suit to Serbia. A banker based in Geneva but working in London for the week needs his navy double-breasted linen before dinnertime, so it is decided Rebecca will take it round to Claridge's on a hanger at lunch.

Next we review which customers are booked to come in. At ten thirty, a first-timer who works around the corner on Sackville Street and has been emailing us with questions for a week needs measuring up. At midday, a Spanish actor and his elder brother, a surgeon visiting from the Upper East Side, are due for forward fittings for a suit and three sport coats between them. At two, an American property tycoon with extremely tricky shoulders is trying on two classic business suits on the go. At three fifteen, another American, this one a retired businessman and avocational fashion designer, hopes to collect a patchwork coat of his own invention. And at half-four, I am due to see my father, for whom I have made a double-breasted grey pick-and-pick he plans to wear to my sister's wedding at the end of the month. Five appointments in a day is about average, but what with impromptu punters also pitching up it can stretch to eight, in which case I can go into the fitting room at half-nine and not come out again until three.

When we have confirmed the readiness of every garment to be fitted, picked up and dispatched, Rebecca and I then review her list of jobs to strike and trim and decide which bundles must be ready for handing over to Horace when he comes to collect next week's basting. Horace works in Hackney and only comes in once a week, so we do not want any urgent orders to miss the slot.

At nine, the shop opens.

At two past nine, a handsome Indian man in a dark grey suit and white shirt comes briskly through the door, checking his wristwatch.

'I need a tie,' he says urgently. 'A plain. Red. *Tie*.'

Brian, who has been reviewing next month's American itinerary, ushers the man down the back, where our ties sleep rolled-up on their sides in wooden cubbyholes, while I turn my mind to the day's first cutting job — for Prince Edochie, a South African polo enthusiast who called late yesterday to order a new double-breasted grey worsted he needs in three weeks' time. This is not the Prince's usual style; his long-time pattern is a single-breasted model, so I must convert the existing coat pattern; i.e., produce a new one using the original as my guide. A successful balance has already been achieved, so the coat's sleeve and back patterns will remain the same, but I need to create a new forepart by marking around the old one, increasing the front edge by an inch and three-quarters and changing the shape of the lapel from notched to peaked. Left alone to do nothing else, I could accomplish this in ten minutes — cutting an entire suit pattern without interruption takes more or less an hour, depending on the customer's figuration — but today no sooner have I begun to sharpen my chalk (on a wooden box lined with tiny razors to look something like an ancient tribal torture device) when the shop phone rings and the receiver is passed to me by Clive.

The caller is a new customer, a young London-based barrister referred by his uncle and whose pattern I finalised about a fortnight ago. He is now ready to confirm his first order: a single-breasted blue linen winter business suit, for which I suggest a fourteen-ounce navy from Scabal. While the man runs this by his wife I watch the Indian tie-seeker and Brian emerge from the back of the shop empty-handed. The man is just about out the door when Brian spots a length of crimson silk among the ties entwined around a dummy next to the fireplace and the sale is saved.

The barrister returns to the phone to affirm the fabric suggestion, which Clive pops next door to order while I return to my forepart conversion. By five past ten the new piece has been marked out, cut and handed over to Rebecca along with the rest of the pattern for striking — at which point I have only ten minutes before my first appointment, so instead of starting on another pattern I join Brian in reviewing our American itinerary. We now visit the States three times a year, usually every September, January and May — so that our customers know when to expect us and can plan accordingly. In order to accommodate my sister's wedding, however, we have pushed this year's autumn trip back to early October, when we will spend three days together at the Carlyle in order to meet with approximately twenty customers there. It is decided Brian will go on alone to the Jefferson in Washington (two days), the St Regis in Houston (one), the Fairmont in Chicago (two), the Regent Beverly Wiltshire in Beverly Hills —

The phone rings again and this time it is Mark Henderson, chief executive of Gieves & Hawkes and chairman of the Savile Row Bespoke Association, wishing to discuss the association's plans for an international show next spring. Simultaneously, my ten thirty has arrived, so Brian takes the call while I head down to the front of the shop to receive Sebastian Green. He is a young man, in his early thirties, about six foot one and maybe a pound or two over fourteen stone, and he wants to wear his first Savile Row suit to a wedding in January in Melbourne. But it is already mid-September, and Mr Green is leaving for Australia at the end of November; will there be time? Ideally the process would be afforded eight weeks from measurement to finished suit, but this can be juggled to an extent, and — I can see no difficult figuration right off the bat — in this case I think we should be fine.

So we start talking cloth. Mohair, I say, is a South African fabric that springs back nicely, will be good in Australia's hot summer climate, and will also perform well over time. What colour? Mr Green wants blue, but not solid blue — blue with some texture to it. We look at pinstripes, rain and cable, then some nailheads, birdseyes and herringbones. A couple of the birdseyes catch his fancy and he pulls the swatches aside. For comparison's sake, we also look at some Super 150s, which have a softer handle and come in herringbone as well, but he prefers the birdseyes — although he is uncertain about how much definition he wants to the pattern. I pose the question of weight: more definition will take the weight from eight up to nine ounces, which might be too hot. Ultimately, a nine-ounce navy worsted birdseye from Holland & Sherry's Perennial range is pronounced the winner, and its lining he elects to choose when he comes back to try on the baste.

Now, single- or double-breasted? One in four suits I cut is double-breasted, I say, and Mr Green asks whether the choice is of generational significance. No is the answer; many young men actually prefer double-breasted for being a more formal look, while single-breasted generally does more to thin and elongate the figure. Mr Green opts for single-breasted, with sleeves that, like mine, show a good width of cuff — and button-fly belt-buckle trousers with straight hems.

He has come in a T-shirt and jeans, so in order to take his coat-on measurements I run my tape around his chest and ask Rebecca to fetch a forty-two-inch block coat from the ready-to-wear rail — and when I have helped Mr Green into it I can immediately see it is too short. I locate his natural waist and take his coat-on numbers, calling them out to Rebecca who calls them back and jots them down; then I take my coat-on figuration notes: Mr Green's left hand hangs lower than his right; indeed, like most of us (men and women) his right shoulder is lower, his right hip higher, and the whole of his right side a tiny bit larger overall. This means the block coat's right sleeve is slouching and gathering under the arm. Now I take his coat-off measurements, his trousers measurements and his trousers figuration: he stands with his toes at eleven and one on the clock, so to fall along the centre of each leg his pleats will have to be rotated out slightly. Otherwise he has a confident stance and a sturdy, athletic build, so I have all the information I need now, and, following a bit of chat about our respective football teams, Watford and West Ham, we say our farewells. Up front Brian takes Mr Green's deposit, schedules him for a baste fitting in three weeks' time, and, after some tie-browsing by the fireplace, Mr Green leaves.

I have missed a call from a young investment banker evidently up at dawn in New York; he ordered two suits just yesterday and when I return the call he says he forgot to ask that each of them contain a Blackberry pocket. (Requests such as these are fairly common; another Savile Row patron, one with a rather public heroin problem, once asked his tailor to line the inside of his coats with syringe loops.) The young banker is left-handed, so the pocket should go on the right. When I have made this note on the client's ticket, I then pass the two Prince of Wales checks Clive is preparing to pack up for Cheshire (both are fine) as well as a cavalry twill Eugene adjusted late yesterday (back of the neck needs squaring up).

At quarter to midday a small BBC crew arrives for an appointment booked with Brian last night — they are running a spot this evening about Barack Obama's upcoming trip to Europe and want to know what we think of his wardrobe. His is a very loose-fitting, American style, I say — flattering as it fits both his slim frame and cool character. At midday on the dot the Spanish actor and his brother arrive and Rebecca fetches their clothes to be forward-fitted. The actor is trying on a grey worsted single-breasted suit and two black sport coats, a micro and a serge, and he has ordered his brother a blue cotton pinpoint coat as a gift. These men are relatively new customers, the actor referred by a male stylist who, like Faye, sends a good number of his charges our way, and while the actor prefers a slightly less fitted style than our house line, we seem to meet somewhere in the middle and the end results please us both. Both of his sport coats look good, but the suit trousers are a quarter inch too long and his brother's cotton pinpoint needs some fullness taken out of the right shoulder. The actor is due to commence filming in Italy in ten days and his brother's London holiday is up at the end of next week, so it is agreed the suit and pinpoint will be ready for final fit Wednesday next.

When the brothers leave I mark up the garments needing adjustment and put them in hand with Eugene. Meanwhile Ben Glazier, our PR man, has arrived to discuss the forth-coming American trip — which cloths and styles to promote and how to format the brochure — but a young woman is milling about the front shop untended because Clive has popped out for a sandwich. I leave the brochure to Ben and Brian and ask the young woman if I may be of help. She is looking for a gift for her fiancé, she says — maybe a tie, or some cufflinks, or . . . what would I suggest? I ask whether her fiancé is a relatively style-conscious guy, in which case I might suggest a gift certificate. It is easy to mistake ties and cufflinks as ideal gifts because they are generally elegant and do not require trying-on — but, in fact, for some men they are a matter of such personal and narrow-ranging taste that if chosen by someone else they will be worn once or twice and then relegated to the drawer.

As it turns out, I know the woman's fiancé:

he is a young and exceedingly amenable university professor for whom I have already made two suits, a blue linen and a grey worsted. While I am selling the woman a cobalt blue-and-grey striped knitted tie, James Fox, the American tycoon with the tricky shoulders, arrives for his first fitting in over a year. A client inherited from Hammick, Mr Fox broke his collarbone after falling from a horse as a boy and as a result has protruding bone to the right side of his neck and irregular shoulders consisting of various lumps and bumps running from neck to end. Indeed, the sartorial campaign to counteract these protrusions has gone on for so long I am beginning to think it would be less expensive all around if we just paid for him to have an operation. I have been experimenting with possible solutions for years, trying various combinations of canvas, wadding, styrofoam — even my children's plasticine, which I brought into the shop to try to replicate Fox's lumps on a mannequin. Back in my reprobate days at St Michael's, I got some good press for successfully evading a woodworking exam — news of my audacious protest spread quickly and went some way to impressing Fran — but now whenever I am working on Mr Fox's shoulders I wonder whether some basic woodworking technique might have come in handy after all.

My most recent potential solution involves a shoulder pad designed to lodge the protruding bones in precisely positioned depressions, and I have inserted a pad made according to this mould into each of the two suits Mr Fox is trying on today. They are both classic single-breasted business suits, a blue spot and a grey nailhead, and when I passed them yesterday on myself and then also on the plasticine-enhanced dummy, both looked fine. But this has happened before: I try on a coat equipped with my latest shoulder-levelling contraption and it looks good; then Mr Fox comes in, puts the same coat on, and no matter how beautiful the rest of the suit looks, his eyes go straight to the shoulders and he frowns. His disappointment is never with the coat, or so he says — indeed, he takes great care to express awareness and appreciation of my boundless dedication to the cause — but rather with his own physique, which I gather is an enduring personal bane.

Today, however, we have some joy. When I have eased him into the blue spot and together we inspect the shoulders, our eyebrows raise in synchronised approval. The results are not bad. In fact, the coat's shoulders seem to have successfully camouflaged the ones underneath; the only thing needed now is to raise the front button slightly, for the padding has lifted the coat by about a quarter inch. The grey nailhead is equally successful, so it is agreed this latest shoulder model should be unofficially patented and the coats adjusted for pickup next Wednesday, just before Mr Fox is scheduled to return to Washington.

Now I pour a cup of tea and unwrap a sausage sandwich Granger has brought me back from the café around the corner — but I should know better, for, just as when one waits ages for a bus, it is only a freshly lit cigarette that prompts three to pull up simultaneously — the first bite of a sausage sandwich inevitably summons the arrival of three customers at once. Today they are a lanky chap enquiring about a bespoke shirt; Edward Wingler, our patchwork designer, who is apologetically early; and, on Mr Wingler's heels, the Duke of Aspremont, carrying a coat cut by Hammick nineteen years ago and whose elbows he would like patched with brown suede. Brian handles the Duke while Clive shows the extra-tall gentleman some shirting and I wipe my mouth and take Mr Wingler into the back. He has arrived straight from Heathrow, and while

I am helping him out of the coat he is already wearing (a navy worsted cut by Hall), he informs me, with equal gall and astonishment, that he was the only man in first class wearing a tie.

Possibly our most fanatical clotheshorse, Mr Wingler came across a magazine advertisement some weeks ago — a picture of a young man in a patchwork tweed coat winding up to throw an American football — and he liked the coat so much he tore out the photo and brought it to me to ask whether I could not cut him one just like it. I was extremely keen, so together we set about selecting tweeds from a harmonious Shetland range, Rebecca cut dozens of squares from the different bolts, Eugene patched them together into something like a big quilt, and from this I struck the pattern — a long-established single-breasted template. The result was so smart that in addition to Mr Wingler's original we made a model to put in the shop window and have since taken orders for ten more.

And now the original is very nearly done. When Mr Wingler puts it on I can see that all it needs is the right sleeve lengthened by a quarter inch, so I offer to have the adjusted coat sent to him next week, as he is only in London through the weekend. Before leaving, however, he also wants to look at some samples for yet another coat he has in mind — a ruby red velvet dinner jacket — as well as some silk swatches for a tie to match. Clive sets him up with some books on the sofa and Reina brings me his windowpane check to pass, which this time I do; he then moves on to altering the left sleeve length on a £17,000 vicuña overcoat for Mr Agassi, our Iraqi entrepreneur.

While Brian and Christine review the billing and Clive fetches additional swatches for Mr Wingler, the phone rings again and it is Simon Cundey, of Henry Poole's, calling to report some logistical details about the Merchant Taylors' biannual Golden Shears competition, which, along with three other bespoke tailors, I am slated to judge. When Simon and I hang up the phone rings again, and this time I am told by the caller, a Frenchman, that he has read about us online and would like to come by when he is next in town to be measured up for a blue or grey double-breasted pinstripe, he has not yet decided which. After offering to email him some photographs showing the possibilities in both straight and diagonal patterns, I hand the phone to Clive to book the appointment — and just as I do my mobile goes off.

It's Faye, who wants to know whether I can

make one of her singers a double-breasted overcoat for a video shoot — something in a military style, a là Kitchener's Valet.

As ever, there's a catch.

She needs it by Monday.

After promising an answer ASAP I hang up to call Carmelo Garofalo, another one of my off-site tailors, and Francesca Galeone, a finishing tailoress, to ask whether they will be available to work through the weekend in order to meet a Monday morning final press. They will. Meanwhile, Clive has run around the corner to the cloth supplier William Bill, on New Burlington Street, to check that they have the eighteen-ounce black wool we need. They do. Brian is willing to come in early tomorrow to put the struck material in hand with Carmelo, so I ring Faye back to accept and schedule the pickup.

While I wolf down what is left of my sandwich, Brian, just finishing his early shift, begins gathering up his papers and leather jacket to leave. His departure for Kent at around half-four each afternoon is my signal to start looking at tomorrow's diary — which customers and tailors are due, which dispatches are expected, which coats should be passed, which jobs to cut and put in hand to keep everything moving smoothly. Today, while I am doing this, Nick Demetriou,

357

whose workshop is just over on Berwick Street, comes in to swap two basted fittings and three pairs of finished trousers for four straight finishes needed in three weeks. And as Nick leaves my father arrives — looking rather like he did the day he escorted me to Huntsman in a snowstorm more than twenty-five years ago, except that now he is a little whiter on top. His grey pick-and-pick for my sister's wedding still needs a bit of tightening across the shoulder blades, but otherwise is done, so we look at some shirting he is also considering having made up for the occasion, then he pores over the cufflinks for a minute or two and asks how the book is coming along. Good, good. Nearly finished. And when am I next off to America? Would I like him to pick me up from the airport upon my return? We agree to speak closer to the date and he hurries off to catch the five twenty from Euston to Tring.

Just inside half an hour I have cut the pattern for Faye's overcoat and — because Rebecca is busy striking Prince Edochie's double-breasted grey worsted, which needs to be given to Horace before the end of the day for basting — I set about striking the cloth from William Bill myself. This means switching shears, from my paper-cutting shears to the larger, heavier, cloth-cutting shears I inherited from Hall and which were made over a hundred years ago in Newark, New Jersey — and cleaning them, which one does simply by running them through the hair on the back of one's head, so as not to disrupt their balance. Ideally this does not involve taking an ear off, or dropping the blades altogether — for, so the superstition goes, dropping one's shears heralds the imminent death of a tailoress. ('Whoops,' Lakey used to say whenever his hit the floor. 'There goes another one.') While I am unrolling a length of the heavy wool across my board, Andreas Velissariou, our alternate presser who works over in Soho on Lexington Street, comes in to pick up a batch of finished suits to be pressed while Granger is on holiday next week.

At twenty-five past six, my Japanese interpreter Hiro and his colleague Kikuchi, who are in town for a few days, arrive for a preprandial conference. I abandon my shears for the customary round of smiling bows and pull a chair down to the front shop so that the three of us can sit around the sofa under our current window model, which the two Japanese men seem to admire — it is a camel-coloured ladies' coat with chocolate-brown lapels — and talk about the last trunk show, whether we should consider adding

359

some new fabrics to the custom line, the latest design theme, and the weekend-by-weekend schedule for next March in Shinjuku. En route to The Wolseley for dinner, we pass the Royal Arcade, where Cleverley is, which reminds me to mention that Richard Anderson Ltd is in the process of starting up its own custom shoe line, perhaps another international licence arrangement of interest — a comment that seems to move Kikuchi, over asparagus soup and Wiener schnitzel, to enquire politely about business in general. How are we weathering the economic storm? Knock on wood, I say: the plunging pound-to-dollar exchange rate has actually encouraged an uptake in American orders and, since breaking even five years ago, we have been consistently profitable. In fact, we now have about as much business as we can handle without hiring another cutter — a road I am not quite ready to go down, but soon may have to consider. We shall see. When dessert is finished and the cheque paid, I help Hiro and Kikuchi hail a cab for St Georges and then backtrack past the Royal Arcade, the chic Old Bond Street boutiques, the Burlington Arcade, aromatic Abercrombie & Fitch and the Royal Academy of Arts . . . then left onto Savile Row and right once again into the now-empty Number 13 — which, incidentally, Faye tells me is lucky in her family — where I finish striking the wool overcoat, bundle it up with the ticket order and a cheque for Carmelo's pickup from Brian in the morning, change out of the candy-blue mohair and back into the older and warmer hopsack, lock up, catch my own cab to King's Cross in time for the twenty-three eighteen to St Albans — and, at five to midnight, unlock the Hexagon and ride the last half-mile to Marshalswick in the dark.

Dispatched

be·spoke [bi-**spohk**]
— *verb*
1. a pt. and pp. of bespeak.
— *adjective*
2. *British*. a. (of clothes) made to individual order; custom-made: *a bespoke jacket*. b. making or selling such clothes: *a bespoke tailor*.
3. *Older Use*. engaged to be married; spoken for.

be·speak [bi-**speek**]
— *verb (used with object)*, -**spoke** or (*Archaic*) -**spake**; -**spo·ken** or -**spoke**; -**speak·ing**.
1. to ask for in advance: *to bespeak the reader's patience*.
2. to reserve beforehand; engage in advance; make arrangements for: *to bespeak a seat in a theater*.
3. *Literary*. to speak to; address.
4. to show; indicate: *This bespeaks a kindly heart*.
5. *Obsolete*. to foretell; forebode.

The Random House Unabridged Dictionary

In July 2007, a new suitmaker named Sartoriani opened on Old Bond Street and appealed to prospective new customers with an offer of one 'Bespoke Suit Uniquely made according to your personal measurements & specification from our extensive range of finest Italian Super 120's quality fabrics £495 (Regular price £995)'.

This 'limited introductory offer' prompted the lodging of an anonymous complaint with the British Advertising Standards Authority (ASA), arguing that the wording of the offer was 'misleading' and therefore in contravention of the Committee of Advertising Practice's 'truthfulness' code.[1] The basis for this argument was that Sartoriani, whose slogan promises 'each suit as individual as its wearer', does not actually produce suits in conformation with the definition of 'bespoke' that has been accepted by a legion of Savile Row practitioners for over two centuries. Traditionally, a 'bespoke' garment is not merely made of cloth 'spoken for' by its customer; nor even is taking a customer's measurements into account while making the garment a sufficient additional criterion. Critically, to meet with the traditional trade definition of 'bespoke', a garment must also: 1) be made according to a pattern created

---

[1] Which states, in part, that 'No marketing communication should mislead, or be likely to mislead, by inaccuracy, ambiguity, exaggeration, omission or otherwise.'

and cut uniquely for that customer; 2) assembled by hand, with machines used only for the long seams; and 3) fitted on the customer an indefinite number of times from baste to finish such that the most successful and individualised fit can be achieved. By contrast, Sartoriani's offer was for suits made with cloth chosen by the customer who would also be measured up on the company's premises, but then the cloth and measurements would be sent abroad to be cut and assembled by machine, based on a template. Once constructed, the suit would then be sent back to Old Bond Street, where its buyer would try it on and, if necessary, it would be adjusted accordingly. So a suit made by this process differs in at least two critical ways from the traditional classification of 'bespoke' long celebrated and associated with the Golden Square Mile: it does not involve a unique pattern and its cloth is not cut and sewn together virtually entirely by hand.

Sartoriani contested the complaint with several counterarguments, one of which was that while its method of suit-production deviated from the traditionally accepted definition, the collective English lexicon has evolved to include several variations on the meaning of 'bespoke', including the Oxford English Dictionary's minimalist definition:

'made to order'. *The Random House Unabridged Dictionary* is much more expansive with its entries, but even the most relevant one above — 'made to individual order; custom-made' — does not get to the heart of what it means to have an authentic bespoke garment made on Savile Row. And the ASA saw fit to agree with Sartoriani's argument — on the basis that a majority of people understand 'bespoke' and 'made to measure' to be synonymous with 'made to order' and therefore distinguishable from ready-to-wear clothing. In other words, a suit may qualify as 'bespoke' even if its purchaser had personally preordained nothing more than its buttons.

In fact, this debate is nothing new. Sartoriani was hardly alone in coopting 'bespoke' according to this logic; for years, the word has been thrown around by tailors of every calibre in reference to garments made by a variety of techniques and of wide-ranging integrity and durability. Sometimes it seems as though they believe the word alone can do the work, as though its very utterance will magically 'bestow a good figure where nature has not granted one'. Some 'bespoke' houses put their sleeves and shoulders in by machine, which can compromise a garment's longevity; some fuse their chest canvas with a synthetic adhesion that (unlike padding inserted by hand) does not mould as well to the wearer's body and over time can cause unsightly corrugation in the lapel; some, like Sartoriani, do not even cut unique patterns. Indeed, anyone who can afford a lease may set up shop on Savile Row; anyone can put a half-made suit full of white basting stitches on his website or in his shop window — even if the process by which that shop's suits are made does not involve a baste fitting at all.

The ASA's ruling over 'bespoke' versus 'made to order' is not regrettable because it might draw business away from the true traditionalists. The traditionalist's clientele represents a fairly consistent minority — of long-time supporters who can easily afford the justifiably high price of a true bespoke suit and are too discriminating to settle for anything less. These patrons are immune to hollow marketing tactics. Moreover, by virtue of his rarity, the traditional bespoke tailor who dedicates himself to providing good and reliable services should be able to attract and retain as much business as he can handle. Rather, the ASA's ruling is unfortunate for another reason, which is its apparent indifference to distinctions even on the *non*-commercial level — the implicit message that even in the symbolical, historical and socio-cultural sphere there is no reason to insist upon the distinction of pure bespoke. And such an unnuanced adjudication would seem to invite extinction of the true and original craft.

★ ★ ★

Hammick called me Young Richard until he died.

Hall died the following year, in 2008, but Lakey is still very much with us, and still comes by in his beautiful three-piece suits to say hello. He and I discuss what has changed since his halcyon days — there is no more smoking, for one, although on occasion a customer will ask to light up and I have to cross my fingers when he stands under the fire sprinkler and ignites a massive Monte Cristo.

As for Huntsman: since the company's flirtation with liquidation in 2004, it has been rescued by a new team of investors headed up by a seemingly dedicated bespoke enthusiast named David Coleridge, who dismissed Trevor Swift and, with the help of Peter Smith, an earnest veteran of the old Huntsman guard and now the company's general manager, could very well be on his way to turning the firm around. What it will take, I dare say, is what every true bespoke tailoring house must always seek to cultivate: a committed and talented cutting team who can attract and retain the confidence of customers over time. It is not enough to lure people in the door just once, with fancy marketing and special one-off offers. To ride out recessions, depressions, rent hikes, steep pension governances and rising material costs, one needs a core clientele who know and trust that they cannot get better quality clothing elsewhere — indeed, that their tailoring house will do the job to the absolute best of its ability *every single time*. And if a cutter wants his company to survive him, to endure not only his own passing but that of his loyal clientele as well, he must identify someone young, talented, hardworking and game to learn his system of bestowing good figures for the benefit of a new generation — and start training his would-be inheritor as soon as circumstances permit.

So, what with all this talk of future generations: what do my own children make of Savile Row?

Tom, who is now sixteen, has long claimed no interest whatsoever, although for my sister's wedding he recently acquired his first suit — not bespoke, because he would have outgrown it within six weeks, but still a rather nice Calvin Klein model in which he was fitted by me for adjustments in the shop — and I dare say the process occasioned a glimmer of curiosity, if not about my participation then at least regarding his own potential as a handsome wearer of the livery.

Molly, thirteen, took one look at me in a recent BBC documentary about Savile Row and pronounced that on telly I have 'a big fat tomato face'. Shortly prior to this, I had come home one evening to report over dinner that Richard Anderson Ltd had won the 'Best Bespoke' category in the London Fashion Awards — in response to which Molly said: 'Dad, no one likes a gloater.'

For Mai, ten, the intimate fact that her father dresses people she sees routinely on television is a source of acute embarrassment. A year or so ago, an extremely well-known prime-time personality ordered half a dozen bespoke shirts that I wanted to soften and re-press so their collars would lie more naturally around the neck. And, of course, the most efficient way to soften cotton is to give it a wash — so, in a sort of tribute to Lakey, I brought the shirts home and, while they were taking a spin in the washing machine, Mai came into the kitchen for a glass of milk. When I told her whose shirts were tumbling round in our washer she went bright red and left the room with her face in her hands.

And then there is George.

George, the pincushion of all my dynastic hopes, came to me one day shortly after his eleventh birthday to say that what he would really like is to be a professional footballer someday, but he does not think he is good enough — so he has been thinking that instead he will 'just take over the shop'. He reckons this will prove a fairly straightforward transaction: we will simply scratch 'Richard' off the front window and replace it with 'George'.

As for Fran: ever since our first date twenty-seven years ago, when I invited her along on an errand to exchange some stay-press trousers, she has been unfailingly supportive of my sartorial ambitions and allegiance to Savile Row — and yet said support does not necessarily always translate into mutual agreement on personal preferences of attire. When it came time for Molly's first holy communion, I put on a pale yellow voile shirt, my Cartier cufflinks and a brand-new navy pinstripe cotton suit, which I love, but it was such an unseasonably baking-hot day that for the life of me I could not bear the idea of encasing my feet in a pair of socks and proper shoes. Fran had already taken Molly and Tom to the church and I was running late in getting myself plus George and Mai there also in time, so I hurriedly slipped into a pair of smart leather flip-flops I had bought recently in New York and off we went. At Sts Albans and Stephen, I made it all the way across the car park, down the aisle, and into my pew before Fran looked down to see my bare toes — and gasped. Two years later, when it came time for George's first communion, I was thoroughly inspected from tip to toe before allowed out of the house, and no sooner had I stepped out of the car downtown than a couple of acquainted parishioners hurried over to elbow me gleefully in the pinstripes and say:

'What, no flip-flops this year, Richard?'

Ah well.

What do they know.

They don't work on Savile Row.

My Tailor is Rich

Select Tailoring (and Non-Tailoring) Terms

-A-

Abercrombie & Fitch — Named for founders David Abercrombie and Ezra Fitch, a fashionable clothing chain dealing in, among other items of 'lifestyle clothing', leather flip-flops and pre-torn jeans. Founded in 1892, in New York, Abercrombie & Fitch began as a small factory store specialising in quality camping, fishing and hunting gear. Prominent historical clientele is rumoured to include Theodore Roosevelt, Clark Gable, Amelia Earhart, Katharine Hepburn, John Steinbeck, the Duke of Windsor, Dwight D. Eisenhower, John F. Kennedy and Ernest Hemingway, who allegedly shot himself with an Abercrombie & Fitch gun. In 2007, the company opened its London flagship shop at the top end of Savile Row — at 7 Burlington Gardens, a Grade II-listed building built in 1725.

Abiti — 'Clothes' in Italian.

Accordion pleats — Narrow, straight pleats.

Acetate — A synthetic material made of cellulose acetate and which is comprised of very finely spun strong fibres that take to dye more readily than some natural materials.

Alpaca — The soft, silky fleece (or fabric or yarn made from the fleece) of a South American hoofed mammal related to the llama. Its colour is typically grey, russet or brown. Alpaca was first introduced to England by Benjamin Outram, of Halifax, who spun a rough yarn with it and wove it into rugs and shawls.

ASA — Advertising Standards Authority.

-B-

Back stitch — A hand stitch in which the needle is 'backed up' and inserted at the end of the previous stitch.

Back strap — A strap across the back of a garment, such as on a waistcoat.

Back tacking — Reverse stitches at the beginning and end of a seam to give it strength.

Balance — Usually used in reference to the relationship between the front and back of a garment: the ideal harmony among sections of a garment and its wearer's figuration.

Balance marks — Notches, nips or threads in garment parts and which help to preserve the balance of the garment during assembly.

Bar tack — Side-by-side stitches used at the ends of button-holes, pocket corners and belt loops for reinforcement.

Barathea — A soft fabric of silk, rayon, cotton or wool in a hop-sack twilled weave and having a pebbled or ribbed surface. Worsted barathea is often used to make fine dress evening coats in black or midnight blue, whereas silk barathea is often used to make neckties.

Baste — To sew a garment together temporarily with long, loose, provisional stitches, usually in white thread (for easy spotting during removal), early in the construction and fittings process.

Batiste — A fine, often sheer fabric, constructed in either a plain or figured weave and made of any of various natural or synthetic materials. Named after Baptiste of Cambrai, who was supposedly its first maker.

Bearer — Atop the fly, a piece of cloth stitched into the waistband of trousers for reinforcement and to bear the weight of the trousers when fastened.

Bedford cord — A smooth corded fabric with

cords running lengthwise. Probably came from the town of Bedford.

Bespoke — See p. 365.

Bias — A line running diagonal to the warp and weft threads of a cloth. True bias is at forty-five degrees and is the angle of reference in cutting an undercollar.

Bicycled — Slang adjective for work done on a sewing machine.

Birdseye — Woven fabric having an all-over pattern of tiny geometric shapes reminiscent of a bird's eye.

Blazer — A single- or double-breasted sport coat often with metal (e.g. gilt or silver) buttons and sometimes an insignia indicating affiliation with a company or club.

Blend — A yarn obtained when two or more staple fibres are combined in a textile process for producing spun yarns — or a fabric containing a blended yarn of the same fibre content in the warp and weft.

Blind fly — A fly fastened down rather than left open between each button.

Blind stitch — A stitch by hand or machine that does not penetrate all the way through the cloth.

Block pattern — A generalised paper template for marking out the parts of a garment on cloth.

Bluff edges — Finished edges in which no

stitches are visible on the garment's exterior.

Bluffing — Stitching together the canvas and front facings of a coat.

BMG — Bertelsmann Music Group.

Board — The long, broad, table-like surface on which a cutter or tailor works, standing or sitting.

Bodkin — A small plastic pen-shaped tool with a softly pointed tip used for piercing cloth, ripping down basted garments and rounding out the eyelets of hand-worked buttonholes.

Body — A term applied to textiles, suggesting compactness, solidity and richness of handle in the raw, semi-manufactured or manufactured state.

Bolt — An entire length of cloth from the loom, rolled or folded. Bolts vary in length.

Boot — Old-fashioned slang for money. Bootmakers called money 'boot'; grocers called it 'sugar', milkmen 'cream' — all usually on account of work started but not finished. Thus some boot would be asked for by a tramp tailor at the end of the day, to pay for his meal and bed, and then deducted from his reckoning on payday.

Botany — Originally merino wool grown near Botany Bay, Australia. More modern usage is to call raw goods merino and, once they are processed, Botany.

Botany twill — A twilled mixture made of Botany wool.

Bouclé — A novelty yarn and finish effect produced on cloths whereby very small, drawn-out curly loops in the individual threads appear on the surface. The name is from the French *bouclé*, meaning buckle or ringlet.

Bound edge or *bound seam* — A seam whose fabric edges are bound by thread or lining to prevent fraying or grinning.

Break — On a coat, the point at which the bridle ends, usually just above the top button.

Breeches — See *Britches*.

Brick stitch — Stitches resembling brickwork.

Bridle — A narrow strip of material, usually cotton, added to the canvas inside the lapel in order to hold its roll, as a bridle restrains a horse.

Brilliantine — Wiry fabric, like alpaca, but of higher lustre, made from Angora goat hair.

Britches or *breeches* — Calf-length trousers of a durable fabric (such as whipcord, Bedford cord or cavalry twill) flaring at the sides of the thighs and fitting snugly at the knees so as to be worn with boots while hunting or riding.

Broad silk — Silk a yard or more wide.

Brocade — A fabric with decorative woven figures or patterns, often floral. Made on a jacquard loom.

Brother — A sewing machine made by Brother Industries Ltd. The brand was born in 1908, when the Yasui Sewing Machine Co. was established in Nagoya, Japan. In 1954 Brother International Corporation USA became the company's first overseas sales affiliate and today also manufactures label printers, typewriters, fax machines, printers and other computer-related electronics.

Brushed fabrics — Cloths with a nap finish.

Buckling — A fault in weaving because of tight threads and uneven tension.

Buggy — Lining across the back of an otherwise unlined coat — reminiscent of buggy carriages that have an awning but no 'lining' on the front or sides.

Bumping table — A slightly inclined table designed to be shaken or 'bumped' laterally to aid in the amalgamation or separation of metals.

Burberry — Registered trademark name for weatherproofed cotton garments or fabric.

Button stand — The distance from the finished edge of a garment to the centre of a button.

Buttonhole twist — The thread used for the stitches around a buttonhole.

Cabbage — Like mungo, material leftover from garment making.

Calico — A cotton material whose name derives from Calicut, India, where the cloth was first printed with wooden blocks by hand.

Cambridge grey — See *Oxford grey.*

Candy blue — A very vivid, pure, almost metallic shade of blue.

Canvas — A cloth originally made of hemp yarns and named from cannabis. The term has since come to refer to rough, heavy fabric woven of flax and cotton and sometimes jute. Inserted (and, ideally, hand-stitched) into a coat's collar and chest, it gives a coat its shape and support. Canvas is also used as a verb to describe the assembly of such interfacing.

CAP — Committee of Advertising Practice.

Cashmere — The soft, fine, lightweight, downy yarn and fabric made from the wool at the roots of the hair of the cashmere, or Kashmir, goat.

Casualty book — The book in a tailoring house in which botched jobs and replacement fabric orders are recorded.

Catch — A backing of material providing reinforcement to an opening such as a trouser fly.

Cat's face — Once upon a time: slang for a small shop opened by a journeyman just starting out — sometimes just the front room of a residence. As in, 'Mr Strickland has opened up a cat's face.'

Cavalry twill — A strong cotton, wool or worsted fabric of double twill and having a distinctive diagonal weave, often used to make hunt coats.

Centreline cut — A style of cutting trousers in which the pattern is drawn using the front pleat line or crease as one's starting and reference point.

Chain stitch — A flexible, stretchable, ornamental stitch commonly used in the legs and seat seams of trousers. Its thread interlopes to look like a chain.

Chalk stripe — Classic business suit pattern in which solid, broader-than-pinstripe stripes (i.e. at least one-eighth of an inch) appear against a contrasting background.

Check — Term given to a chequerboard appearance produced on a fabric by employing a weave of two or more colours of warp and weft specially arranged to give this appearance. See also *Windowpane check*.

Chest piece — A combination piece of canvas and felt inserted into the chest of a coat to give it strength and shape.

Chiffon — A thin, gauze-like fabric with a soft or sometimes stiff finish.

Chuck a dummy — Slang for 'to faint', in the manner of a dummy falling on its face. The term was also used by soldiers, perhaps in part because so many tailors wound up in the military.

Clapham Junction — Slang for a pattern draft having several alterations or additions.

Clapper (also called a *beater, striker* or *pounding block*) — An oblong or rectangular piece of hardwood wielded like a paddle to flatten parts of a garment.

Clip — 1. All of the wool taken from a flock. 2. A small straight cut made into a seam allowance so that the seam will lie flat around curves.

Cock — Once upon a time: slang for a master who minutely examines a finished garment.

Cocksparrow — A wing-like effect at the back of a coat.

Cod — Slang for booze. See also *On the cod*.

Codge — To repair a garment badly, unskilfully.

Codger — An alteration tailor for old suits.

Collar interfacing — Stiff, firmly woven linen fabric sewn between a collar's surface and its undercollar.

Corduroy — A strong, ribbed, velveteen fabric made of cotton and whose name is the anglicisation of the French phrase *corde du roi*, i.e. 'cord of the king'. The material was originally made exclusively to clothe the huntsmen of the Bourbon King of France.

Counts — The number of yarns or threads per inch.

Crêpe — Thin, crimped gauze made of silk or cotton.

Crimp — The natural waviness of the wool fibre. It varies with the fibre's diameter.

Crimplene — A thick, polyester yarn used to make a wrinkle-resistant 'wash and wear' fabric of the same name. Developed in the mid-fifties by ICI, it was named after the Crimple Valley, where the company was located.

Crinoline — Originally a stiff fabric made of horsehair and cotton for holding out a lady's dress; later a petticoat expanded with hoops of whalebone or steel or a kind of hat frame made of horsehair (real or imitation), stiffened and shaped. From the Latin *crino* for horsehair plus *lino* for flax.

Crooken on — To bring the fabric of a coat's shoulder closer to the neck point, closing or eliminating the gap visible between the coat and shirt just beside the collar.

Cross-bred — A term applied to wools

obtained from sheep of mixed breed. The bulk of wool manufactured is cross-bred; it is strong, but lacks fineness.

Cross jet — The small, typically horizontal hem on a coat's inside or outside breast pocket.

Cross pocket — A horizontal pocket.

Cross stitch — An ornamental hand stitch that looks like an X.

Crushed beetles — Once upon a time, slang for poorly made buttonholes.

Crutch or *crotch* — Point at which the inside leg seams meet. Also *fork*.

Cub — Once upon a time: slang for an apprentice, learner.

Curly — Once upon a time: slang for troublesome, supposedly from a cloth curling problematically. E.g. 'Granger's getting curly.'

Curtains — The strips of material that hang below the trousers' waistband. Usually made of the same material used for the waistband, e.g. Ermazine or silk.

Cutter — The person responsible for measuring the customer, assessing the customer's figuration, cutting a paper pattern, and fitting the garment on the customer in its various stages of make, until finished.

Cutting turf — Working in a conspicuously

unskilled or clumsy manner, i.e. making more bodily movement than the job warrants, presumably to hide what is lacking in precision and craftsmanship.

Cutting your own flap — Looking out for yourself.

-D-

Damask — A figured cloth originally from Damascus.

Damp rag — A wet pressing cloth or depressing person.

Darkey — A sleeve board.

DDI — Direct Dispatch International, an international courier service based in London.

Dead horse — A job one continues to work on although it has already been paid for.

Denim — A coarse twill, today used to make jeans (and other garments, including suits). Its name comes from *de Nîmes*, as in *serges de Nîmes*.

Dice — Small squares of different colours: a pattern used for the edging of dresses, stockings and tartan for the bands of Highland bonnets.

Dogtooth — A woven fabric pattern reminiscent of canine teeth.

Donegal tweed — A coarse, plain or

herringbone Irish tweed with coloured slubs, i.e. flecks.

Double-breasted — Term to describe a coat, jacket or similar garment having two parallel columns of buttons, a wide overlap of fabric and a more formal peaked lapel.

Dupion silk — A lustrous silk often woven from two different colours of threads, so that the fabric shimmers or changes colour in the light.

-E-

Ease — An even distribution of fullness in fabric, created without perceptible gathers or tucks.

Ermazine — A light, well-ventilated lining alternative to silk, typically used in fancier coats.

Estrato — A stretchable worsted fabric woven from merino wool and created by Trabaldo Togna, an Italian mill in Biella, to be flexible and wrinkle-resistant.

-F-

Facing — A garment's covering or lining in places such as the silk lapels on a tailcoat.

Fell — To sew or finish a seam with the raw

edges flattened, turned under and stitched down.

Figuration — A bespoke cutter's notes on a customer's physique, particularly any bodily idiosyncrasies — such as a stoop, a paunch, arms of dissimilar length or uneven shoulder blades — that affect how a garment hangs. The bespoke cutter uses these observations to individualise the customer's pattern such that it both fits precisely and is maximally flattering. For example, if a cutter observes that his customer has a hunched back, he will generally cut a coat pattern that is shorter than average in the front, longer than average in the back, and smaller and tighter around the neck in order to keep the balanced back and foreparts in place. An off-the-peg or indeed a badly made bespoke coat breaks down in three areas on a hunched body: the back of the coat strains on top and collapses below, its collar bunches up, and the front hangs long and loose from the body. But in a bespoke coat made according not only to careful measurements but also practised figuration and Rock of Eye, once one area is adjusted, the others start to fall into place.

Findings — Padding and interfacing

materials used to reinforce and structure a garment.

Fishtail — On the back of a pair of trousers requiring braces: the slightly higher cut tab with a V-shaped opening to which braces are attached and which resembles a fish's tail.

Fitting — One of the two, three or more stages in the making of a suit or other bespoke or custom-made garment during which it is donned by the customer and assessed by customer and cutter together for necessary adjustments.

Flannel — A soft and slightly napped fabric of wool or cotton combination and usually used for the making up of suits. Probably a variant on the Middle English *flanyn*, or *sackcloth*; in turn from the Old French *flaine*, for a coarse kind of wool.

Flash basting — Superfluous basting stitches put into a garment at the fitting stage (or for display in a shop window or website photograph) to impress the customer.

Float — Excess material, e.g. approximately one-eighth of an inch of surplus where the sleeve of a coat meets the scye.

Floating canvas — The canvas inside a hand-canvassed coat. It 'floats' between the facing and forepart rather than is adhered into place by chemical means.

Fly — An inner flap on trousers, overcoat or indeed any other garment to conceal a row of buttons or zip. In trousers the fly is on the crutch opening in front of the left side and is stitched on to conceal the method of fastening. It is made up and has buttonholes worked into it before being fastened onto the left topside.

Fly catch (or *button catch*) — The counterpart of the fly, seamed onto the right topside. The buttons on the catch are what fasten the fly parts together.

Flyline — The line up the centre of the front from the seat to the waistband.

Flyline cut — A style of cutting trousers in which the pattern is drawn using the fly as one's starting and reference point.

Fork — The point on a pair of trousers where the legs join. Also *Crutch* or *crotch*.

Forward (or *advance*) *fitting* — The second or subsequent stage of a garment's assembly, after it has already been basted, fitted once on the customer, and ripped down and re-cut if necessary according to the adjusted pattern.

French tack — A chain of thread that connects the hem of a lining to the garment hem.

Fresco — A cool, well-ventilated, high-quality plain-weave worsted fabric patented in

1907 by English manufacturer Hudders-
field especially for the making up of
business suits and other necessary clothing
worn in hot climates.

Fusing — A method of securing canvas in
place in the collars and chests of coats
using chemicals whose adhesive qualities
are awakened at high temperatures. Fusing
is a cheaper and less time-consuming
method of securing canvas, but it does not
last as long as comprehensive hand-
stitching and can lead to a corrugated
appearance over time, especially if the
garment in question is treated repeatedly to
dry-cleaning.

-G-

Gabardine — A sturdy, smooth-finish fabric
of worsted, cotton, polyester or other kind
of fibre having a tight twill weave and being
fairly resistant to creasing. Gabardine is
most often used to make up trousers and
blazers.

Gimp — Heavy cord made of silk, cotton or
wool strands with a wire core, used to
reinforce the edges of hand-worked buttonholes.

Glen check, Glen plaid or *Glenurquhart plaid*
— A classic plaid pattern of muted colours

or black and grey or white, often with two dark and two light stripes alternating with four dark and four light stripes, horizontally and vertically, forming a crisscross pattern of irregular checks. Named after Glen Urquhart in Invernesshire, Scotland.

Gorge line — Line made by a diagonal seam joining the collar end to the lapel top.

Grain — The direction of threads in a woven fabric. The warp forms the lengthwise grain while the weft forms the crosswise grain.

Grinning — The straining or pulling apart at the seams of fabric that has not been sufficiently reinforced.

Guanashina — A rare, specially commissioned blend of the three finest fibres in the world: Andean guanaco, pashmina and yearling cashmere.

-H-

Haircloth — A wiry, resilient interfacing fabric made from a mixture of strong cotton fibres and tough horsehair.

Ham — A firm, ham-shaped cushion with built-in curves that conform to various contours of the body and which is used for pressing garment areas that need special shaping.

Hard finish or *clear finish* — The surface of a

fabric that has no nap, either naturally or because the nap has been sheared off.

Harris tweed — Heavy, hand-woven tweed from the Outer Hebrides.

Hermès — A French, Paris-based high fashion house with a shop on London's New Bond Street and which specialises in leather, ready-to-wear, lifestyle accessories, perfume and other luxury goods. The company's products, extremely prestigious by virtue of workmanship, reputation and price, are often recognisable by the brand's Duc carriage-and-horse logo and the orange letter *h*.

Herringbone — Worsted fabric with a chevron pattern, most often used to make up suits and overcoats.

Hip stay — One's wife.

Hipple — Good pay for an easy job.

Hopsack — Coarse, loosely woven cotton or wool (or other, jute-like fibres) whose texture resembles that of burlap.

Horsehair canvas — One of the types of canvas used in building the inner construction of a coat, to give the chest and upper forepart shape and support.

Houndstooth — A distinctive check pattern comprised of what look like tiny lightning bolts. Generally two different colours of thread are woven together in equal measure, so there is no dominant back-ground or foreground colour; when the colours are very contrasting, the pattern is very dramatic. A common choice for sporting garments.

House of Parliament — A meeting of tailors' assistants and apprentices in the shop to address some serious matter.

Hunter's pink — The standard colour, a vivid scarlet, that melton intended for frock and dress coats for riding with hounds is dyed.

-I-

ICI — Imperial Chemical Industries PLC. Formed in 1926 from the merger of four British chemical companies to challenge the rest of the world's chemical producers. Now part of AkzoNobel, a leading chemical supplier and the largest coatings manufacturer in the world.

In breast — A pocket on the inside breast of a coat.

In the drag — Behind in work.

Inauguration cloth — A heavyweight, super-fine black and unfinished twill worsted fabric for double-breasted frock and morning coats. Named as such in honour of American President McKinley's 1897 inauguration suit, the fabric for which was made by a Connecticut mill amidst a debate over tariff regulations likely either to liberate or strictly hinder the American textile industry.

Indigo — A vegetable substance extracted from the leaves and stems of certain tropical and semi-tropical plants and from which brilliant and durable blue dyes are obtained.

Interfacing — Fabric sewn between two layers of garment fabric to stiffen and strengthen different parts of the garment.

Interlining — An inner lining placed between the lining and outer fabric of a garment for extra warmth or bulk.

Irish duck — A stout linen cloth used for overalls.

Irish tweed — A fancy tweed cloth with homespun yarns.

Iron tailor — An old name for a sewing machine; used derogatively when machines were first introduced.

-J-

Jacket — A short coat whose name supposedly originated with the French name Jacques, a common nickname for a male peasant.

Jacketing — Fabric for jackets or coats.

Jacquard — A simple method of weaving intricate designs into fabric, invented by the Frenchman Joseph Marie Jacquard.

Jeannie — Calf-length slacks.

Jeff — Once upon a time: a small-business master who cut his garments and also made them up.

Jigger button — The button placed inside the left forepart of a man's double-breasted coat or waistcoat (or the right side of a lady's; see p. 304) to keep the underneath forepart in position.

-K-

Kapok — Soft light fibres from the seed-pods of the kapok tree and which are used for interlining materials.

Kelt — Scottish name for the cloth made of natural black and white wool mixed and spun together.

Kersey — A thick woollen cloth similar to melton but felted, napped and finished dull.

Keyhole buttonhole — A buttonhole with one rounded end, such that it looks like a keyhole. This is often an indication that the buttonhole is machine-made, and therefore sometimes gives its garment an impression of being of inferior quality.

Keyhole lapel — A lapel with a keyhole buttonhole.

Khaki — An Urdu word for the colour of the earth — or, in some people's opinion, dung.

Kick — To look for work.

Kink — A snarl or curl produced by a hard-twisted thread receding upon itself.

Kipper — A tailoress.

Knickerbocker yarns — Yarns spotted or striped, usually in several colours.

Knitting — The process of making fabric by interlocking series of loops or one or more yarns.

Knot — 1. A fault in a cloth, caused by the joining of broken warp or weft. 2. A snugly looped tie.

-L-

Lad of wax — A tailor or apprentice who models clothes so perfectly still and expressionlessly they appear modelled by a lad made of wax.

Lamb's wool — A fine yarn composed of the fine wool shorn from young sheep in their first year.

Lapthair — A type of canvas inserted in the chest area of a coat to give it body and shape.

Laventine — A very thin silk fabric usually

used to line sleeves.

Lightweights — Lightweight fabrics (such as an eight- or nine-ounce mohair) used for clothing to be worn in warm climates or interiors.

Linen — Fabric and yarn made of flax fibres.

List — The edge or selvedge of a piece.

Listed — A defect in the list or edge of a garment, such as the edge being torn away, stained or frayed.

Liverpool pocket — A ticket pocket with a welt inside.

Llama — A South American mountain animal resembling the camel, but smaller. Cloth made with an admixture of the animal's soft, furry hair is quite luxurious and often used for formal wear.

-M-

Mackinaw — Coarse, heavy-weight fabric with a large check pattern of many colours and usually used to make the topcoats or belted jackets of the same name. Once popular among north-western American lumberjacks.

Made-to-measure — The term used to describe a garment made according to the customer's measurements (and sometimes with cloth chosen by the customer) but which is then cut and assembled in a factory according to standard block patterns and then adjusted. A less individualised (and therefore less expensive) alternative to a true and traditionally made bespoke suit.

Madras — A type of soft fabric (muslin) usually with fancy patterns used in shirting.

Make your coffin — Overcharge for a garment.

Matcher — Once upon a time: a trotter or young girl who would go out to find matching materials.

Melton — A heavily milled woollen in which the fibres have been made to stand straight up and then the piece cut bare to conceal the weave. Made with a cotton warp and a woollen weft. Used for overcoats, hunting jackets, etc., particularly on the underside of collars. Named for the town Melton Mowbray.

Merino wool — The best (softest and lightest) quality wool from sheep originally bred in Spain; used for suits.

Micro — Microlite fabric, which is 70 per cent wool, 30 per cent microfibre; a lightweight alternative to 100 per cent natural fabrics, good for hot climates.

Micron — The unit of measurement used for wool fibre diameter. One micron = 1 millionth of a metre.

Mohair — The fine, soft, silky hair of the angora goat. It has a slight sheen, is crease-resistant and ideal for summer suits and dresswear. Imitation mohair made of wool and cotton combinations is detectable because its fibres cling closely together, whereas the fibres of mohair are clearly separable.

Moleskin — Sturdy and heavily napped twilled cotton fabric that resembles the skin of a mole and is often used for casual, sport and working trousers.

Morning coat — A tailcoat typically made of black herringbone fabric and worn at formal events such as weddings and races e.g. Ascot.

Mounting — A tightly woven fabric cut in the shapes of the main pieces of a garment and attached to these pieces before the garment is sewn together. Used usually for women's garments.

Mouse in the straw — An unsociable board colleague or nonunion worker.

Mulesing — The surgical removal of strips of wool-bearing wrinkle skin from around the breech of a sheep. Mulesing is a common practice in Australia as a way to reduce the incidence of flystrike on merino sheep in regions where this is common.

Mungo — Material remnants too small or inferior in quality to be used for garment-making and which cutters and tailors use to practise technique or as rags. The word also once referred to longer lengths of fabric made up of the smaller remnants, which tailors would bring to shops that specialised in recycling them.

Muslin — An inexpensive, plain-woven cotton fabric used for making prototypes of garments as an aid to styling and fitting.

-N-

Nailhead — A subtle geometric fabric pattern wherein a solid background colour is offset by many small nailhead-sized depressions at regular and very small intervals. The background colour tends to dominate, but the nailheads' colour can be brought out with a tie or shirt of the same colour.

Nap — A fabric's short surface fibres that have been drawn out and brushed in one direction, such as on velvet or corduroy.

Natural waist — One's torso circumference where it intersects with the small of the back. Positioning the front button on a single-breasted coat at the natural waist will have the optical effect of thinning and elongating the wearer's figure.

Needle — A pointed rod with an eye used for sewing, either by hand or with a machine — also used generally as a verb meaning 'to irritate', supposedly after the sensation of having a sewing needle run into one's finger.

Ninth part of a man — It used to be that funeral bells tolled in spells of three for a child, six for a woman and nine for a man. The resulting expression 'Nine tellers make a man' became corrupted as 'Nine tailors make a man.'

Noble — A general term for fine wool and other luxury animal fibres, e.g. mohair, alpaca, vicuña.

Norfolk coat or *jacket* — A loose, belted single-breasted coat with box pleats for a gun and cartridges; worn in the country for game shooting.

Notch — A V- or diamond-shaped marking made on the edge of a garment piece as an alignment guide. Also a triangular cut into the seam allowance to enable it to lie flat.

Notched lapel (also called a *step lapel*) — A lapel sewn to the collar at an angle, such that the junction looks like a step. Notched lapels are standard on single-breasted suits, blazers and sport coats. The size of the notch varies; a small notch is called a fishmouth.

Nothing at the neck point — The point on a shoulder immediately next to the collar. 'Nothing' refers to the distance away from the collar or neck point.

Nothing at the top — The point on a line or seam immediately next to its top. 'Nothing' refers to the distance away from the top of the line or seam.

Notions — Items such as buttons, hooks and zips required to finish a garment.

Nylon — A man-made synthetic material having a chemical composition akin to that of proteins (e.g. silk, hair and wool) but which has no exact counterpart in nature.

-O-

Off-the-peg — Made in standard sizes and available from merchandise in stock. Synonymous with 'ready-to-wear'.

On the back-seam — An elegant euphemism for 'on one's backside', as in, 'to fall on one's back-seam'. Also to lie down on one's tailoring board for a short siesta.

On the cod — Drunk.

On the double — On both the front and back.

Operation — A patch, especially on the trousers' seat.

Outbreast — A pocket on the outside breast of a coat.

Overcheck and *overplaid* — A pattern effect made by the super-imposition of one check over another check; often seen in the tartans of Scottish clans.

Oxford grey — A dark grey fabric made of mixed dyed black and white wools. A lighter version is called 'Cambridge grey', a distinction corresponding to the two universities' colours: Oxford's is dark blue while Cambridge's is light blue.

Oxfords (and *pinpoint Oxfords*) — A style of leather shoe with enclosed lacing and which originally appeared in Scotland and Ireland, where they are occasionally called Balmorals. Oxfords with ornamental pinpoint-like perforations in the leather are pinpoint Oxfords.

-P-

Padding — A stitch or addition of materials to an area of a garment to give it shape.

Paisley — Patterns reminiscent of those in shawls originally made in the Scottish town of Paisley.

Pantaloons — Skin-fitting leg garments that run from the waist down and over the feet. 'Pants' is a diminutive of pantaloons.

Pashmina — A luxurious soft wool from the pashmina goat, bred in northern India and commonly found in the deserts of Tibet and Kashmir at an altitude of more than 16,000 feet.

Pass a coat — What a cutter does to check whether a coat is progressing well and properly in the making-up process. He puts the coat on himself (or a fellow employee, if the coat is too small for his own frame) and scrutinises its reflection in a mirror to confirm that in every last respect it meets his standards before it proceeds to be fitted on the customer or dispatched.

Pass up — To rip open the side seams and move the back panel up to create more length in the back.

Peaked lapel — The most formal style of lapel, which peaks upward at the junction of lapel and collar. Peaked lapels are standard on double-breasted jackets and formal coats including tailcoats and morning coats.

Pencil stripe — Akin to pinstripes, an effect on cloths whereby contrasting threads are woven in lines suggestive of having been drawn on by a pencil.

Pick-and-pick — Textured plain cloth made up of single filling threads in different colours.

Pig, pork — A garment miscut beyond

rectification and which therefore must be killed, in which case the cutter is said to have 'made pork'. See also *Pork Rail*.

Pile — A fabric having a surface made of upright ends, as in fur.

Pin check — An effect on suiting material, often in grey and white, where the small checks of the pattern are a size almost that of a pinhead.

Pinstripes — The classic English suit fabric distinguished by its very thin stripes. The lines in 'true' pinstripes are solid lines, 'rain pinstripes' are comprised of tiny unjoined dots, and 'cable' pinstripes look like tiny braids.

Piping — A narrowly folded strip of garment fabric usually used to finish the top and bottom edges of a pocket opening.

Plaid — Fabric having the checked and lined pattern of Scottish tartan cloth.

Plain weave — A weave in which the yarns are interlaced in a simple chequerboard fashion.

Plugging — Fastening purely ornamental buttons onto fabric by forcing the button's shank through the cloth and securing it on the other side with a plug of linen or other material so the button lies flat against the garment.

Plus 2s — Three-quarter-length trousers that

buckle under the knee (technically two inches below the knee) to look like baggy breeches and typically worn when hunting or shooting.

Plys — 1. Layers of cloth. 2. The strands twisted together to make yarn, rope or thread.

Pocketing fabric — Silk or tightly woven twilled cotton fabric with a satiny finish and which is used to line pockets.

Point presser (also called a *seam* or *tailor's board*) — A narrow hardwood board used for pressing open small seams in hard-to-reach places and for pressing open seams on hard fabrics.

Poplin — A finely corded fabric made of cotton, rayon, silk or wool; so named for coming originally from the papal city of Avignon.

Pork Rail — Where porked garments hang. See also *Pig, pork*.

Pre-shrink — To shrink fabric to an irreducible degree before cutting it.

Press mitt — A thumbless padded mitten used to press small curved areas that do not fit over a tailor's ham or regular ironing board.

Presser foot — The part of a sewing machine that holds down fabric while it advances under the needle.

Pressing cloth — A piece of fabric, usually

cotton, placed between the iron and garment while pressing.

Prince of Wales check — Similar to a Glenurquhart check but with a coloured overcheck and larger pattern. Popularized by the Duke of Windsor when he was Prince of Wales, but reputedly originally designed by King Edward VII when he was Prince of Wales.

Puff cut — A short cut made in the canvas inserted in the breast panels of a coat to prevent the outer material from stringing.

Pyjamas — Sleeping clothes whose name is said to come from the Persian for 'leg clothing'.

-R-

Rain pinstripes — Pinstripes comprised of tiny unjoined dots that look as though they are raining down the material.

Ranter — To sew a seam such that it is invisible, or nearly so.

Raw edge — An edge that has not been hemmed or turned in. Only practicable with meltons and other materials that do not fray or unravel.

Ready-to-wear — Made in standard sizes and available from merchandise in stock. Synonymous with 'off-the-peg'.

Regatta stripe — Lightweight or woollen suiting (e.g. flannel) with a neat fancy stripe effect.

Reinforce — To strengthen a seam with additional stitches or to add an extra layer of fabric to a stress area.

Rip down — The removal, typically using a bodkin, of the stitches from a basted garment so that it can be adjusted and reassembled more formally.

Rock of Eye — The faculty that allows a cutter to draw and cut a pattern practically freehand, unguided except by basic measurements and the cutter's cultivated instinct that it 'looks right' and will accommodate the customer's figuration in the most comfortable yet flattering way.

Roll line — The pattern marking along which the collar and lapel are turned back.

Roped — Describes a sleeve that has been attached too high on the armhole of a coat and therefore puffs up at the shoulder.

-S-

Satin — A warp or weft surface cloth in which the intersections of warp and weft are so arranged as to be imperceptible.

Savile Row Bespoke Association — An association established in 2004 to protect and develop the craft of bespoke tailoring as well as its continued residence on Savile Row and its Mayfair surrounds. At writing, members include Anderson & Sheppard, Davies & Son, Dege & Skinner, Hardy Amies, Henry Poole, Huntsman, Meyer & Mortimer, Norton & Sons, Ozwald Boateng, Richard Anderson Ltd and Richard James.

Saxony — High-grade wool, yarn and worsted cloth produced from the merino sheep of Saxony.

Scale, tailoring — A wooden device marked with fractions to identify relative dimensions and ratios of reduction or enlargement and used in the drawing of patterns.

Scroop — The feel associated with silk and which is given to rayon and other synthetic sateens by chemical means.

Scye — A contraction of the words 'arm's' and 'eye', scye is the round opening in a coat into which a sleeve is inserted. The 'depth of scye' measurement is the distance from the armpit to the shoulder line.

Seam — A line of junction between two edges.

Seam allowance — The fabric that extends outside a seam line.

Seat allowance — The quantity allowed for expansion of a trousers' seat when the wearer is seated.

Seconds — Pieces of cloth containing visible faults.

Seersucker — A lightweight fabric with crinkled stripes that may be laundered without ironing.

Selvedge — The narrow, lengthwise finished edge of a woven fabric that prevents it from unravelling.

Serge — Term for all fabrics of a twill character and of a rough make, distinguished from the finer make of worsteds.

Shading — An optical effect produced by different colours or qualities of material or weave combined together, e.g. an illusion of darkening caused by the misalignment of pieces of patterned (usually checked) cloth.

Shadow stripe — A stripe pattern wherein the stripe has only a very subtle difference in texture or shade from the background colour (e.g. medium grey on dark grey). Shadow stripes are generally solid lines, as opposed to cable or rain pinstripes.

Shank — The link of buttonhole twist (thread) between a button and the fabric onto which it is sewn, or the small pillar on a button to be fastened to a garment by plugging.

Shawl lapel (also called a *roll* or *shawl collar*) — A lapel with a continuous curve. Original to the Victorian smoking jacket,

412

shawl lapels are now given occasionally to dinner jackets and tuxedos in which a slightly less formal look is desired.

Shirting — Cloth recognised as being suitable for the making up of shirts.

Silesia — A lightweight, smoothly finished, twilled cotton for garment linings, e.g. in coat pockets. The name is said to have originated with the wife of Joseph Ferguson, who invented the process of 'beetling', i.e. beating cotton goods down to have a silky finish. His wife called his goods 'Silesias', the name of a region of Poland, because the couple was sympathetic to Poles averse to the partitioning of their country by Germany, Austria and Russia.

Silk — The filaments created by the silkworm in spinning its cocoon.

Single-breasted — Term to describe a coat, jacket or similar garment having one column of buttons and a narrow overlap of fabric.

Single-stitch — The clear, single stitch that appears along the edges of a coat, e.g. on the lapels. In the case of tweed garments this stitched area would be slightly 'swelled', i.e. set in slightly to create a wider margin, just for style.

Sittin' drums — Old clothes.

Sizing — A finishing process in which a

413

substance (e.g. glue or starch) is added to the yarn and cloth to give it additional strength, stiffness, smoothness or to increase its weight.

Skein — A strand of yarn or thread wound around a spool in a series of crossings.

Skiffle — A rushed job.

Slanted patch pockets — Pockets external to the body of a garment or accessory and patched on at an angle to the garment's centre line.

Sleeve caps — Strips of cotton wadding or lambswool fleece placed around the tops of sleeves to create a smooth line and to support the roll at the sleeve top.

Sleeve cushion — A long, flat pad with a sleeve-like silhouette and which is inserted into a completed sleeve during pressing to prevent wrinkling and unwanted creases.

Snob — A verb to describe when a tailor has produced unskilled, unfinished work. As in: 'He snobbed the job.'

Soft finish — A fuzzy nap on the surface of a fabric. The nap may be natural or created artificially by brushing a smooth fabric with steel combs.

Sport coat — Typically a single-breasted patterned jacket worn with contrasting trousers.

Stay — An extra piece of fabric sewn into a garment to reinforce a point of possible wear, such as a crutch, heel or trouser pocket.

Stay stitch — A line of regular machine stitches, sewn along the seam line of a garment piece before the seam is stitched.

Strike — To cut cloth.

Stringing — Undesirable pleating or creasing in fabric, usually between the shoulder and breast.

Suit — Originally, and formally, a three-piece outfit consisting of a matching coat, trousers and waistcoat.

Suiting — Fabric for suits.

Super 100s/120s/150s — Types of cloth whose numbers refer to the maximum worsted count of yarn to which that particular type of wool can be spun. The higher the number, the finer the cloth.

Swatch — A strip or square of cloth, loose or bound in a swatch book, used for sampling.

Synthetic — Man-made material produced from chemical elements or compounds.

-T-

Tack — Several stitches made in the same place to reinforce a point of strain or to hold garment parts permanently in position.

Taffeta — A plain, closely woven, smooth

crisp fabric. Originally a rich silk used in England in the seventeenth century.

Tailcoat — A man's fitted coat, usually black and cut away at the hips and descending in a pair of tapering skirts behind. Tailcoats tend to have silk facings and covered buttons and are worn to white-tie events.

Tailor — The general term for an artisan who works at a tailoring house. Not a cutter but the worker who assembles the cloth cut according to the cutter's pattern; nevertheless, the word comes from the French *tailler*, 'to cut'.

Tailor's thimble — An especially sturdy industrial thumb protector, made of metal and open at the top.

Tartan — An old name for plain woollen army wear, as well as the checks-and-lines pattern made distinct by the Highland clans of Scotland.

Texture (or *handle*) — The surface effect of cloth.

Ticket pocket or *ticket right cross* — A small subpocket (to accommodate tickets, traditionally) within the right outside breast pocket on a coat.

Top — A continuous strand of partially manufactured wool, which previously has been scoured, carded and combed; an intermediate stage in the process of worsted yarn.

Top-stitching — A line of machine stitching on the visible side of the garment parallel to a seam.

Trim — To cut away excess fabric in a seam allowance after a seam has been stitched.

Trimmings — The accessories required for the making and ornamenting of any article of dress: canvas, silk, buttons, buttonhole twist, etc.

Tropical syddo — Canvas inserted in the length of the front of a jacket to give it body and shape.

Trotter — A tailor's assistant whose chief duty would be to take work to outsourced staff and to bring back bastes and finished work for fittings and to be dispatched.

Trouser curtain — A strip of soft, durable fabric that extends below the waistband of trousers to keep the waist area from stretching, hold pleats in place and conceal interior stitching.

Trousering — Cloth recognised as suitable for making up into trousers.

Tulle — A fine lace-net fabric, one of the first such man-made materials.

Turn-ups — Hems, or rather cuffs on the bottom of trouser legs, usually one and five-eighths inches deep and referred to as

'PTUs', 'Permanent Turn-Ups'.

Tuxedo — American term for a long-tailed dinner jacket said to have been conceived originally by Henry Poole's on Savile Row for Pierre Lorillard, whose son Griswold first wore it in 1886 to the Tuxedo Park country club in New York.

Tweed — Woollen goods, plain or twilled, felted or rough-finished, woven with dyed yarns and typically made into suits, skirts and overcoats. Originally tweeds were twilled cloths woven of Cheviot wool with a heavy nap, but the name is now applied to woollen cloths of a light make almost indiscriminately, so that there are Harris tweeds, Donegal, Irish, handwoven tweeds, fancy tweeds, and an almost infinite variety of colours and patterns. The word is said to derive from 'twirls', possibly a corruption owed to sloppy handwriting.

Twill weave — A fundamental weave admitting of many variations, including serge and denim, and in which the intersection of yarn forms lines running to the right or left diagonally across the fabric.

Twist — An alternate term for thread, or the number of yarns about its axis per unit of length of a yarn or other textile strand.

Twist is expressed in turns per inch (tpi), turns per metre (tpm), or turns per centimetre (tpcm).

-U-

Ums, Umsie, Umses — A tailor's term for an anonymous newcomer into a workshop until his name would be made known (and could be remembered).

Undercollar — The part of the coat collar one sees when one lifts the collar up.

Undercollar fabric — The fabric that is sewn to the collar interfacing to form the underside of the collar. In women's clothing, it is often of the same fabric as the rest of the garment. In men's, it is typically melton in a colour complementary to the rest of the coat.

Upturn — See *Turn-ups*.

-V-

Velcro — The brand name of a popular two-ply, self-adhesive hook-and-loop fabric invented by a huntsman and Swiss engineer, George de Mestral, who in 1948 got the idea for it from the tiny hooks on the burdock burrs he had to pick out of his clothes and his dog's fur whenever

419

they came in from hunting in the Alps. The word *Velcro* is a portmanteau of the French words *velours* ('velvet') and *crochet* ('hook').

Vent — The slits or openings in the back of a coat between its tail flaps that allow its hemline to move when the wearer bends or reaches into a trouser pocket.

Vest — The correct term for a waistcoat, always worn with a suit until after the Second World War.

Vicuña — The South American vicuña goat (a relation of the guanaco, but smaller), inhabiting the higher regions of Bolivia and Chile. Its long, silky hair is of the highest textile quality and when first used was made into fine broadcloth, but as the vicuña has become endangered its wool is now extremely rare.

Voile — Lightweight, semi-sheer fabric of wool, silk, rayon or cotton constructed in plain weave.

-W-

Wadding — Shoulder pads, often a grey, multi-flecked felt-like substance cut into a half-moon and shaped into plys, with collar canvas inserted for strength.

Waistband interfacing — A strip of strong,

canvas-like fabric used for reinforcement around the waist.

Warp — Threads running lengthwise in a piece of cloth.

Weasel — 1. The board on which journeymen tailors used to work when sitting cross-legged at their benches. 2. A long thin pressing iron, the most easily dispensable of the presser's tools and therefore usually the first to be 'popped' or pawned in hard times:

> A penny for a cotton ball
> A ha'penny for a needle
> That's the way the money goes
> Pop goes the weasel

Weave — The interlacing of warp and weft.

Weft — Threads running crosswise in a piece of cloth.

Welt — Strips of cloth or other reinforcements sewn or otherwise fastened to an edge, pocket or border of a garment to strengthen or adorn it.

Welt pocket (or *Liverpool pocket*) — An interior pocket that opens to the outside, finished with a horizontal band of garment fabric that covers the opening.

Whipcord — Hard-wearing cotton, woollen or worsted fabric with a steep, diagonally ribbed surface, similar to cavalry twill; used for trousers and military uniforms.

Whipping the cat — What a cutter or tailor does when he takes his tools to his customer's house.

Windowpane check — A check pattern in which the checks are quite large.

Wool — The hair from sheep, lamb and certain other animals and which is spun, woven, knitted or felted into fabric for clothing.

Woollen — Fabric made from short, uncombed fibres of wool, characteristically soft to the touch and often finished with a nap. Woollen fibres are not parallel but crossed in what appears to be a haphazard arrangement. Not necessarily synonymous with 'all-wool'.

Worsted — Clear, smooth-handled fabric in which the structure and colour are clearly defined owing to the smoothness of its yarns and interlacing. Gabardine and serge are worsteds.

-Y-

Yarn — Made from the fibres taken from sheep. Once they have been sorted, washed and combed they can be woven into fabric.

-Z-

Zephyr — A fine, light cotton fabric generally woven with dyed yarns in a variety of fancy patterns.

Acknowledgements

With thanks to rising star Lisa Halliday for her hard work, dedication and friendship throughout. To Clive and Brian: Brian what an extraordinary journey we are on. It has been an honour and a privilege. To Fred Seidel, for keeping the faith; to Jim, Robert and Rupert for their unwavering support and constant wise counsel; to Faye Sawyer, stylist to the stars; and of course to the three men who shaped me, Colin Hammick, Brian Hall and Dick Lakey. I salute you all!

We do hope that you have enjoyed reading this large print book.

Did you know that all of our titles are available for purchase?

We publish a wide range of high quality large print books including:
Romances, Mysteries, Classics
General Fiction
Non Fiction and Westerns

Special interest titles available in large print are:
The Little Oxford Dictionary
Music Book
Song Book
Hymn Book
Service Book

Also available from us courtesy of Oxford University Press:
Young Readers' Dictionary
(large print edition)
Young Readers' Thesaurus
(large print edition)

For further information or a free brochure, please contact us at:
Ulverscroft Large Print Books Ltd.,
The Green, Bradgate Road, Anstey,
Leicester, LE7 7FU, England.
Tel: (00 44) 0116 236 4325
Fax: (00 44) 0116 234 0205

Other titles published by
The House of Ulverscroft:

TELL ME WHERE IT HURTS

Dr Nick Trout

It's two forty-seven a.m. and vet Nick Trout is woken by an urgent telephone call. Sage, a twelve year-old German shepherd dog, has been rushed into surgery with a serious stomach condition that could kill her if she isn't operated on immediately. Over the next twenty-four hours, we follow the progress of Dr Trout, Sage, and his many other patients as he battles disease, unravels tricky diagnoses, deals with desperate owners, and reflects on the heartache and humour that are part and parcel of life as an animal surgeon.

AROUND THE WORLD IN 80 TRADES

Conor Woodman

He's sold his house to finance the trip, and by trading Sudanese camels for Zambian coffee, coffee for South African red wine and then to China to buy jade with the proceeds — he stands to return with a lot of money, new friends and many tales. Whether trading teak or tea, surfboards or seafood, Conor makes deals in the world's most hotly contested markets. But will a business analyst's expertise mean anything in the deserts of Sudan? Part *The Undercover Economist*, part *Apprentice* challenge, *Around The World In 80 Trades* reminds us that making a living is about exactly that — living.

GIRL IN BLUE

Anne Ramsay

Girl in Blue is Anne Ramsay's story of the fourteen years she spent in the police, first as a WPC and then as a detective. On the beat she would never know if she was about to face a violent criminal, a burglar funding his heroin habit, or even a corpse. Life as a police officer could involve catching drug dealers, watching a post-mortem or solving murder cases. But eventually she was exiled from the 'biggest gang in the world', as differences between life on Scotland's toughest streets and life inside the force itself were sometimes hard to see.

BLADE RUNNER

Oscar Pistorius

Oscar Pistorius was born with no fibulae. His parents' decision to have both his legs amputated was to give him the best chance of a normal life. His mother wrote him a letter: 'A loser is not one who runs last in the race. It is the one who sits and watches, and has never tried to run.' Running on prosthetic legs, he's now a world-renowned athlete, winning three gold medals at the 2008 Beijing Paralympics, breaking a Paralympic record for the 200m and a world record for the 400m. His ultimate fight now is to compete at the 2012 Olympics.

THE MUSIC ROOM

William Fiennes

William Fiennes' childhood, spent in a moated castle, is the perfect environment for a child with a brimming imagination. Whilst the house is alive with history, beauty and mystery, young William is equally in awe of his brother Richard. Eleven years older and a magnetic presence, Richard suffers from severe epilepsy. His energy influences the rhythms of the family and the house's internal life, and his story inspires a journey, interwoven with loving recollection, towards an understanding of the mind. *The Music Room* is a song of home, of an adored brother and of the miracle of consciousness.

APL			
Cen		Ear	
Mob		Cou	
ALL		Jub	
VH		HE	
Ald		el	
Fin		Fol	
Can		STO	
Til		HCL